The Chicago Athenaeum: Museum of Architecture and Design

"an instant classic" - Fast Company Magazine

2013 GOOD DESIGN AWARD

www.carloaiello.com

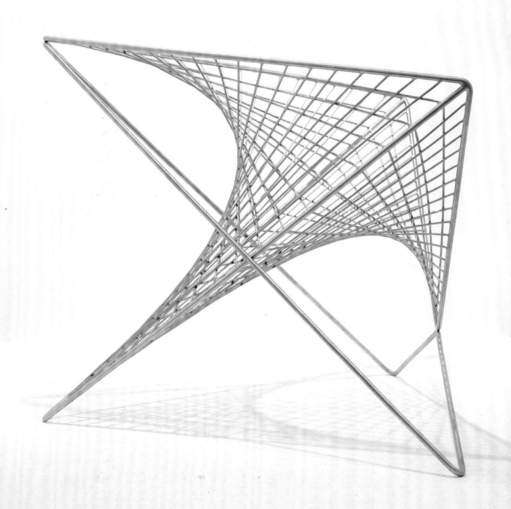

Performing Arts.

At Luminaire, it's not enough that an object look beautiful.
It must fulfill its role in life beautifully, too. Whether a
sofa or a teapot, a cabinet or a lamp, every object in our
collection reflects our obsession with good design that
performs at the highest level. Brilliant design statements
that take exception to the axiom: 'art for art's sake.' For
each also displays a clear sense of purpose.

It is this unique and unwavering perspective that has helped
make Luminaire the leading purveyor of fine contemporary
furnishings in the country. It is a journey that began more
than 30 years ago, born of an understanding that the best
way to earn the trust and loyalty of our customers is to
keep them abreast of the ongoing replenishment of design
ideas that serve to constantly transform our industry.

Luminaire.
Sitting, dining, sleeping, working — standing for the very
best in contemporary design.

Flap Sofa designed by Francesco Binfaré

YOU CREATE
WE DISTRIBUTE
THEY PUBLISH

the property congress 2014

17-18 SEPTEMBER | THE STAR, SYDNEY

ENGAGE YOUR SENSES

SEE IT — SYDNEY'S BEST SIGHTS AND PROJECTS

HEAR IT — AUSTRALIAN AND INTERNATIONAL KEYNOTE SPEAKERS WITH ROBUST DISCUSSIONS

TASTE IT — WORLD CLASS VENUES AND CUISINE

TOUCH IT — INTERACTIVE NETWORKING LIKE NEVER BEFORE

SMELL IT — SUCCESS!

REGISTER NOW using the code INTERNAT to claim your discount

thepropertycongress.com.au

FOLLOW US ON SOCIAL MEDIA

 PropertyCouncil   @PropCongress   /theproperty congress   PropCongress

Iconic design.

MONDAINE

Swiss ✛ Watch

www.mondaine.com

LARGENT™

MICROCORE™

Advanced LED Technology
for Outdoor Lighting

More Info: www.aal.net/products/largent

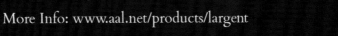

AutoCAD, Autodesk Maya,
Rhinoceros, Maxwell Render, Vray
for Rhino, Autodesk 3Ds Max,
Grasshopper, Adobe Premiere,
Adobe After Effects, Adobe
Photoshop Adobe Illustrator

Project Management, Office
Management, Collaboration and
Communication Skills

UNCOVER THE TALENT

**Archinect's *Talent Finder* connects firms with
the most talented architecture job seekers**
archinect.com/talentfinder

Use code "evolo12" for 50% off the regular subscription cost (limited to 100 subscribers)

Cesar M. Rodriguez
Chicago, IL

Karen Miller
San Francisco, CA

Steven Wong
New York, NY

Full Time, Part Time, Freelance

Full Time

Full Time, Part Time, Freelance

Full Time, Part Time

9 Years of Experience

3 Years of Experience

1 Year of Experience

15 Years of Experience

6 Years of Experience

Design, Large project
coordination, Design and Project
Management Strategies, Client
Liaison, feasibility studies, Town
Planning - Consultant
Coordination Documentation and

3D modeling & rendering,
(+3years) Cinema 4D, (+ 3 yrs)
AutoCAD, (+ 3 yrs) Rhinoceros,
(+3 years) Adobe Creative Suite,
(+1 yrs) Autodesk Revit

Rhino 4.0, Maya, 3DSMax,
Sketchup, Grasshopper, V-ray,
Mental-Ray, EcoTec, AutoCAD,
Revit 2012, Photoshop, InDesign,
Illustrator, Ms Project, Excel,
Hand Sketching Physical Model

(8+years) AutoCad, (+ 3 years)
Maxwell for Rhino, (+2 years)
Autodesk 3Ds Max, (+ 3yrs) Vray,
(+ 3 yrs) Rhinoceros, (+ 3years)
Google Sketchup, (+ 10yrs)
Microsoft Office & the Adobe

(+ 5yrs) AutoCAD, (+ 5yrs)
Photoshop, Creative And
Professional Writing, Graph
Design & Presentation, (+1 y
Adobe Illustrator, Accurende
4/NXT Autocad 3D

LIGHTVAULT 8

✳ Bluetooth® Wireless Adjustable Aiming & Dimming.
This is Kim Lighting.

KIM LIGHTING

http://www.kimlighting.com/ltv8/

 **HUBBELL** Lighting

The **Bluetooth** word mark and logos are registered trademarks owned by Bluetooth SIG, Inc. and any use of such marks by Kim Lighting is under license.

A Archinect.com/jobs

CONNECTING THE TOP TALENT WITH THE TOP EMPLOYERS SINCE 1997

Architectural Association
School of Architecture
Visiting School Programmes 2014

LOS ANGELES
Machining Adaptive Living
Monday 16 – Friday 27 June 2014

PUERTO RICO
Play With Your Food
Monday 30 June – Friday 11 July 2014

SAN FRANCISCO
Post-Industrial Landscapes
Monday 14 – Wednesday 23 July 2014

NEW YORK
Embedded Intelligence
Monday 21 – Wednesday 30 July 2014

CALIFORNIA – PACIFIC HIGHWAY ONE
Windscreens
Wednesday 13 – Sunday 24 August 2014

EUGENE
Marking the Forest
Thursday 14 – Sunday 24 August 2014

HOUSTON
Interscaless Border City
Galveston Island
Monday 11 August – Friday 22 August 2014

ACADIA 2014
DESIGN AGENCY
USC, LOS ANGELES, CALIFORNIA

DESIGN AGENCY will bring together the spectrum of research and creative practice currently occurring within the ACADIA community through the combined support of the research networks of the University of Southern California, University of California Los Angeles and Southern California Institute of Architecture. Questions the capacity for computation to inform or challenge traditional design processes; computation as design operation - the capacity, condition, or state of acting or of exerting power, and/or computation as design instrumentality - the design mechanism through which power is exerted or an end is achieved.

ACADIA is an international network of digital design researchers and professionals. ACADIA supports critical investigations into the role of computation in architecture, planning, and building science, encouraging innovation in design creativity, sustainability, and education.

find more info at:
http://2014.acadia.org/
tw: @ACADIA2014
fb: facebook.com/ACADIAconference

Important Dates:
Call for Papers: 1st of April
Research and Design Poster: 10th May
Workshops + Hackaton to be announced.

CONFIRMED KEYNOTES:

WILL WRIGHT
Creator of SimCity, the Sims, StupidFunClub

CASEY REAS
Creator of Processing

MARC FORNES
Principal, TheVeryMany

additional keynotes to be announced.

CHAIRS:

DR. DAVID GERBER
Assistant Professor, USC School of Architecture

ALVIN HUANG
Assistant Professor, USC School of Architecture
Principal, Synthesis Design + Architecture

JOSE SANCHEZ
Assistant Professor, USC School of Architecture
Principal, Plethora Project

SPONSORED BY:

HOSTED BY:

IO∆ INSTITUTE OF ARCHITECTURE

UNIVERSITY OF APPLIED ARTS VIENNA

ARCHITECTURE FACULTY

HEAD
Klaus Bollinger
MANAGEMENT
Sabine Peternell
PUBLICATIONS/PR
Roswitha Janowski-Fritsch

STUDIO ZAHA HADID
"Tectonic Articulation: Making Engineering Logics Speak"

HEAD: Zaha Hadid
TEAM: Mario Gasser, Christian Kronaus, Jens Mehlan, Robert Neumayr-Beelitz, Patrik Schumacher, Hannes Traupmann, Mascha Veech, Susanne John (Organisation)

STUDIO GREG LYNN
"Vast Empty Room"

HEAD: Greg Lynn
TEAM: Parsa Khalili, Martin Murero, Maja Ozvaldic, Bence Pap, Diana Geisler (Organisation)

STUDIO HANI RASHID
"Deep Futures: Über Port"

HEAD: Hani Rashid
TEAM: Brian De Luna, Jörg Hugo, Sophie Luger, Sophie Prix, Reiner Zettl, Andrea Tenpenny (Organisation)

TECHNOLOGY

STRUCTURAL DESIGN
HEAD: Klaus Bollinger
TEAM: Andrei Gheorghe, Florian Medicus
"Advanced Structural Methods and Analyses"

ENERGY DESIGN
Brian Cody, Bernhard Sommer

BUILDING CONSTRUCTION
Karin Raith, Anja Jonkhans, Franz Sam
"Applied and Integrated Building Construction"

DIGITAL DESIGN AND DIGITAL PRODUCTION
Peter Strasser, Armin Hess, Jörg Hugo

BUILDING INFORMATION MODELING
Torsten Künzler

EXPERIMENTAL DIGITAL DESIGN METHODS
Jens Mehlan, Robert Neumayr-Beelitz

DIGITAL DESIGN AND FULL SCALE STRATEGIES
Andrei Gheorghe

ENERGY DESIGN STRATEGIES
Bernhard Sommer

CNC (COMPUTER NUMERIC CONTROL)
Ivan Tochev

THEORY AND APPLIED THEORY

THEORY AND HISTORY OF ARCHITECTURE
Liane Lefaivre

SCIENCE AND ART
Matthias Boeckl

COMPARATIVE THEORY OF ARCHITECTURE
Sanford Kwinter

THEORY OF SCIENCE AND THEORY OF SOCIETY
Reiner Zettl

THEORY OF LIVING SPACES
Andrea Börner

APPLIED GEOMETRY AND MATHEMATICS
Georg Glaeser

STRATEGY OF REALIZATION AND COMMUNICATION

LEGAL CONDITIONS OF ARCHITECTURE
Petra Rindler

CONSTRUCTION MANAGEMENT
Hans Lechner

PLANNING MANAGEMENT
Holger Hagge

STRATEGY OF COMMUNICATION
Wojciech Czaja

SPECIAL TOPICS IN ARCHITECTURE
Anton Falkeis

[APPLIED] FOREIGN AFFAIRS
Baerbel Mueller

INSTITUTE OF ARCHITECTURE   UNIVERSITY OF APPLIED ARTS VIENNA
OSKAR KOKOSCHKA-PLATZ 2, 1010 VIENNA, AUSTRIA
+43 (0)1 711 33-2331, ARCHITECTURE@UNI-AK.AC.AT, WWW.I-O-A.AT
WWW.FACEBOOK.COM/IOA.INSTITUTEOFARCHITECTUREVIENNA,
WWW.YOUTUBE.COM/IOAANGEWANDTEVIENNA

dı:'ɑngewɑndtə

Universität für angewandte Kunst Wien
University of Applied Arts Vienna

JANGIR MADDADI
DESIGN BUREAU

"Never Content with the Ordinary"

JANGIR MADDADI

DESIGN BUREAU

www.jangirmaddadi.se

Media Partners:

KCRW eVolo

MACHINING ADAPTIVE LIVING
16-27 JUNE 2014

We seek, in the spirit of the Case Study project and its antecedents, to go beyond re-mastering current attitudes driven by contemporary issues of parametric design, new materialization and digital fabrication, sustainability, and hypothesize future modes of living, informed by the present. How will they relate to the recently institutionalized redefinitions of what constitutes a family? What are the new demographics and lifestyles to consider? Where will our society lead us and how can architecture forestall negative trends in a redemptive drive to once again instill its role in a projective practice.

The AA Visiting School is a worldwide network of design workshops and other programmes organized by the Architectural Association School of Architecture.

Programme directors:
Alvin Huang
Kevin McClellan
Programme coordinator:
Danielle Rago

Hosted by:

USC

Lecture Series
Neil Denari   **NMDA**
(Additonal speakers to follow)

Design instructors:
David Freeland   **FreelandBuck**
Marc Fornes   **THEVERYMANY**
Alvin Huang   **Synthesis Design + Architecture**
Adam Marcus   **Variable Projects**
Kevin McClellan   **TEX-FAB**
Jenny Wu   **OylerWu**

Design writing instructor:
Danielle Rago   **Writer and curator**

About/Register: losangeles.aaschool.ac.uk
Email: losangeles@aaschool.ac.uk

"The Holcim Awards appeal to students, to professionals, to everybody who has an interest in sustainable construction and design. All can stand together and talk as equals in the arena."

Reed Kroloff, Director, Cranbrook Academy of Art, USA.

4th International Holcim Awards for sustainable construction projects. Prize money totals USD 2 million.

Renowned technical universities lead the independent juries in five regions of the world. They evaluate projects at an advanced stage of design against the "target issues" for sustainable construction and allocate additional prizes for visionary ideas of young professionals and students. Find out more about the competitions at www.holcimawards.org

The Holcim Awards is an initiative of the Swiss based Holcim Foundation for Sustainable Construction. It is supported by Holcim and its Group companies and affiliates in around 70 countries. Holcim Ltd is one of the world's leading suppliers of cement and aggregates.

OPEN NOW FOR ENTRIES
www.holcimawards.org

Holcimawards
for sustainable construction

lab07
www.lab07.mx
architecture
consultant

Finally Connected

LAUNCHING SUMMER 2014

Join our private beta at **tower.io**

FOURTH DIMENSION PAINTINGS

THE ART OF
SERGEY BAGRAMYAN

WWW.ASBART.COM · SBAGRAMIAN@GMAIL.COM · (818) 422 54 2

David Trubridge

Eco-conscious lighting inspired by the myths,
legends and beauty of New Zealand
www.davidtrubridge.com

wakaNINE
North American Distributor
info@wakanine.com // 512. 354. 7889
2125 Goodrich Ave #C, Austin TX 78704
f y in ⓟ /wakanine

Photo by Will Fuller

JANGIR MADDADI
DESIGN BUREAU

www.jangirmaddadi.se

Rendering Software for Visionaries

v-ray.com

CHAOSGROUP

v·ray

ARTWORKFLOW

artwork by Factory Fifteen

**CREATING LOVE
THROUGH DESIGN**

M&J
MARQUES & JORDY

ART
-Special Art Commissions
-Sculptures
-Paintings
-Curating

DESIGN
-Product Design
-Bespoke Furniture
-Chandeliers & Lamps
-Graphic & Branding

ARCHITECTURE
-Commercial & Retail
-Residential & Hotels
-Masterplanning
-Interior Design

www.marquesandjordy.com

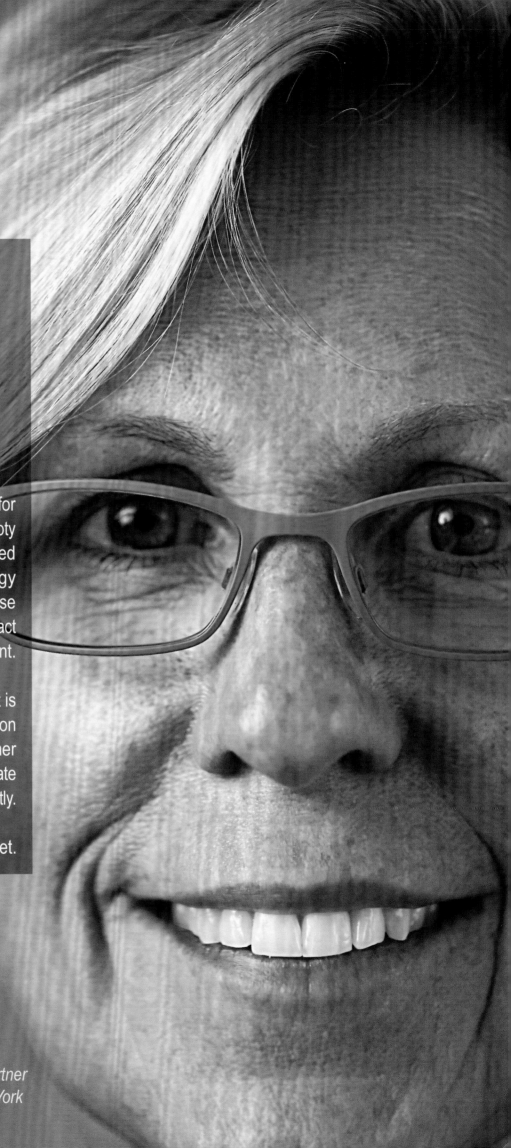

YOUR VISIONS. PERFECTLY REALIZED.

Vectorworks is software that is built for people like award-winning architect Coty Sidnam. People who are committed to employing material and energy resources to their maximum end use and efficiency in order to limit the impact of our built work on the environment.

Sidnam's visions are guided by what is best for the planet, and she relies on Vectorworks software to capture her ideas, develop them, and communicate them … easily, accurately, and efficiently.

Learn more at www.vectorworks.net.

NEMETSCHEK
Vectorworks

Coty Sidnam, AIA, Founding Partner
SPG Architects, New York, New York

CONT

FNTS

CREDITS

EDITOR-IN-CHIEF / CREATIVE DIRECTOR

Carlo Aiello

EDITORS

Paul Aldridge

Noémie Deville

Anna Solt

Jung Su Lee

CONTRIBUTORS

Benjamin Ball

Philip Beesley

Marcos Betanzos

Francesco Brenta

Dongyan Chen

Brandon Clifford

Raffaello D'Andrea

Cristina Díaz Moreno

Efrén García Grinda

Nataly Gattegno

Mark Goulthorpe

Michael Hansmeyer

Alvin Huang

Lisa Iwamoto

Jason Johnson

Alex Kaiser

Christoph Klemmt

Jan Knippers

Andrew Kudless

Magnis Larsson

Ilona Lénrd

Caroline Littlefield

Xiaodu Liu

Iain Maxwell

Wesley Mcgee

Yan Meng

Achim Menges

Andrew Michler

Kristine Mun

Gaston Nogues

Arthur Olson

Kas Oosterhuis

David Pigram

Steffen Reichert

Benjamin Rice

Craig Scott

Rajat Sodhi

Doris Sung

Ming Tang

Geoffrey Thun

Skylar Tibbits

Kathy Velikov

Dihua Yang

GRAPHIC DESIGN

HI (NY) Design

COVER

P_Wall by Andrew Kudless

EVOLO IS PUBLISHED BY:

EVOLO, INC. – LOS ANGELES
6363 Wilshire Blvd. Suite 311
Los Angeles, CA 90048

EVOLO, INC. – NEW YORK
570 West 204 Street, Suite 1B
New York, NY 10034

ADVERTISING
magazine@evolo.us

NEWSSTANDS
Export Press
dir@exportpress.com

DISTRIBUTION + RETAIL SALES
Actar D
orders@actar-d.com

EVOLO 06: DIGITAL AND PARAMETRIC ARCHITECTURE
ISSN: 1946-634X
ISBN: 978-1-938740-06-0
2014

www.evolo.us

eVolo ©2014. All rights reserved.
No part of this publication may be reproduced
in any form by any electronic
or mechanical means without permission
in writing from Evolo, Inc.

Printed in China

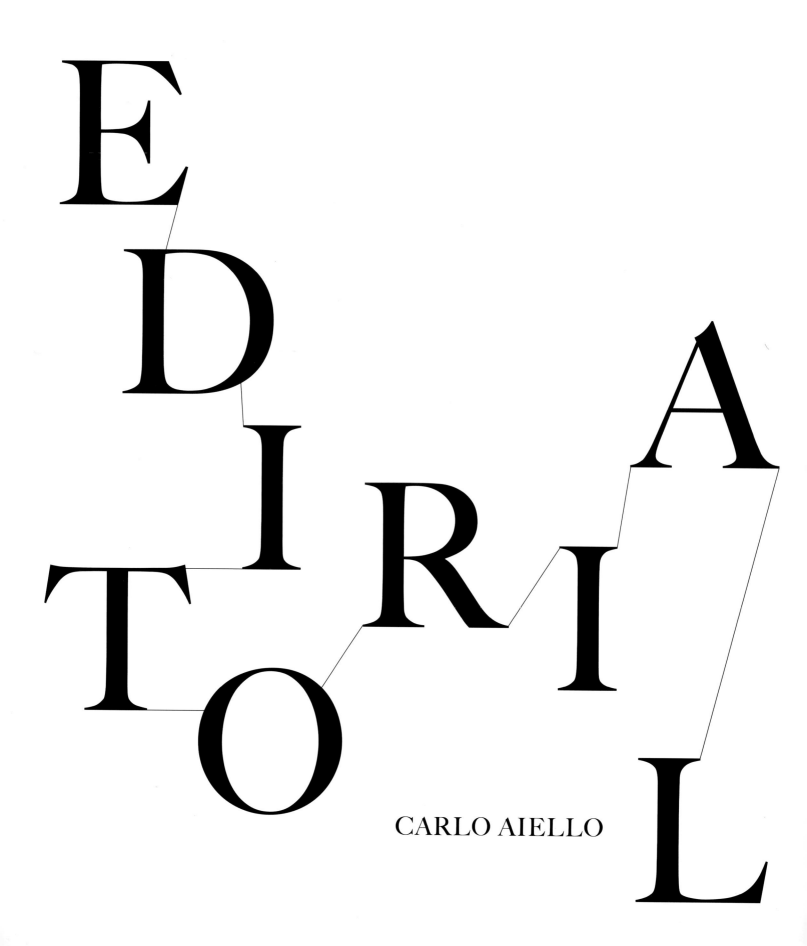

EDITORIAL

CARLO AIELLO

The last twenty years have seen a radical transformation in the designing and making of architecture. Before the1990's, architectural design was developed through analog tools such as freehand sketching, physical model making, drawing on drafting boards, and manual rendering techniques. What started in 1992 at Columbia University as the Paperless Studio, with the use of computers to design, represent, and produce architectural ideas has evolved into the norm today.

Digital and Parametric Architecture explores the development of the latest digital tools including advance-modeling software and computer aided design. It is a journey through the most fascinating projects, digitally designed and fabricated, during the second decade of the 21st century. Some projects use these technologies to analyze tectonic operations such as sectioning, folding, contouring, and tessellating while others explore "climate responsive architectural systems that do not require sensory equipment or motor functions." Another group studies the use of algorithms and computation to generate form where complexity is a result of a simple generative system. Designing algorithms of building processes and the interaction between components and space is the main research of other ideas that seek the possibility of constructing architecture with flying robots, free from the touch of human hands –"conceiving spatial relationships and contextual behaviors through programming." Mathematical analysis is also used to simulate stress driven material growth and organization where "data flows and components are self-organized into design outputs". Many other projects explore other fascinating topics such as kinetic buildings with cellular pneumatic skin, emotional responsive structures, biomimicry, and self-organizing cities.

It is a great time to be an architect! No other period in human history has seen this speed in the advancement of architectural design. With the continuous development of new technologies and its rapid integration into the design fields it is only possible to imagine what the future of our built environment will be in the next few decades. These projects, which vary in scale and location, offer a true insight into our new world.

NEWS

MODERNICA CARRIES ON THE LEGACY OF MID-CENTURY MODERNISM

Carlo Aiello

Southern California is the epicenter of mid-century modernism, a period from 1930 to 1965 characterized by important developments in modern design and architecture. Some of the most relevant figures including John Lautner, A. Quincy Jones, and Richard Neutra, to name a few, made of Los Angeles their home and research lab. The city has always been a place of confluence where ideas are imagined and materialized, from Hollywood movies, to theme parks, to novel design.

Los Angeles has a rich history of experimental design and manufacturing and no other designers represent this period in time like Charles and Ray Eames. The Eameses identified the need for affordable, yet high-quality furniture for the average consumer. Although they designed many objects, their chairs in molded plywood, fiberglass, wire mesh, and cast aluminum have transcended time and are considered masterpieces of modern design.

Modernica is now manufacturing their fiberglass chairs with the original materials and specifications. The story of Modernica is the story of an American company that values first-class affordable furniture entirely produced in the United States. We recently had the opportunity to visit their factory located in downtown Los Angeles where they fabricate all of their products. Modernica started out of the passion of Frank and Jay Novak for mid-century design after purchasing 12,000 discarded Eames fiberglass shell chairs from Century Plastics in 1989 after Herman Miller discounted the line - they also purchased all the original equipment in 2010.

What started as a small operation twenty-five years ago has grown into a very successful company that sells more than 30,000 fiberglass chairs per year, among many other mid-century inspired furniture and lamps. What makes them relevant is their attention to detail in every piece produced. This is possible because their factory operates like a series of European workshops - small teams of five to ten people that specialize in a part of the process. The workshops are distinct families, each with their own schedule, rhythm, and vibe; we refer to them as such because the atmosphere was that of a family reunion.

The first one of these units is a triple-height small building, separated from the main complex, where the Eames fiberglass chairs are produced -there is a sense that something important is happening. The space is divided in two areas; the first one is equipped with the original machines used by Century Plastics, including the preform machine invented by Sol Fingerhut in 1960 for Herman Miller. The second area is where the bases and shock mounts are placed.

4

5

The second and largest workshop is the woodshop where traditional carpenters work along high-end CNC machines to produce iconic design like Hans Wegner's Papa Bear chairs and ottomans. Along with these classics, Modernica also manufactures its own original furniture including the Case Study line. Jay Novak has been awarded a federal design patent for the Alpine Bed of "fluid lines of molded layered wood handcrafted and engineered to last for generations." The third workshop is the upholstery area where skilled workers finish their furniture with the most comfortable and beautiful fine fabrics and leathers.

We highly commend Modernica's ability to continue the legacy of mid-century furniture and make it affordable to the average consumer. Modernica is the story of a successful American company that believes in the quality and people behind American made products. We have teamed up with Modernica to give away one Eames fiberglass chair and one Papa Bear chair to two lucky readers. Please send you comments to magazine@evolo.us to be entered in a raffle.

6

Image captions

01 Chair mold for fiberglass preform machine
02 Hand-crafted refinement of fiberglass shell
03 Original press used by Century Plastics
04 Application of resin to fiberglass shell in press
05 Fiberglass shell in preform machine
06 Pressed fiberglass shell
07 Completed chairs
08 Papa Bear Chair structure
09 Fiberglass chair produced by Modernica. Designed by Charles Eames in 1950
10 Fiberglass rocker chair produced by Modernica. Designed by Charles Eames in 1950. (send your comments to magazine@evolo.us for a chance to win one)
11 Papa Bear Chair produced by Modernica. Designed by Hans Wegner in 1951 (send your comments to magazine@evolo.us for a chance to win one)
12 Case Study Alpine Bed produced by Modernica. Designed by Jay Novak in 2009

NEWS

JANGIR
MADDADI
DESIGN
BUREAU

Head designer Jangir Maddadi, born in Kurdistan and now a Swedish citizen, is fervently prolific in designing cutting-edge furniture for both private and public use. In just a few short years since the establishment of his company in 2008, his collections have been received with great admiration worldwide. He won the Swedish Entrepreneur Award presented by the King of Sweden 2010, and has catered to clients such as the Kennedy Family, US Ambassador to Sweden Matthew Barzun, Unibail-Rodamco (France, Netherlands), Columbia Pictures for their set of Men in Black III, Arlanda Airport in Stockholm, Aruba Airport, and Harrods London.

The Jangir Maddadi Design Bureau began with the birth of the now-classic Union Family, a convention-defying take on the public bench, offering high quality freedom to its users. The array of sizes and materials - fiberglass, leather, teak or concrete are offered in this extraordinarily versatile family of indoor and outdoor public and private seating options.

Following the Union Family came the groundbreaking Compound Collection, a series of four benches whose clear, refined forms are designed to fit together in virtually infinite seating arrangements. With the Compound Collection, the designer creates his own puzzle; the pieces are there for the choosing. Like the Union Family, the Compound Collection is available in a variety of materials, including fiberglass, leather, teak and concrete.

②

③

4

5

After conquering the conventions of public seating, Maddadi set his sights on lighting options. His Droid Lamp, born from his fascination in the future, outer space, and the 1950's Space Race, is so crisp in detail it may has well have been a NASA commission. With LED lighting, double dimmer switches and gel-colored lighting options, the Droid Lamp is a labor of love. Made to last, it is available in black, white and rusted steel.

Maddadi's next collection, the Butler Family arose from one seemingly radical question: What if waste bins were beautiful? The Butler Bin's elegant, sweeping form brings interior design to a whole new level. Composed of a steel skeleton covered by a fiberglass shell, the Butler Bin offers a rare kind of functional perfection. Taking out the trash has never been this elegant. The Butler Bin expanded to the smaller Office Butler, and the Butler Flowerpot, offering clients a well-rounded collection of options.

The largest addition to Maddadi's luxury furniture collection came with the Flight Pot, a piece that can't be missed - literally. Standing at an impressive 165 cm tall with a 155 cm round diameter, the Flight Pot is a giant public planter, perfect for adding substantial greenery to any open space.

Originally a custom design for the Aruba Airport, the inspiration for Flight Pot came from the majestic, streamlined shapes of the casing armor for jet plane engines. The unique curvature of their fiberglass shapes gracefully complements the Jangir Maddadi bench collections. Sculptural and unique, the Flight Pot is a testament to the boundary-breaking forms that Maddadi is known for.

The Swarm Lamp is the latest product by the Jangir Maddadi Design Bureau. Inspired by the transient, organic movements of nature, the Swarm is a fresh take on the traditional pendant lamp.

6

⑦

⑧

Jangir Maddadi developed the Swarm Lamp based on his own visualization of the firefly, nature's brightest organism. While the design itself is aesthetically simple, its conceptual complexities are vast. Maddadi's intent was to create a zoomorphic form whose minimalistic qualities rendered an archetypal organic design, allowing users of the lamp to interpret and experience its shape as they choose.

Giving new meaning to the word enlightened, the genius of the Swarm Lamp lies in its ability to attain a feeling of suspended motion, each lamp tethered in a perfect harmony of light. Playful yet earnest, the bulbs emanate a sensual glow.

Specially rounded, 125 centimeter 60 Watt light bulbs reveal a sculptured pattern of entwined filament that is near-entrancing. Connected to a body of custom-cut oak wood, the Swarm Lamp reveals a distinct Scandinavian quality, and a respect for woodcraft that hearkens back to a simpler, pre-industrial time when the creative process was just as important as the end product.

The Swarm Lamp, like all Jangir Maddadi products, is designed for individual style: The angle of each Swarm can be adjusted to a broad spectrum of positions, and each lamp can be purchased as one, a group of three, or a group of five, giving people the freedom to choose the light in their lives. The Swarm Lamp brings together three simple materials: glass, wood, and metal, and creates a piece so organic that it could have been designed by nature itself.

Ever the perfectionist, Jangir Maddadi's creative momentum is turned at full speed. The next project in development at Jangir Maddadi Design Bureau addresses the technologically connected, fast-paced world in which we live, and offers a forward-thinking design for the needs of the public right now, and for the future.

All Jangir Maddadi Design Bureau products are produced in Sweden and shipped worldwide. Visit www.jangirmaddadi.se for more information.

Image captions

01 Designer Jangir Maddadi
02 Union Bench. Two seater
03 Union Panorma
04 Compound Collection
05 Butler Bin
06 Droid Lamp
07 Droid Lamps
08 Swarm Lamps

NEWS

LUCEPLAN: ONE OF THE BRIGHTEST DESIGN COMPANIES IN THE WORLD

In 1978 a group of three Italian architects, Ricardo Sarfatti, Paolo Rizzatto, and Sandra Severi founded Luceplan, one of the world's most creative lighting companies. The company emerged from its founders experience at Arteluce, Gino Sarfatti's legendary firm specialized in lighting and interior design – an international reference in the 1950's for modern lighting fixtures.

Luceplan has been in the front run of lighting innovation for more than 30 years and their products are regarded as art pieces for the 'public at large', some of them included in the permanent collection of the Museum of Modern Art in New York, MoMA. Since its inception, the company believed in experimentation, research, and quality. Today, Luceplan has a wide range of lighting products from table lamps to floor, wall, and ceiling fixtures conceived by the most celebrated designers and architects of our time such as Francisco Gomez Paz, Ross Lovegrove, and Odile Decq.

For many years, Luceplan has received some of the most recognized awards in the industry. In 2009, Francisco Gomez Paz and Paolo Rizzatto conceived 'Hope', a unique suspension lamp that reinterprets the traditional glass chandelier for the 21st century. The glass pieces are replaced in 'Hope' by thin polycarbonate Fresnel lenses that glitter as thousands shards of light. The celebrated design received the Reddot award, the Good Design Awards, and the Compasso d'Oro award.

In 2012 Luceplan unveiled another innovative design, one perfect for architects and designers, 'Otto Watt'. A desk lamp, created by Alberto Meda and Paolo Rizazatto that allows the user to adjust the light temperature for warm and cold white tones. The lamp's perforated sculptural head decreases the hot surface and swivels 360 degrees for the perfect adjustment. Sleek and elegant, 'Otto Watt' is the prefect companion for relaxation and work.

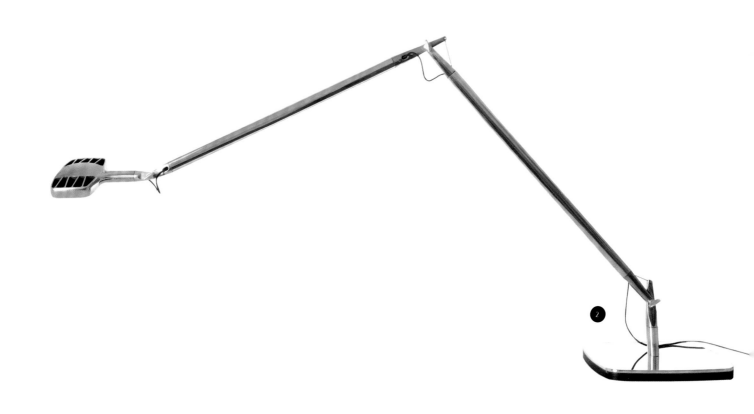

INTERVIEW WITH GIUSEPPE BUTTI, CEO LUCEPLAN USA

Interviewer: Carlo Aiello, eVolo (CA)
Interviewee: Giuseppe Butti, CEO Luceplan USA (GB)
Place: New York, New York. 2013

CA: Could you explain to our readers Luceplan's transformation from a small company at the beginning of the 1980's to one of the industry leaders nowadays?

GB: Well, let's say that the company grew with a strong goal. The goal of designing, producing, and bringing to the market lighting fixtures that provides something new to the consumer. Also having in mind that every single product has to be analyzed in every aspect from its conception to its material research and realization. We have the willingness to not only introduce new ideas, but also new materials.

CA: What are the main differences between the company's past and present?

GB: Our philosophy has always been the same since the three Italian architects created the company in the 80's, to design the best quality and innovative lighting fixtures. Of course today we have more possibilities to research the universe because of the advancement in technologies. As well, the communication is much easier than it was at that time.

CA: Do you think the time between the conception and the materialization of a new product has been shortened because of new technologies.

GB: I would say that the time remains the same. If you look into our entire collection, our portfolio, and you look into our competitors you will see that we don't have a large number of products. The reason behind this is that from the beginning, when a designer comes with an idea, to the time that it hits the market we have a lead time of at least two years; mainly because of the research of new materials, technologies and their possibilities – it really takes more time to create an innovative product. The advantage of this, of course, is that our products last much longer in the market. I have been with this company for thirteen years and every year we only present two or three new products. Only once we presented six, which was an exceptional year.

CA: It is evident that the investment of time has paid off. For example, your 'Hope' lamp has received the most important awards in the industry. 'Hope' is a brilliant idea about using a new material to produce a beloved shimmering effect – a traditional chandelier with a new twist.

CA: How do you start a new project?

FB: We can go in two different directions. The first one, it is our company that knows what we are missing in our portfolio and we talk to our in house designers to start the development of it. The second one, many outside designers approach us with new ideas within the philosophy of Luceplan.

CA: Among your designers there are some of the most celebrated figures in the design world, how do you select one among so many talented individuals?

FB: The main consideration is to see if the designer understands our general philosophy and if he is working in that direction. We like to work with designers from all over the world: Italian, French, Scandinavia, American, etc. At the same time we don't want to go in every direction because we lose focus. It amazes me when I walk through the aisles of design shows and there are companies that try to do everything.

CA: Thank you for your time and for giving away an 'Otto Watt' lamp to a lucky reader. We will be patiently waiting for your new wave of products.

Image captions

01 Hope. Designed by Francisco Gomez Paz, Paolo Rizatto
02 Otto Watt. Designed by Alberto Meda, Paolo Rizatto
03 Otto Watt. Designed by Alberto Meda, Paolo Rizatto
04 Curl. Designed by Sebastian Bergne

GB: This is a clear example of our philosophy. When we met with our CEO, Ricardo Sarfatti we discussed the possibility of designing a chandelier because at the moment we didn't have one. But what we needed is nothing traditional but the Luceplan chandelier, something modern, creative, spontaneous, and exceptional. At the end, after a long work and a lot of investment, the designer came out with the idea of 'Hope'.

CA: What are Luceplan's goals for the 21st century? How do you see the evolution of lighting design?

GB: Well, that is a good question. The most important evolution in the last years has been the light source. You know that in Europe all the incandescent bulbs have been banned from the market and it also going to happen pretty soon in the United States. No one was expecting to something like this to happen so rapidly and most of our new products are based on the new technology. For example, a few years ago the quality and efficiency of LED's was not ready yet to be used in our products, but this has recently changed.

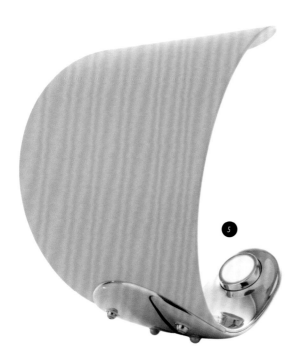

NEWS

THE FOURTH DIMENSION ART: ABOUT SERGEY BAGRAMYAN'S CREATIVE WORK

Sergey Bagramyan, a remarkable painter of today, has managed to create his own, unique and inexhaustible world existing at the turn of Millennium and looking into the future.

His paintings-books, paintings-stories which have no analogues are characterized by a complicated and subtle structure. They are saturated with information and are read like books. Each image representing one and integrate whole is composed of multiple characters, artistic symbols-words.

Sergey Bagramyan's realistic, tangible images are woven from abstract geometrical figures and lines which are beautiful in themselves and create a unique rhythm, a peculiar musical intonation of his paintings in which the micro and macrocosm are organically conjugated. The canvases bear the stamp of decorativeness, ornamentalism, but this ornamentalism is very special, a lot of symbols and meanings are ciphered in it, and in the process of contemplation, they gradually reveal themselves before the spectator. Many ancient symbols live on the master's canvases. The artist often resorts to the images of a turtle, dragon, and fish. The turtle is a symbol of long age and wisdom. The Oriental dragon is a symbol of happiness, power, and kindness, and the fish – of overpowering love.

Laconism and clarity of composition, of artistic expressions allow creating live subjects, which often reveal themselves with dramatic power and persuasiveness.

The canvases are characterized with a soothing, well-balanced color scale usually featuring soft, non-aggressive shades, while the painter's plane-like presentation creates a special lightness of images.

Each of his creations contains a fairy-tale world. All characters, images, and objects are humanized. The distinct character of the images, sometimes raised to the point of grotesque, would have been impossible without the element of caricature, cartoon. There is almost always humor, sometimes even a light irony in the paintings. Each painting has its past, present, and future, it exists in time, talks to you. We as if feel the live sequence of an intriguing animation film.

In his creative work, the painter builds up a new spiritual and everyday-life world of objects, in Malevich's words, realizes "development of the world's new covenant that existed in the past and was going to us, and will go further leaving thousands of years of symbols behind". The artist pays great attention to eternal subjects. The apocalyptic tonality of "The Divinity's Punishment" makes the onlooker think of the higher moral values, the inevitability of responsibility to one's own conscience and the Almighty who is shown sitting with his devoted followers in a heavenly bark – a cloud symbolizing a ship of salvation.

Another manifestation of the human morality subject is the cycle created in 2008 and exposing various vices: envy, greed, pride, wrath, despondence, and gluttony, lust. These vices are presented as repulsive scaly-gray monsters touched with morbid accents of red.

A separate page of Sergey Bagramyan's creative work is the cycle of illustrations to the books of J.R.R. Tolkien, in particular, to his novel "The Lord of the Rings". This cycle of graphical manner reveals the artist's outstanding craftsmanship and, in some respect, has something in common with the stylistics of Renaissance, Albrecht Dürer's prints, and dying Boromir cannot help recalling associations with the typical for the Renaissance epoch motive of Saint Sebastian's death. Only using two-color scale means, the painter brilliantly conveys everything – the movement, a breath of wind, fire, feelings and sensations of his characters, the human soul, body movements, and even the voice.

Having given original interpretation to the best traditions of the world art in his creative work, Sergey Bagramyan has managed to create his own, unique, unlike anything else Universe. He spiritualized this Universe and, like a true creator, gave it an opportunity to live in time on its own, independently from the creator. It is wisdom, humor, and love that reign in his fantastic, fairy-tale world.

2

INTERVIEW
WITH
SERGEY BAGRAMYAN

Interviewer: Carlo Aiello, eVolo (CA)
Interviewee: Sergey Bagramyan (SB)
Place: Los Angeles, California. 2013

CA: What inspired you to become an artist?

SB: I think the environment I grew up in had a lot to do with it… well, and probably the genes I inherited from my father, a famous and very talented artist Alexander Bagramyan. I have been painting as long as I can remember myself. At the age of 1.5 years I was making drawings of people on the walls of our apartment above the plinth, as high as my height would allow me. I also remember my physics and mathematics notebooks in school were full of drawings of dragons, dwarfs and all kinds of imaginary creatures…and what came out of all of that is for the public to judge.

CA: Can you summarize your way of approaching art?

SB: Art reflects life, and my life is art.

CA: What has been the evolution of your art?

SB: Inspiration just comes to me, and the source of that could be different things-people, animals, memories or just a simple desire to portray something that flashes in my consciousness. Those "bright pictures" appear out of nowhere, without a warning, like flashes. It could happen when I am taking a walk through interesting and beautiful streets, I was especially inspired by Prague, which I recently visited, and now I have ideas for new art work. I can also wake up in the middle of the night like I have been stung by a bee and start making sketches, but best time for me to start working is early in the morning with a fresh head. Sometimes I just paint things that worry me, but of course it happens in a format that is true to me, in a form of allegory. Let's just say I would like to portray gluttony, it's unlikely that I will paint a fat man stuffing his face.

CA: What or who do you consider the strongest source of your inspiration when it comes to the ideological meaning of your art?

SB: I think the strongest source of inspiration served the desire to better myself and on a daily basis reach something I was not able to do yesterday through hard work and effort and, of course, the talent given to me by mother nature. I truly think that my desire to know and to learn about the great masters, plain people, nature of human existence, human sufferings and joy, finding things in people or things that others don't see has a lot to do with it. I would summarize all of this by saying that I consider my life the strongest source of inspiration to the ideological meaning of art.

CA: Do you see a relationship between your art and architecture?

SB: Yes, of course. Painting people, animals and other things involves some sort of architecture-architecture of movement, expression of human body. If you mean architecture in specific as it is, I can tell you, that it is quite present in my illustrations of The Lord of the Rings-castles, fortresses, and bridges.

CA: Have you considered doing a series in which architecture plays the main role?

SB: I won't give away all of my secrets, but I can say that I am going to work on a series of artwork where I will use elements from architecture of Prague. How successful that would be, we will see in 2013. I am a big fan of architecture and one way or another it could be found in any painting.

CA: With so many artists moving to the digital realm, what would you say is the future of analog / traditional painting?

SB: I welcome digital technology, I am a big fan and use graphic programs myself, but it is my opinion that digital paintings are better suited for illustrations or for creation of computer games. I do not think that digital paintings will ever push back traditional art and graphics. I personally cannot imagine my art without a canvas or watercolor paper, acryl, ink, etc. It is very important to me to feel and sense the brush or the pencil in my hand, mix the mediums on a palette, feel the thickness or the transparency of the colors which I mix, to penetrate into the texture of the canvas or the watercolor paper.

CA: Have you done any three-dimensional work such as sculpture or an installation?

SB: I used to do interior designs and would also design stages for performers, and back then the knowledge of 3Dimension programs helped me a lot. But later I realized that my passion is art and graphics. I love sculptures, but I have not tried myself in that area. Maybe I should?

CA: Having lived in many different cities how would you describe the main differences in the art scene?

SB: I think that in United States as well as in Europe and Asia there are people who have taste and people who don't, but as they say tastes differ. I agree. Some people prefer portraits, others still life and some others prefer landscape. To me a pink mermaid painted on the background of a blue wave with a palm tree in the back is honestly very tasteless. In Europe they are very careful calling art giclees printed on canvas signed by artists. In United States it is acceptable. Europeans enjoy abstract art and installations. In puritan America art that can be "understood" is very much appreciated, for example western art. Of course, it would be rude and wrong to generalize, but in any case art is different everywhere and it is usually presented with elements of national pride. That's a good thing. I also would like to say that all of the original and amazing will stay; everything mediocre and tasteless won't be around for long…well, at least I would like to believe that.

CA: Can you share with us your other passions, what else do you enjoy?

SB: Quite a lot, and that helps me to create. I enjoy travelling, discovering other cultures for myself. I am very passionate about London, and overall countries of the Old World. I also enjoy the eastern culture; it is impossible to fully comprehend it even if you spend your whole life there. I like to read, I very much enjoy truly good movies. I am a big fan of Federico Fellini. I love and enjoy my son Robert and very much hope that he will grow up a good and a kind man; I will try to help him with that. I adore my wife Lilit who makes me a better person with each day. I love my father and best friend Alexander Bagramyan who has a big input in me becoming an artist. And of course, I love my mother. Without her I would not be born and do what I do now and will continue to do the same as long as I live.

Inquiries: www.asbart.com

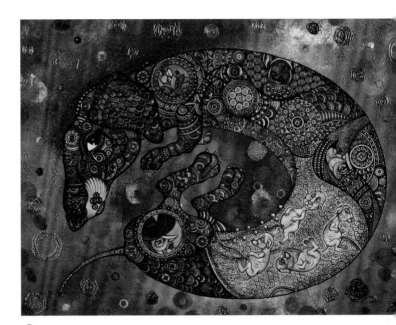

5

Image captions

01   Royal Cat.
02   Three Horn Turtle, Which Swallowed Three Hogs
03   Fear
05   Approaching Democracy
04   Sixty Days

1

NEWS

#BORDOS100 DWELLINGS AS DELATOR: PRETEXT AND DENUNCIATION

Marcos Betanzos   *Translation: José Muñoz-Villers*

*"I am not talking about making ugly houses, what I am saying is:
let's suppose that we build a house that is not only a "happy home"
but that is at the verge of being mysterious, that defines the sublime,
an element that is uncertain, an perhaps that terrifies. Something
that is beyond beauty"* - Peter Eisenman

HYBRID
QUESTIONING

What is a house? Before we have a definite answer according
to our academic background or our personal experiences, it is
important to notice that the formulation of this question evidently
embodies many lines of exploration within its apparent or
simulated simplicity. It is worth to ask a question and try not to
answer it – it is appropriate to analyze every possibility that an
open-ended process of thinking offers, rather than arriving to a
first hand conclusion.

If questioning confirms ignorance it is also true that it ignites
reasoning in multiple trajectories that reveal new information, an
emergence of ideas, which might not be found within the original
question.

What is the role of an architect? What is the purpose of
architects' obsession for a building to be useful, sound, and
beautiful? What is the role of architecture when sometimes it only
seems to be a tool to materialize dictatorial economic and political
desires? What does sustainability mean in this polluted scenario?
Why 90% of what is built worldwide is done without architects?

What is a house? Is it possible to obtain endless answers
through the analysis of the urban configuration of existing cities?
Are there physical and mental frontiers where architecture tests its
own limits, where there is no opportunity to transcend beyond the
discipline, its function, and aesthetic.

Spanish architect Iñaki Ávalos hints to an answer when he
stated that a house could be an instrument of vision and a tool to
critique domestic life in the 21st century. Expanding on this idea,
it is possible to carry on the premise and question architects and
their vision of what should a dwelling be and how it influences the
life of its inhabitants.

Andrés Jaque asserts that a dwelling is not a place to detach
from society but rather a mechanism where we establish links or
ties with it. A dwelling can also be a small and particular territory
where ideological academic meaning confront a particular reality
often ignored. A house is pure ideology, a formal paradigm, a
fantasy, and an entity built by the collective imagination. For the
architect a house could be an experimental laboratory, but for
society it is a delator.

How could architects formulate answers to a community
they don't belong to? Perhaps the only vehicle is through pure
speculation inherent in a design process that feels noxious and
asymptomatic.

PARALLEL READINGS
ON A FAILED PROJECT

Based on the idea of questioning and to formulate a critique
on the architectural production processes and their creators,
the #BORDOS100 project takes shape; a reinterpretation of
a project proposed by Ai Weiwei and Herzog & de Meuron
in Inner Mongolia: Ordos 100. #BORDOS100 is a research
about lifestyles and living conditions deployed through different
techniques of space appropriation, its domain and accumulation

of objects all take place inside a garbage dump in Netzahualcóyotl City – a few miles east of Mexico City. A photographic essay recorded the architecture of one-hundred houses (out of five-hundred houses) located on the site and analyzed the ways in which objects, discarded by the inhabitants of Mexico City, configure and build an informal and clandestine city apparently invisible to the general population and government.

The new City of Bordos is an imaginary settlement, a society that knows how to reuse instead of consume; it is a city with an architecture that moves away from traditional architectural thinking through sheds without attributes, and simple and generous envelopes that demonstrate programmatic improvisation and heterogeneous materiality.

#BORDOS100 reveals that recycling waste owns an aesthetics that can be perverse or sophisticated within an urban landscape that is chaotic and decadent, where aspiration to intimacy vanishes among city fragments: doors, windows, water tanks, tires, cars, shoes, bottles, etc. Paul Auster's words open the door to the valorization of the recycled matter that produce this new inhabitable spaces: "things themselves, like utensils of an ancient civilization, do not mean anything; however, they tell us something, they still remain but not like simple objects, but rather, like vestiges of thought, awareness; emblems of solitude."

Mirroring the work process in Ordos, a fictitious character named Ay Güeywei invited 40 Mexican architectural offices to participate in a project to design a house inside the garbage dump, a game of speculation and possibilities - an invitation to see different ways of living while confronting a conventional architectural practice.

Convinced that garbage would be the only archaeological trace of our future; those who participated were asked if it would be easier and equally attractive to design a house in a garbage dump, more precisely in a place known for the public realm (City of Bordos) to be as remote and with the same lack of infrastructure and identity as Ordos. Thirty offices accepted the invitation but only nineteen delivered a proposal. Among the invited offices four offices specialized in sustainability – none presented a project.

From the firms that also participated in the Ordos City Project, just one delivered a project: Taller Territorial de Mexico (Arturo Ortiz Struck in collaboration with Alba Carbonell).

The proposals go beyond a showcase of attractive ideas; further than designing a house out of garbage. What achieved is a collection of arguments and discourses that provokes a revision of different scenarios and territories where architects feel more comfortable working in, a clear and direct confrontation against snobbism where is more relevant to define the limits of the architectural profession rather than strengthening the idea that the discipline can transform reality.

With a powerful dose of irony, #BORDOS100 makes clear that the uncommon polarizes the space; that the reinterpretation of social events can enrich the architectural practice once the role of the architect, as a dictator, is put aside. That the city can be understood as a cluster of objects to consume and willing to be appropriated by external agents that inject new codes of beauty. It is clear that just as Asger Jörn stated, "dirt is a component of reality and its existence cannot be disguised by the obsession for cleaning."

7

8

9

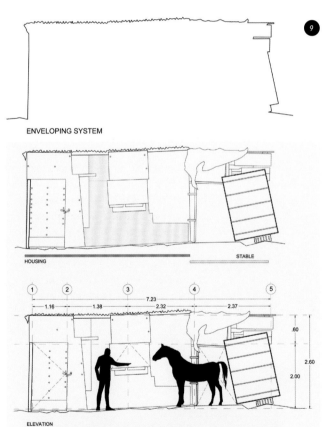

ENVELOPING SYSTEM

HOUSING   STABLE

① ② ③ ④ ⑤

1.16   1.38   7.23   2.32   2.37

.60

2.60

2.00

ELEVATION

#BORDOS100 is not about issuing immediate judgments on the paradoxical, contradictory, and hesitant attitude of the architectural practice; it is about producing enough energy to motivate reflection that goes beyond the conception of a project, positioning us in a more adequate place to question if it is possible to disrupt not only our production systems but also our systems of thought. The irony remains open and constitutes the last opportunity before enclosing ourselves into cynicism.

It is now worth asking, at which point a house stops being a house? When the roof falls down? When the windows are removed? When the walls crumble? When it becomes a pile of rubble? A house is a manifestation of life that establishes a negotiation with space, an approach to different realities, a platform or observatory to reveal the work of anthropologists that architects have rejected. It is an excuse to demonstrate how shallow and ridiculous can be to select 100 world architects to design houses, homes in a place where neither users nor inhabitants exist.

@MBetanzos #BORDOS100

Biography

Marcos Betanzos (Mexico City, 1983) architect by the Escuela Superior de Ingeniería y Arquitectura del Instituto Politécnico Nacional, photographer and writer, member of the Editorial Board of Domus Magazine Mexico, Central America and the Caribbean, fellow of the National Fund for Culture and Arts, faculty at the School of Architecture at UNAM and ITESM.

Image captions

01 A facade of green architecture.
02 The life inside the City of Bordos.
03 A chair inside a house, the domestic.
04 Open air kitchen.
05 Dropping a system (represented by a house). Ink on paper.
06 Human waste.
07 The difference.
08 Frame from short film #BORDOS100 directed by Marcos Betanzos.
09 Study Casa (House No. 100). Ink on paper.
10 Clase A (Bordos) by Victor Betanzos and Guillermo González.
11 House with stable by Eduardo Audirac
12 Circular house by Sindy Martínez and Erik Carranza
13 #BORDOS100 by Taller 5

NEWS

THE ECO BOULEVARD IMPASSE: THE FAILED CONTEMPORARY ARCHITECTURE OF POVERTY

Andrew Michler

Spain's embrace of new architecture is legendary and distinctive. Coupled with a constitutional right for housing, inflated housing market and a privatized system (1) the social housing design movement flourished. It seems most architecture practices have one or two vivid public housing projects in their portfolio, for some their first large commission. This makes for a remarkable laboratory for the architecture of poverty which has been a perplexing problem for generations. Each new eager age of architects formulates a blueprint to encode ethics and function to serve the traditionally underserved communities through the built environment. This is the promise of Eco Boulevard, a development started in 2004 and still under construction on the fringes of Madrid, Spain. It is a signal of intention that creating alluring public places and environmentally minded building topographies will be the core to revitalizing a community. As a response to the chaotic and claustrophobic development trends of the area that went unchecked for a couple of decades it joins a significant list of new bespoke public housing projects to bookend the vast, faceless apartment blocks of greater Madrid.

Madrid's growth is in the form of the classic concentric rings, clearly punctuated by the highways looping around the city's ancient core. A speculative housing boom crammed characterless projects along the outer edges of the city, pressing into the raw plains. The old neighborhood of Vallecas is one of the many quickly metastasized but poorly planned blue collar communities which shares an industrialized area on Madrid's southern edge. While maintaining a high density, typical of Spanish heritage, the community lacks both a center and green space for its residents. This stands as counterpoint to Madrid as a city renowned for its outdoor lifestyle, where the sidewalks become living rooms and dining rooms for the wealthy and poor alike. The proposal of the Eco Boulevard in the mid 2000's was a great leap by Vallecas and Madrid's Municipal Housing Corporation, with euro backing of EU's LIFE program. An open competition resulted in a dramatic and environmentally sophisticated proposal by the then unknown firm Ecosistema Urbano Arquitectos.

Perhaps taking a cue from the many roundabouts of the city or echoing the industrial nature of the community the design is anchored with three substantial tank shaped pavilions dubbed Air Trees which buttress a nascent forested open space. Trees, playgrounds, common areas, and even a community media space embedded in one of the Air Trees adds to the ideals of the social engagement of design. The 550 meter long Boulevard de la Naturaleza is ringed with an assortment of contemporary architectural urban housing schemes. Each one is a pronounced and colorful observation on new residential program with Olalquiga Arquitecto's recently completed white shuttered Social Housing tucked in the northwest corner.

While the park's trees grow, the immediate need for a cool public space led to the thought of creating the artificial 'trees' ringed in elevated plants and showering fresh, naturally conditioned air from above using the solar panels crowning the towers. A diagrid skeleton supports a three story tall atrium but each Air Tree uses a differing technique based on the evapotranspiration of plants to achieve a pool of temperate space. The silver skinned version is equipped with sensor triggered fans that push the air downwards through the vegetation and into the base. Rubberized floors made from recycled tires line the surroundings, encouraging play and relaxation. A dramatic motif of steel, vegetation and solar panels encompass the view to the sky from within, becoming a natural place of congregation.

4

5

The project's intent is to reintroduce a dense forest into the urban fabric. Vast stretches of hardscape makes the city a sponge of excess solar heat in the summer, pushing the residents indoors and turning the typical residential towers into brick ovens, reliant on the graces of air conditioning to keep them habitable. Eventually, after the planted trees mature, the Air Trees can be uprooted to a new location, starting the green urbanization growth process once again. Hailed as elegant urban planning which covers all the needs of a 21st century population the project has instead been a sobering failure.

6

7

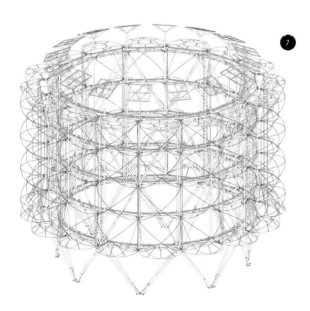

I spend only five days in Madrid, most of them were on my feet, walking from impoverished but bustling neighborhoods to the core of the capital infused with the life and culture that makes Madrid a magnet for the young and cosmopolitan. Indeed Madrid is a city for walking, where social hubs and eateries lace the thoroughfares and neighborhoods everywhere. Eager to explore the concept of the Eco Boulevard first hand as I am researching for a book on the great successes of environmental architecture, one of the architects I visit states that that the space is essentially deserted. With this forewarning I approach the site tepidly, not able to reconcile the glowing narrative from websites and the bleaker first hand depiction of it.

The Eco Boulevard is in fact an island, disconnected from the throbbing city beyond the M-40 circular highway. It breaks from the metrodome of the vast Madrid grid, losing pace with the city's bustling streets punctuated by double parked cars, winding scooters, round-a-bouts and subway stations. Cut off by the highway to the north, broken promises of skeletal developments to the west, and the high central Spanish plains to the south the Eco Boulevard has no place to go. Created to discourage the use of cars along the plaza the master plan is also lacking any direct route, meaning one would need to go out of one's way to find it. That loss of spontaneous connection runs counter to the vast linkages that Madrid offers its citizens.

Among the dozen cinder block walled retail spaces I find a single bar that would struggle to cater to more than a handful of patrons at any one time. Perhaps the buildings are actually vacant, as a couple are still being built? After all, Spain's housing glut is well-known as further south the landscape is festooned with empty buildings, vividly displayed in an episode of Top Gear racing in an abandoned airport and town center (2). In fact there are signs of life here, a dog poking his head out an apartment window and a smoker hovering near another, a family crossing the boulevard to their car, and a mother taking her baby in a stroller through the gated entrance of a complex. Her home is a pixilated and corrugated steel wrapped series of low slung apartments with open public spaces inserted in the center and bottom. The weed infested community space on the ground level was intended to be fully porous, but now is layered in severe rebar fencing, cinder block walls, and security doors. The democratic design intent subverted by security. Olalquiga Arquitecto has learned this lesson and their work faces inwards instead, towards a gated court. The transformation is chilling.

From above the development is a brilliant architectural treasure trove, vivid in color, geometry and material. From the street the space is a human desert, devoid of retail, traffic, or play. The design looks fun, but like an empty boardwalk without people it is asleep, or as Tom Waits would sing, it is "a town with no cheer".

11

12

In Madrid graffiti is found everywhere, but a closer look shows a deeper pattern of neglect here. The LED illuminated sign wrapping the first Air Tree is now a nonsensical string of red dots and the health of the suspended plants is debatable. The rubberized matt is coming out in large chucks. Fencing and cinderblocks barricade the surrounding buildings. Acting as a gilded green enclosure for the impoverished the development has quickly transformed from an open and walkable topography to one where each building acts as a small island crossed by a treed mote. The lack of even a bus stop, grocery, or restaurant confounds the isolation. Intended to literally bring fresh air to a community the space lacks the oxygen of commerce, services and connections, and being devoid of people on the street individuals become more vulnerable. This is the death of a place in a nation that famously embraces life starting at the front entrance.

Many quiet successes of social housing dot reclaimed urban landscapes but the failures are historically notable edifices that become social gashes in the host cities, eventually torn down from their platitudes of social equanimity. Others stand zombie like, surrounded by, but not a part of thriving communities. Certainly we have learned from the past and will not repeat the mistakes of creating enormous generic and dehumanizing apartment blocks.

We will inspire residents to feel like they belong to a community. The ethics of environmental design will be front and center. The new formulations of contemporary architecture will be democratically embraced and invested in to bring a sense of visual stimulation and engaging program to the people. But that is clearly insufficient.

The account of the Eco Boulevard cannot escape the conclusion that design does not necessarily solve deep fissures in the social-economic fabric and the resulting impoverishment. It is a budding community cut off from the nourishment of the city and already is in decay. While being a part of the much larger demographic osculation during Spain's painful economic recession the lack of diversity in social outlay, not design investment is laid bare.

Perhaps another hint is found in the most famous of failed urban housing projects, St Louis's Pruitt-Igoe, which was first occupied exactly 50 years before the Eco Boulevard came into being. Popularly thought to be emblematic of bad architecture, where centralized and overly dense design embedded plight among its inhabitants, the documentary The Pruitt-Igoe Myth makes a less conspicuous argument. Resources, not design, the film argues are what helped lead to the downfall of the great social public housing experiment. By not having an investment plan in the upkeep of the buildings the evolving decay multiplied the crushing burden of poverty. While many other social factors are involved the argument is clear, taking care of something is as valuable as its design intent. The translation to the Eco Boulevard is that physical entropy breeds communal entropy, and discourages new ventures. Here, the complexity of the design hastens its failure. All the while just down the street the older neighborhood grows restless and life picks up again.

(1) Recent changes in Spanish housing policies: subsidized owner-occupancy dwellings as a new tenure sector? Joris Hoekstra, Iñaki Heras Saizarbitoria, Aitziber Etxezarreta Etxarri, 2009 http://link.springer.com/article/10.1007%2Fs10901-009-9169-6
(2) Top Gear Season 20, Episiode 3, July 14, 2013

15

Biography

Andrew Michler is a sustainable building consultant and writer. His work focuses on low impact materiality, emerging environmental architecture, and Passive House design and construction. He is writing the book [ours] The Hyperlocalization of Architecture due out in late 2014 and published by eVolo.

16

Image captions

01 Boulevard de la Naturaleza
02 Fencing of community space of public housing
03 Social housing unit with retail
04 Air Tree detail by Urbano Arquitectos
05 Air Tree with scrolling LED by Urbano Arquitectos
06 Public housing courtyard
07 Air Tree diagram by Urbano Arquitectos
08 Air Tree by Urbano Arquitectos
09 Air Tree swings by Urbano Arquitectos
10 Boulevard de la Naturaleza
11 Air Tree by Urbano Arquitectos
12 Eco Boulevard urban forest
13 Air Tree by Urbano Arquitectos
14 Eco Boulevard skyline
15 Social housing by Olalquiga Arquitectos
16 Air Tree detail

NEWS

DAVID TRUBRIDGE: NATURE-INSPIRED DESIGN

The story of New Zealand-based designer David Trubridge is that of a man discovering, experimenting, and understanding nature. David's professional journey is linked to his ongoing relationship with the landscape as a source of energy and inspiration.

Trained as a naval architect in England, David Trubridge began his career as what he describes a "craftsman-designer-maker" submerged in the study of materials properties and capabilities. His first furniture designs borrowed from the admiration of artists like Brancusi and the Art Noveau movement – a period in his career of interpretation and translation rather than experimentation.

In 1981 David set sail around the world to finally settle in 1985 in the Bay of Islands, New Zealand. The five-year experience transformed his vision as a designer; he started to focus on the concept and process behind a product rather than the final outcome. This is the story of one of his most celebrated designs, Body Raft, which borrowed from his nautical background. The rocking chaise lounge fabricated in steam-bent American ash and Australian Hoop Pine plywood was exhibited in 2001 in Milan, Italy becoming an instant success among the media and critics. Italian design powerhouse, Cappellini, licensed and began manufacturing the design, which put Trubridge on top of the international design scene.

David Trubridge's second big success, and probably his best-known design, is the Coral – a light fixture conceived in 2003 based on his underwater experiences and the analysis of the geometric patterns of coral. This is a unit-based design that studies the clustering possibilities of a polyhedron. The lamp is the result of combining multiple CNC-cut bamboo plywood five-pointed stars assembled by the end customer with nylon clips. Being able to ship a flat package and reduce the carbon footprint

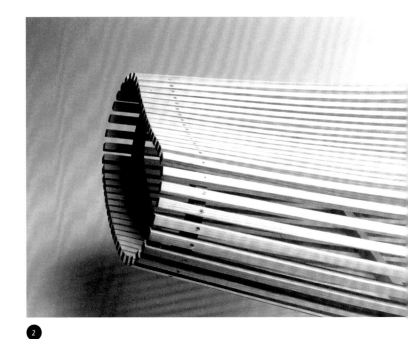

2

of all his designs is one of Trubridge's main goals and what he describes as Seed System – "why fill a truck with one tree, when the cost to the Earth is reduced by packing in boxes of seed?"

Following his success, Trubridge was selected for the Antarctica Arts Fellowship program that enabled him to continue his understanding of nature and in 2007 he was the recipient of a Green Leaf Award presented by the Natural World Art Museum for engaging the public in environmental awareness through his designs. Today, David's pieces have been exhibited worldwide and are part of the permanent collection of museums including the Victoria and Albert Museum in London, the Pompidou Centre in Paris, and the Minneapolis Design Museum.

We have teamed up with David Trubridge and his United States distributor wakaNINE to give away one Coral Light to a lucky reader. Please send your comments to magazine@evolo.us to be entered into a raffle.

3

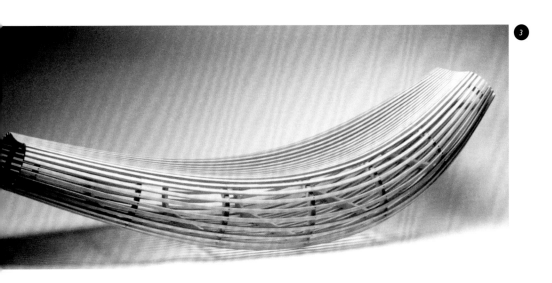

INTERVIEW WITH DAVID TRUBRIDGE

Interviewer: Carlo Aiello, eVolo (CA)
Interviewee: David Trubridge (DT)
Place: Los Angeles, California. 2014

CA: Could you describe your creative process?

DT: I am often asked if I am an artist, designer or craftsman. I am all of these and this is the key to my creative process. I believe that each of these is a process not an object or a profession; and crucially they are each only part of one creative process. We need to work through all these, through the full creative process, to create successful work. So first as an artist I find my spiritual core, that place where my inspiration lies, which for me is the landscape. There I find my voice to speak with, and the vocabulary with which to express myself. If I do not do this then I will have nothing to say, nothing with which to design and my work will be derivative. Then as a designer I compose these into a resolved form, and finally it is made through craft processes. It is only because I have practiced as a craftsman that I can design, because you cannot design what you cannot make - a designer has to have a knowledge and understanding of materials and their limitations.

CA: Your designs heavily borrow from your personal experiences. What tickles you at the moment? Where are your designs headed?

DT: Right now I am fascinated by traditional boats. I have just made a coracle in a contemporary style - it is actually the very first boat that I have designed! I also have other craft on my 'drawing board', which I hope to make. Maybe we will offer these as kit set for the home handy man to make. What interests me about traditional boats is their innate beauty, which defies cultural differences. Probably only we call them beautiful - to the makers they are just the way you build. Aesthetics is not, to them, some rarified and separate philosophy but simply a tool with which to create the perfect form. I see a paradigm here for all aspects of design today. Instead of building ugly forms, which are thrust against the waves by the power of fossil fuels, we can create more beautiful and caring forms that work with Nature, and hence have a future.

CA: What aspects of design terrify you?

DT: The profligate waste of materials and energy in a rampant consumer culture. We are caught in this trap of being sold (often forceably, as in designed obsolescence) more and more stuff, not because we need it, but because they need to sell it ('they' being the miners, the oil companies, the bankers, the manufacturers, the designers, the shippers, the shopkeepers, the advertisers, etc., even the economy we are told!).

CA: We are immersed in a use and dispose culture. How do we change this through design? Are products designed to last a lifetime still relevant?

DT: I think they are really important, but sadly it is not in the interests of consumer culture to encourage them. They will only become more relevant if more people stand up and demand them. Hopefully this will happen as we become more aware of the adverse affects of consumerism, of the pollution on our doorstep, of the exploitation of poor peoples, of global warming, etc. In the meantime responsible designers will do all they can to promote them, and to design with a classic timeless look.

CA: What would your number one piece of advice be to young designers?

DT: Ignore everyone else - be aware of what is going on, but then forget it. Don't try to follow or to fit in with what the market is doing. There is only one of you and your uniqueness is your greatest asset. Speak from your heart, retain your integrity and your work will by default be original and exciting to a discerning audience.

DEPTH

DONGYANG CHEN

the potential of digital architecture

3D
PRINT
CANAL
HOUSE

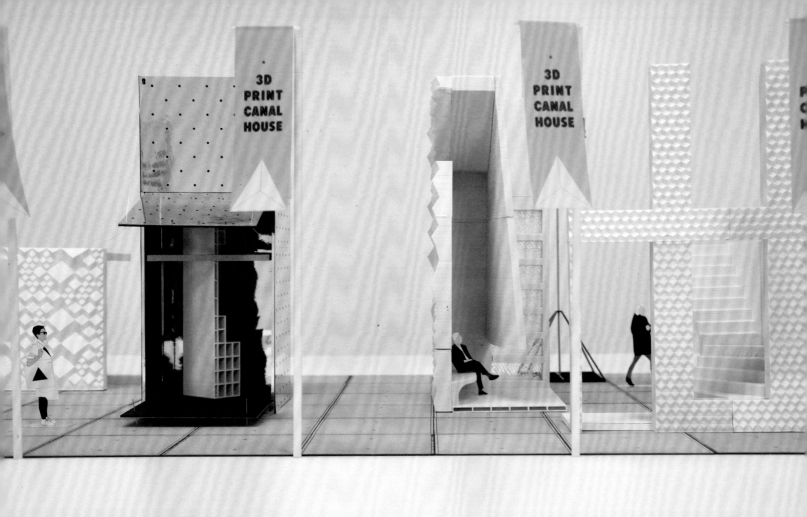

THE POTENTIAL OF DIGITAL ARCHITECTURE

DONGYANG CHEN

Every so often, our world encounters a relentless and unstoppable force that changes everything in every industry, overturning the old and replacing it with innovation. Such were the effects of the Industrial Revolution and are that of Digital Revolution. The Industrial Revolution brought about a radical paradigm shift in manufacturing. The waves set in motion by this new manufacturing process knew no bounds and revolutionized everything from textiles to architecture. Two hundred years later, we are very much in a hurricane of innovation, the Digital Revolution. Much like its predecessor, the widespread effects have altered the very nature of every field and industry across the globe. However, such a complete overhaul of the system does not happen overnight but instead takes significant time to be fully integrated into the design process. The field of architecture has been treading on the road to a complete Digital Revolution since the early days of 2D Computer-Aided-Design (CAD). Primitive CAD systems took advantage of computerized capabilities for precision and repetition to give designer a non-linear, greater consistency, and overall faster turnaround times while allowing multiple copies to be generated, at any stage of the process, with relative ease. However, 2D CAD was fundamentally just a port of the old drafting process to a new technology – an undeniable improvement but at its core, an evolution, not a true revolution. Today, the current generation of CAD programs bridge the gap between 2D CAD and the full potential of electronic computing. The raw calculation power of silicon chips is capable of depicting and representing digital space far more accurately than most people can, thus removing the obstacle of conceptualizing 3D architecture from 2D drawings. This is not just a pathway to more efficient workflow but a whole new way of approaching design. With 3D CAD, the world of design is able to use tools such as CNC, 3D printing, parametric and digital active systems to reimagine the design process.

One of the first applications of 3D CAD was rapid prototyping, especially in the form of Computer Numeric Control (CNC). As early as the 1940s, well before the utilization of CAD, Numeric Control machines existed and were programmed via punch card and later, magnetic tapes. In the 1970s, CAD and CNC were combined to give designers and engineers the rare opportunity to see their concepts materialized at incredible speeds to the prior manufacturing process. This allowed them to physically visualize and understand each components' interactions and operation much earlier. CNC uses a subtractive process in which a tool head mills away at a block of material until the result is the desired objects. The CNC process requires the original material block to be placed on a milling platform where the tooling assembly is attached, which moves on the 3 principal axes. The material block must fit on the milling platform, which is limited to approximately 9 feet and therefore unfeasible for large-scale buildings or structural members. Even though the newer tooling heads can tilt and swivel on auxiliary axes, they are still restricted from accessing material from below. Due to these limitations, architectural usage of CNC is mostly in 3D scaled models, parts assembly, and construction of design elements. Morphosis, a cutting-edge 3D CAD design firms, used CNC mills to produce highly precise and detailed physical models of its Phare Tower project in Paris, France, to be completed in 2017. CNC mills were used to produce the model to accurately curvilinear façade of the building. Beyond scale models, CNC also has applications in real world architecture. Many beautiful design pieces incorporate subtle curves and planes that only CNC can create. Firms such as Min|Day are using CNC machines to fabricate a computer-generated surface of water ripples on a massive wood cabinet that doubles as a headboard. Applications of CNC milling will always evolve, just like the computer and CAD itself. Firms have already taken steps to overcome the material block's size limitations. For instance, Danish architects Entileen have pushed the envelope of CNC milling capabilities by utilizing modular construction. Wood panels, fabricated with a CNC mill, were "snapped" together to form a complete house at low cost, without heavy construction equipment and without the need for a concrete foundation. Another form of rapid prototyping that is gaining popularity is 3D printing. Unlike the subtractive process of CNC milling, 3D printing uses an additive process of layering materials to achieve the final result. While newer than CNC milling, it is showing advantages already. The material etched away in CNC is wasted, whereas the additive process of 3D printing is more resource-conscious. Also, with new and improved materials and milling heads that can utilize multiple materials, 3D printers are capable of more intricate details in less time. 3D printing is also capable of quickly building structures that are inefficient with CNC milling. For example, a concave dome-like structure is difficult to do with CNC, since it cannot directly mill at that location, it must mill thin layers of the material to be stacked together. 3D printing, on the other hand, incorporates the layering step as part of the process, using support material to hold up the cavity, which can be removed when the print is done. Despite these obvious advantages to CNC, 3D printing does have its drawbacks. For one, 3D printers cannot just use any material the designer chooses; in fact, it is the other way around. Each print only allows certain materials to be use; mostly plastic so printing metal is out of the question at the moment. Therefore, materials are not very load-capable and may not satisfy the qualities specified, even during the prototyping stage. Due to the young age of 3D printing technology, it is mostly used in the model making process. Of course, strides are being made in allowing 3D printers to print other materials, such as concrete. One firm, Shiro Studio, has created a 3m x 3m x 3m prototype model of the Radiolaria pavilion using D-Shape's 3D stereolithic printer. The stereolithic printer produces 5 to 10 mm layers of a material that has similar characteristics to Portland cement and allows primary and support materials to be printed at the same time. This combination of materials allows printing of complex shapes that monolithic printers and CNC cannot replicate. Another concept, KamerMaker, from the Dutch firm DUS Architects proposes using a new 3D printer that can spray a variety of materials ranging from concrete to recycled plastic. The printer will be able to make rooms up to 11 feet high and 7 feet wide using only 3D printing. The idea is to create emergency relief shelters for first response units. Overall, it is easy to see the apparent benefit to these rapid prototyping technologies. Digitally enabled architecture offers fast reproduction, a high degree of precision, sustainable design, and a new design process that is unlike anything before. Its potential can lead to anything from economic housing to the extreme environments of outer space.

Digital architecture revolution has not limited itself only to the construction aspect. In fact, it has become an integral way to design for those process the embrace this new technology. One of the key advances in CAD is the move into 3D design from pure 2D drafting. There for if 3D is realizing more potential of CAD, what can realize more potential of 3D design? Parametric processes that inform design are the leading edge of what computers, using it immense computational power, can do with 3D modeling and intense data. The term parametric design is somewhat elusive since it does not restrict itself to one single style or design system. At its core, parametric design uses large sets of data with detailed constraints and algorithms to precisely and quickly automate user-defined tasks, thus generating a design. The result of process could lend itself to being generative, computation, associative and many others. Currently, products of parametric designs are trending, with striking forms and appealing spaces. Firms like Gehry Partners took initiative in parametric design process and are having great success. The ionic Walt Disney Concert Hall is just one of many parametrically designed architecture produced by Gehry. The unique qualities of parametric design are one that crosses cultures and tastes. Architecture such as the Disney Concert Hall can be appreciated by architects and their peers for the amazing marvel of design and process while non-architects can simply enjoy it for its beautiful aesthetics and curves. Of course, parametric design is not without limitation. More and more architects have trended towards generative process, rapidly producing multiple variations of a design. The issue with that and parametric design in general is the resultant form is often felt to exhibit a lack of control. Conditions of the architecture appear to have "happened" rather than been designed. The some of the precise spatial qualities of yesteryear's architecture seem to have disappeared. Perhaps this is just reluctance to move on - or maybe it is much more fundamental. At what point does architecture cease to be an artist's own conception of space and become a technical result of a computing algorithm? The aspects of computer are not only in play at the design level but the post-design status of architecture as well. With the widespread development and popularization of software and digital components, it is now easier than ever to write and incorporate comprehensive active systems that change and adapt a building to its conditions. One exemplar of an active system being integral to the design language is the Institut du Monde Arabe, the Arab World Institute in Paris. The building's south façade is covered by a very sophisticated brise soleil system of photosensitive sensors which control the amount of light and heat gained by the space by opening and closing aperture blades that reside in the voids of the façade. This results in a flickering effect in the interior when these apertures close and open during the course of the day, reminiscent of that in Islamic architecture. This complete integration of mechanized systems that adapt and change according to solar sensitivity is only feasible with the incorporation of digital photosensitive motors. Therefore, the driving force behind the façade is literally the device that communicates the design dialogue. Systems like this and many others have a place in the world as architecture becomes integrated with digital components. Buildings embedded with sensors can adapt and repurpose themselves as conditions vary. As one of the key issues in today's world, the conservation of resources in on everyone's mind, and with smart design and systems, resources can be more thoughtfully planned during design and managed in operation.

3D systems are the next step for specialized computing. The limitations of 2D drafting are no longer present, as space can be conceptualized not only in the mind also visually through CAD. In fact, this new generation of 3D modeling brings a whole question as to what is limiting factor to architecture, what is the barrier, or obstacle causing resistance to create from concept to reality. It is no longer the difficulty of communicating 3D space on 2D drawings, but rather something more fundamental. Perhaps the only factor inhibiting architects from manifesting the designs within their minds is reality itself. This is where the concept of a truly digital architecture can liberate our ideas: architecture that is designed digitally for the digital space and digitally experience. The dreams of architects and people could be fulfilled where they would not or could not be otherwise. Spaces can be exponentially more intricate and delicate. Such a setting would not only exist to satisfy the perfectionist or extravagant desires of a designer but to offer real purpose as well. Building typologies could be used to group and layer for increase efficiency. For example, if there is an office building situated at the corner of two streets, it can only hold a finite amount of occupants in reality. What if this exact building also exists in digital space, where the limitation of the physical reality is no longer present? The concept of only two, three, any number of objccts occupying the same plot of space is not only possible but encouraged. Now, this building is not just a building but also a typology entirely, where people can come to work. These kinds of super buildings offer the efficiency that no counterpart in physical world can. And without the limitations of the physical, the possibilities are limitless.

Architecture as a field has made tremendous progress. Much like the days of the Industrial Revolution, new digital methods and process are always presented to complement the existing system. There will always be room for hand sketches even in the world of digital 3D modeling. It's only the tasks that can be done with greater efficiency and accuracy with the new system that are reinvented. The results are increased efficiency, lower cost, and greater sustainability. In this world of the on-going Digital Revolution, architecture and every other field is finding new uses and better uses for the digital to compliment and aid the existing systems. Digital fabrication, design and operation have been incorporated into architecture and with great success, and with each step further on the march of progress, we are using more and more of the full potential that our powerful computing systems have to offer. Prototype modeling is no longer taking measurements from 2D drawings but rather printing or milling the physical object direct from digital space. CAD is not just a computerized version of the 2D drafting but a completely new system of designing, and perhaps even automating, complete forms in 3D space. The progress made is monumental, but the journey is not over. The Digital Revolution will continue to enhance and guide architecture into the future and the possibilities are truly limitless.

PAGE 41
———
PAGE 42 + PAGE 43
———
PAGE 44
———

1 PHARE TOWER BY MORPHOSIS ARCHITECTS
2 DIGITALLY FABRICATED VILLA ASSERBO BY EENTILEEN ARCHITECTS
3 3D PRINT CANAL HOUSE BY DUS ARCHITECTS
4 CNC HEADBOARD BY MIN|DAY ARCHITECTS
5 DIGITALLY FABRICATED VILLA ASSERBO BY EENTILEEN ARCHITECTS
6 3D PRINT CANAL HOUSE BY DUS ARCHITECTS, STUDY MODELS
7 KAMERMAKER LARGE SCALE 3D PRINTER BY DUS ARCHITECTS, EXTERIOR
8 3D PRINT CANAL HOUSE BY DUS ARCHITECTS, STUDY MODELS
9 KAMERMAKER LARGE SCALE 3D PRINTER BY DUS ARCHITECTS, INTERIOR

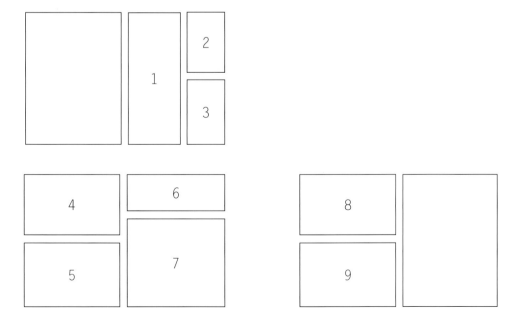

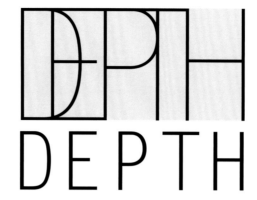

DEPTH

STEFFEN REICHERT

ACHIM MENGES

JAN KNIPPERS

hygroscope: meteorosensitive morphology

icd/itke research pavilion

HYGROSCOPE: METEOROSENSITIVE MORPHOLOGY

ACHIM MENGES IN COLLABORATION WITH STEFFEN REICHERT, CENTRE POMPIDOU, PARIS, 2012

The project explores a novel mode of responsive architecture based on the combination of material inherent behavior and computational morphogenesis. The dimensional instability of wood in relation to moisture content is employed to construct a climate responsive architectural morphology. Suspended within a humidity controlled glass case the model opens and closes in response to climate changes with no need for any technical equipment or energy. Mere fluctuations in relative humidity trigger the silent changes of material-innate movement. The material structure itself is the machine.

The project was commissioned by the Centre Pompidou Paris for its permanent collection and will be first shown in the exhibition "Multiversités Créatives" starting on 2nd of May 2012.

Climate-responsiveness in architecture is typically conceived as a technical function enabled by myriad mechanical and electronic sensing, actuating and regulating devices. In contrast to this superimposition of high-tech equipment on otherwise inert material, nature suggests a fundamentally different, no-tech strategy: In many biological systems the responsive capacity is quite literally ingrained in the material itself.

This project employs similar design strategies of physically programming a material system that neither requires any kind of mechanical or electronic control, nor the supply of external energy. Here material computes form in feedback with the environment.

The meteorosensitive morphology floats in a fully transparent glass case. Within the case the climate corresponds to an accelerated database of the relative humidity in Paris. In this way, the case functions less as a separation from the interior space of the Centre Pompidou, arguably one of the most stable climate zones in the world, but rather provides a virtual connection to the outside, showing the subtle variations in humidity levels that we hardly ever consciously perceive through the system's silent movement. These cyclic changes are interspersed with spontaneous climate events triggered by threshold transitions within a second data set of visitor vapor emission.

The resultant autonomous, passive actuation of the surface provides for a unique convergence of environmental and spatial experience. The perception of the delicate locally varied and ever changing environmental dynamics is intensified through the subtle and silent movement of the meteorosensitive architectural morphology. The changing surface literally embodies the capacity to sense, actuate and react, all within the material itself.

SCIENTIFIC DEVELOPMENT

The project is based on more than five years of design research on climate responsive architectural systems that do not require any sensory equipment, motor functions or even energy. Here, the responsive capacity is ingrained in the material's hygroscopic behavior and anisotropic characteristics. Anisotropy denotes the directional dependence of a material's characteristics; in this case the different physical properties of wood in relation to grain directionality. Hygroscopicity refers to a substance's ability to take in moisture from the atmosphere when dry and yield moisture to the atmosphere when wet, thereby maintaining moisture content in equilibrium with the surrounding relative humidity.

In the process of adsorption and desorption of moisture the material changes physically, as water molecules become bonded to the material molecules. The increase or decrease of bound water changes the distance between the micro fibrils in the wood cell tissue, resulting in both a change in strength due to interfibrillar bonding and a significant decrease in overall dimension. Given the right morphological articulation, this dimensional change can be employed to trigger the shape change of a responsive element.

This enables to employ simple wood, one of the oldest and most common construction materials, as a climate-responsive, natural composite that can be physically programmed to compute different shapes in response to changes in relative humidity.

MICROCLIMATIC MODULATION

The system responds to relative humidity changes within its microenvironment of the glass case. When the humidity level rises, the system changes its surface porosity to breathe and ventilate the moisture-saturated air. The climate changes within the case directly influence the systems behavior.

The Centre Pompidou building is emblematic for a controlled architectural division between interior and exterior climate. In fact, the building celebrates the very technology that maintains the stable interior climate as one of its key architectural features. Within this highly controlled volume of the Centre Pompidou the little glass case serves as a container that allows transferring the continuous unfolding of exterior climatic events to the interior of the building. In this way it suggests how an architecture based on the intrinsic behavioral capacity of a material mediates between interior and exterior climates rather than separating them.

The humidifier and dehumidifier technology enclosed within the case's base regulates the climate driven by two datasets. One is the record of changing relative humidity levels of Paris. The acceleration of these daily climatic variations to hourly changes in combination with the systems surface response allows experiencing the subtle environmental differences and the heterogeneity of microclimatic conditions that usually escape our spatial perception. The second dataset affects the absolute humidity within the case. Based on the number of visitors a proportional amount of the humidity that they emit (approx. 100g per hour per person) will be spontaneously released triggering the unpredictable unfolding of local climatic events, causing nonlinear and complex behavioral response patterns of the system.

COMPUTATIONAL MORPHOGENESIS

For this project the computational design research and the related development of the generative code is as important as the material system research. The way machine computation is used to generate the system is directly related to the way material computation is employed to enable the system's responsiveness. The data for physically programming the behavior of the system during the fabrication process corresponds with digitally programming the code that unfolds the systems morphology. Thus computation and materialization are inherently and inseparably related.

The system consists of custom developed elements made from a combination of quarter-cut maple veneer and synthetic composites. More than 4000 geometrically unique elements are digitally fabricated and the complex substructure is robotically manufactured. The composite system elements can be programmed to materially compute different shapes within variable humidity response ranges by adjusting the following five parameters: [i] the fibre directionality, [ii] the layout of the natural and synthetic composite, [iii] the length-width-thickness ratio and [iv] geometry of the element and especially [v] the humidity control during the production process.

The computational design process is based on these system-intrinsic variables and system extrinsic environmental data. An algorithm iteratively scans various fields of environmental intensities within the simulated environment of the glass case and provides the input data for a custom scripted process of computational morphogenesis. Mimicking the dynamics of ontogenetic a recursive algorithm derives the system through striated linear growth patterns cumulating in cellular arrangements in climatically instable regions.

The emphasis here is not on a linear causality between environmental data and system morphology but rather a tendential intensity mapping to yield significantly different, emergent local behavior in response to climatic events. The algorithmic set-up considers the anatomical specificity of the material and its fibre layout enables the complex movement of the system and yields significantly different local behavior in response to humidity changes.

PROJECT TEAM

Achim Menges Architect, Frankfurt
Prof. Achim Menges, Steffen Reichert, Boyan Mihaylov
(Project Development, Design Development)

Institute for Computational Design, University of Stuttgart
Prof. Achim Menges, Steffen Reichert, Nicola Burggraf, Tobias Schwinn with Claudio Fabrizio Calandri,
Nicola Haberbosch, Oliver Krieg, Marielle Neuser, Viktoriya Nikolova, Paul Schmidt
(Scientific Development, Design Development, Robotic Fabrication, Assembly)

Transsolar Climate Engineering, Stuttgart
Thomas Auer, Daniel Pianka
(Climate Engineering)

PAGE 49

PAGE 50

1 HYGROSCOPE
2 HYGROSCOPE
3 HYGROSCOPE - CLOSED
4 HYGROSCOPE
5 HYGROSCOPE - OPENED

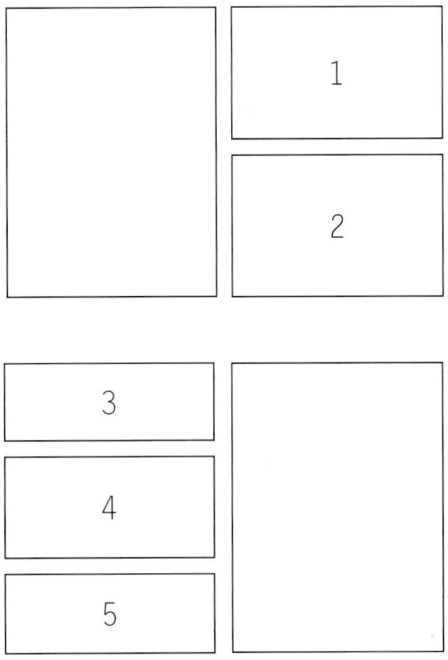

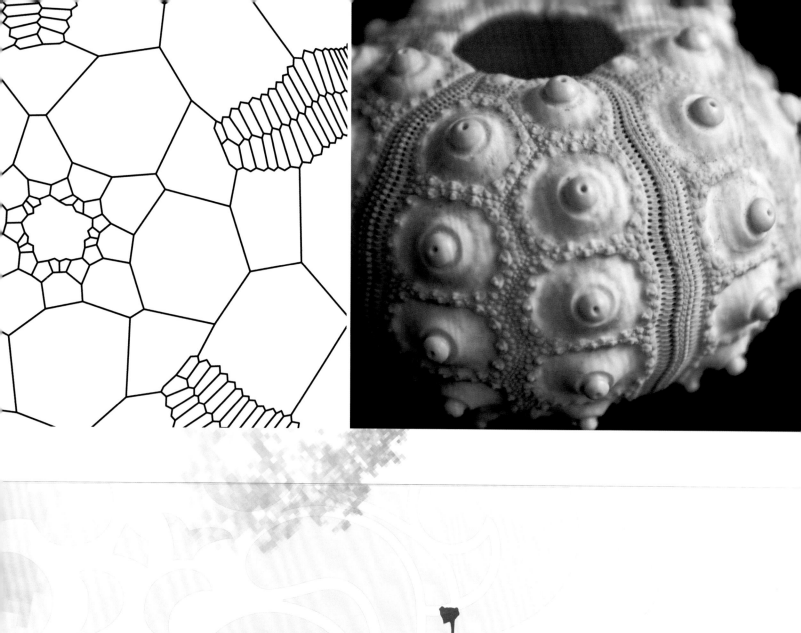

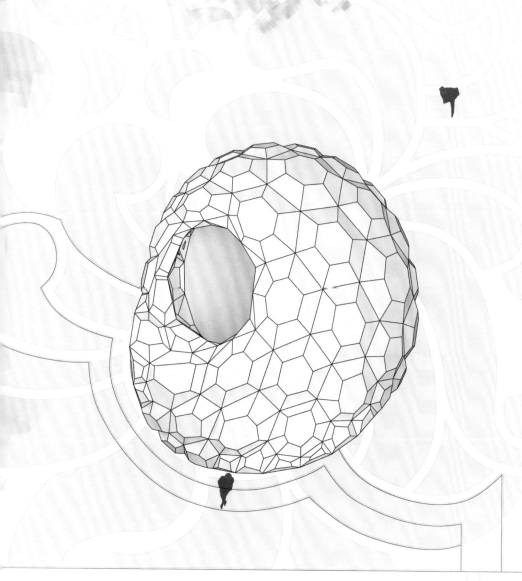

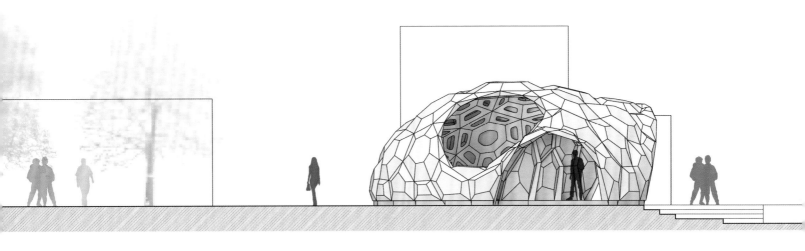

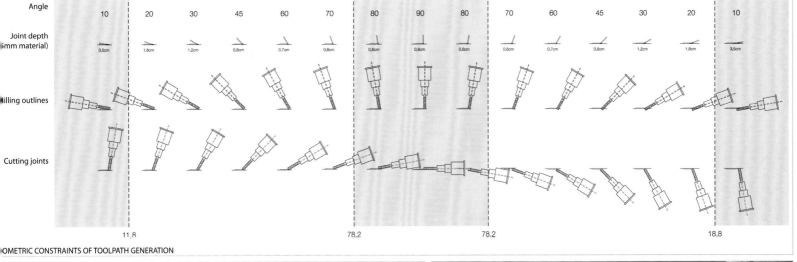

Angle	10	20	30	45	60	70	80	90	80	70	60	45	30	20	10
Joint depth (5mm material)	3,5cm	1,8cm	1,2cm	0,8cm	0,7cm	0,6cm	0,6cm	0,6cm	0,6cm	0,6cm	0,7cm	0,8cm	1,2cm	1,8cm	3,5cm

Milling outlines

Cutting joints

11,8   78,2   78,2   18,8

OMETRIC CONSTRAINTS OF TOOLPATH GENERATION

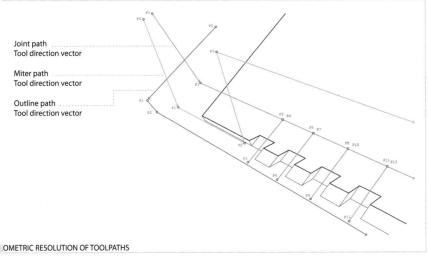

Joint path
Tool direction vector

Miter path
Tool direction vector

Outline path
Tool direction vector

OMETRIC RESOLUTION OF TOOLPATHS

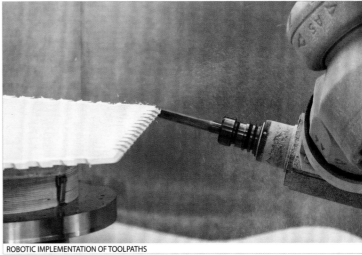

ROBOTIC IMPLEMENTATION OF TOOLPATHS

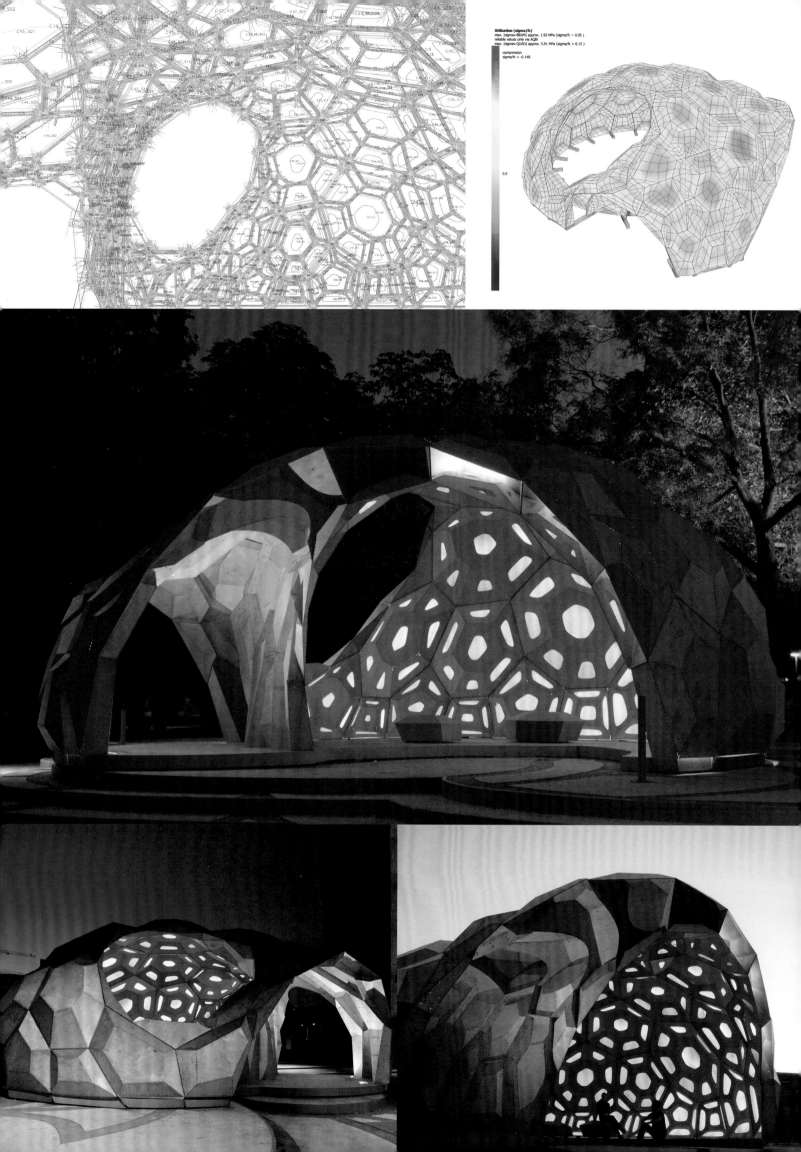

Utilization (sigma/fc)
max. |sigmav-BEAM| approx. 1.92 MPa (sigma/fc = 0.05)
reliable values only via AQB!
max. |sigmav-QUAD| approx. 5.91 MPa (sigma/fc = 0.15)

compression
sigma/fc = -0.148

0.0

ICD/ITKE RESEARCH PAVILION

ICD: INSTITUTE FOR COMPUTATIONAL DESIGN
-PROF. AA DIPL.(HONS) ACHIM MENGES

ITKE: INSTITUTE OF BUILDING STRUCTURES AND STRUCTURAL DESIGN
-PROF. DR.-ING. JAN KNIPPERS

The Institute for Computational Design (ICD) and the Institute of Building Structures and Structural Design (ITKE), together with students at the University of Stuttgart have realized a temporary, bionic research pavilion made of wood at the intersection of teaching and research. The project explores the architectural transfer of biological principles of the sea urchin's plate skeleton morphology by means of novel computer-based design and simulation methods, along with computer-controlled manufacturing methods for its building implementation. A particular innovation consists in the possibility of effectively extending the recognized bionic principles and related performance to a range of different geometries through computational processes, which is demonstrated by the fact that the complex morphology of the pavilion could be built exclusively with extremely thin sheets of plywood (6.5 mm).

BIOLOGICAL SYSTEM

The project aims at integrating the performative capacity of biological structures into architectural design and at testing the resulting spatial and structural material-systems in full scale. The focus was set on the development of a modular system which allows a high degree of adaptability and performance due to the geometric differentiation of its plate components and robotically fabricated finger joints. During the analysis of different biological structures, the plate skeleton morphology of the sand dollar, a sub-species of the sea urchin (Echinoidea), became of particular interest and subsequently provided the basic principles of the bionic structure that was realized. The skeletal shell of the sand dollar is a modular system of polygonal plates, which are linked together at the edges by finger-like calcite protrusions. High load bearing capacity is achieved by the particular geometric arrangement of the plates and their joining system. Therefore, the sand dollar serves as a most fitting model for shells made of prefabricated elements. Similarly, the traditional finger-joints typically used in carpentry as connection elements, can be seen as the technical equivalent of the sand dollar's calcite protrusions.

MORPHOLOGY TRANSFER

Following the analysis of the sand dollar, the morphology of its plate structure was integrated in the design of a pavilion. Three plate edges always meet together at just one point, a principle which enables the transmission of normal and shear forces but no bending moments between the joints, thus resulting in a bending bearing but yet deformable structure. Unlike traditional lightweight construction, which can only be applied to load optimized shapes, this new design principle can be applied to a wide range of custom geometry. The high lightweight potential of this approach is evident as the pavilion that could be built out of 6.5 mm thin sheets of plywood only, despite its considerable size. Therefore it even needed anchoring to the ground to resist wind suction loads.

Besides these constructional and organizational principles, other fundamental properties of biological structures are applied in the computational design process of the project:

• Heterogeneity: The cell sizes are not constant, but adapt to local curvature and discontinuities. In the areas of small curvature the central cells are more than two meters tall, while at the edge they only reach half a meter.

• Anisotropy: The pavilion is a directional structure. The cells stretch and orient themselves according to mechanical stresses.

• Hierarchy: The pavilion is organized as a two-level hierarchical structure. On the first level, the finger joints of the plywood sheets are glued together to form a cell. On the second hierarchical level, a simple screw connection joins the cells together, allowing the assembling and disassembling of the pavilion. Within each hierarchical level only three plates - respectively three edges – meet exclusively at one point, therefore assuring bendable edges for both levels.

COMPUTATIONAL DESIGN AND ROBOTIC PRODUCTION

A requirement for the design, development and realization of the complex morphology of the pavilion is a closed, digital information loop between the project's model, finite element simulations and computer numeric machine control. Form finding and structural design are closely interlinked. An optimized data exchange scheme made it possible to repeatedly read the complex geometry into a finite element program to analyze and modify the critical points of the model. In parallel, the glued and bolted joints were tested experimentally and the results included in the structural calculations.

The plates and finger joints of each cell were produced with the university's robotic fabrication system. Employing custom programmed routines the computational model provided the basis for the automatic generation of the machine code (NC-Code) for the control of an industrial seven-axis robot. This enabled the economical production of more than 850 geometrically different components, as well as more than 100,000 finger joints freely arranged in space. Following the robotic production, the plywood panels were joined together to form the cells. The assembly of the prefabricated modules was carried out at the city campus of the University of Stuttgart. All design, research, fabrication and construction work were carried out jointly by students and faculty researchers.

The research pavilion offered the opportunity to investigate methods of modular bionic construction using freeform surfaces representing different geometric characteristics while developing two distinct spatial entities: one large interior space with a porous inner layer and a big opening, facing the public square between the University's buildings, and a smaller interstitial space enveloped between the two layers that exhibits the constructive logic of the double layer shell.

PROJECT TEAM

Institute for Computational Design - Prof. AA Dipl.(Hons) Achim Menges Achim Menges
Institute of Building Structures and Structural Design - Prof. Dr.-Ing. Jan Knippers

CONCEPT & PROJECT DEVELOPMENT

Oliver David Krieg, Boyan Mihaylov

PLANNING & REALISATION

Peter Brachat, Benjamin Busch, Solmaz Fahimian, Christin Gegenheimer, Nicola Haberbosch, Elias Kästle, Oliver David Krieg, Yong Sung Kwon, Boyan Mihaylov, Hongmei Zhai

SCIENTIFIC DEVELOPMENT

Markus Gabler (project management), Riccardo La Magna (structural design), Steffen Reichert (detailing), Tobias Schwinn (project management), Frédéric Waimer (structural design)

BIOGRAPHY

Achim Menges, born 1975, is a registered architect and professor at University of Stuttgart where he is the founding director of the Institute for Computational Design (since 2008). In addition, he has been Visiting Professor in Architecture at Harvard University's Graduate School of Design (2009-10), at the AA School of Architecture in London (2009-current) and at Rice University in Houston (2004).

He graduated with honors from the AA School of Architecture in London (2002) where he subsequently taught as Studio Master of the Emergent Technologies and Design Graduate Program (2002-09) and as Unit Master of Diploma Unit 4 (2003-06). He also was Professor for Form Generation and Materialisation at the HfG Offenbach University for Art and Design in Germany (2005-08).

Achim Menges practice and research focuses on the development of integral design processes at the intersection of morphogenetic design computation, biomimetic engineering and computer aided manufacturing that enables a highly articulated, performative built environment. His work is based on an interdisciplinary approach in collaboration with structural engineers, computer scientists, material scientists and biologists. Achim Menges has published several books on this work and related fields of design research, and he is the author/coauthor of numerous articles and scientific papers. His projects and design research has received many international awards, has been published and exhibited worldwide, and form parts of several renowned museum collections.

Achim Menges is a member of several international research evaluation boards and a member of numerous scientific committees of leading peer-reviewed international journals and conferences.

PAGE 54 + PAGE 55

PAGE 56 + PAGE 57

1 ECHINOID MORPHOLOGY
2 TOP VIEW
3 ELEVATION
4 FINGER JOINTS TYPOLOGY
5 JOINTS ANALYSIS
6 STRUCTURAL ANALYSIS
7 EAST VIEW
8 SOUTH-WEST VIEW
9 SOUTH-EAST VIEW
10 INTERIOR VIEW
11 CLOSE UP JOINTS

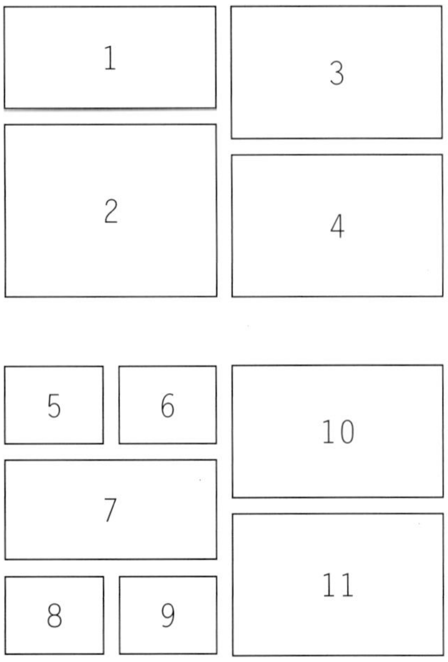

DEPTH

DEPTH

MICHAEL HANSMEYER

subdivided column, hexahedron, dome

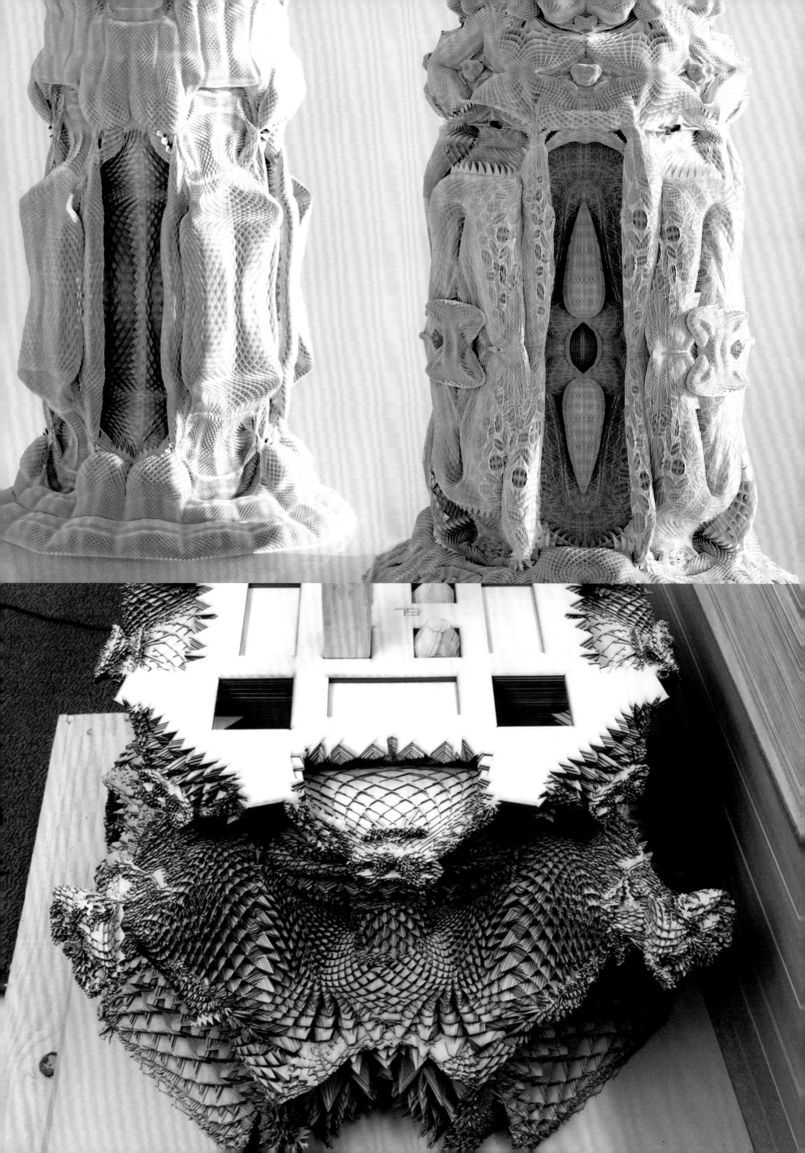

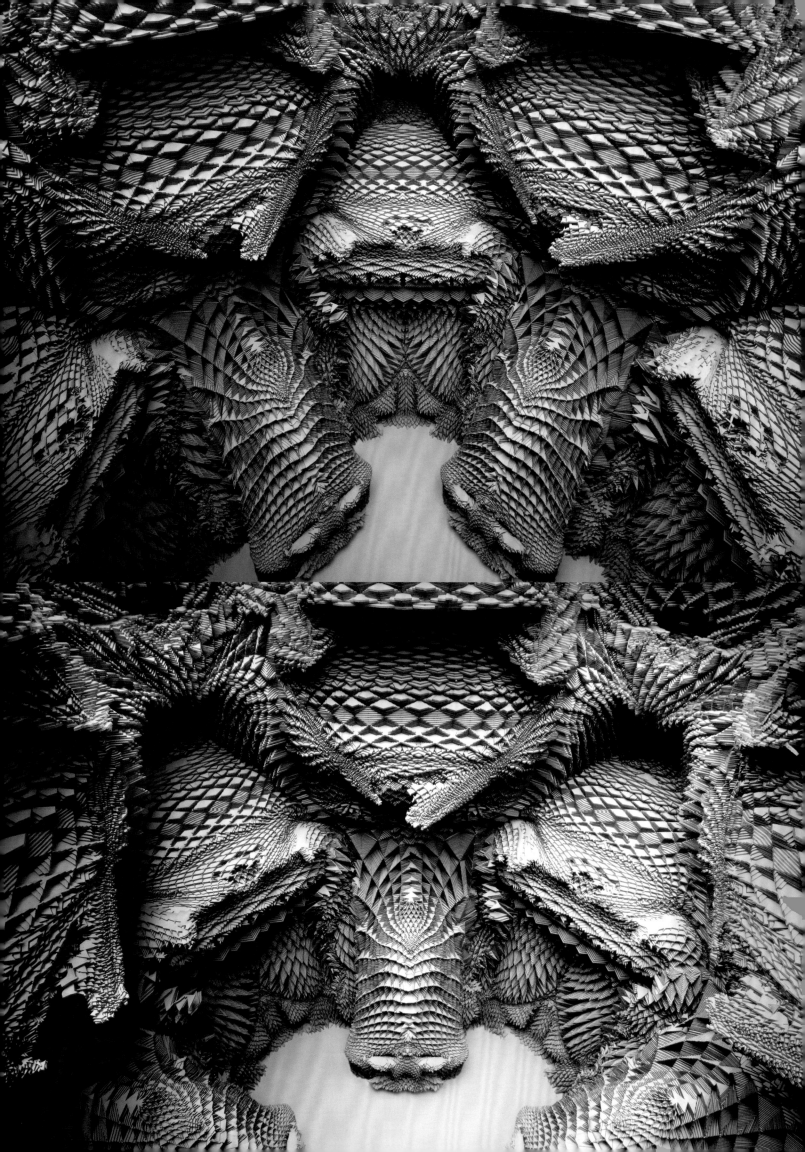

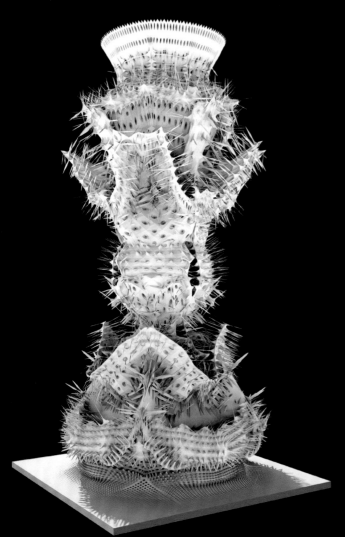
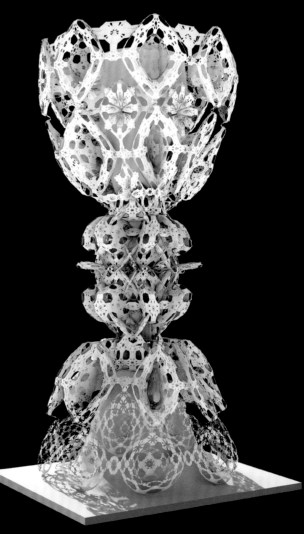

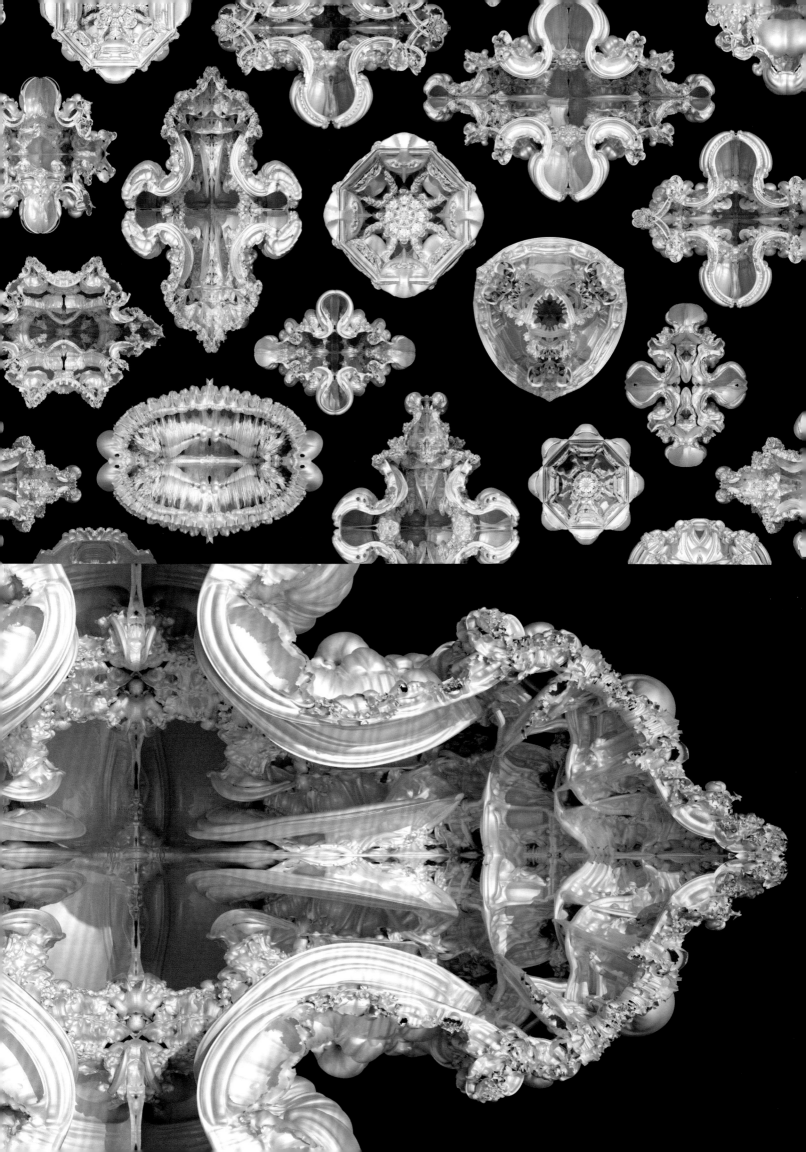

SUBDIVIDED COLUMN, HEXAHEDRON, DOME

MICHAEL HANSMEYER

CONCEPT

The Subdivided Columns project explores the use of algorithms to develop a new language of form. The columns are produced using customized subdivision processes. The allure of these processes is that despite using a very simple input, they can produce something that is extraordinarily complex.

In the case of these column prototypes, the input is an abstracted Doric column. The process functions by taking each face (or facet) of this Doric column and dividing it into four faces. The new faces in turn are further divided again and again until the final form emerges: an intricate column made of 16 million faces.

Each subdivision step adds further levels of detail (or "information") to the form. The first steps of the process influence the overall shape and its curvature; the next steps determine the surface development, while the final steps generate a minuscule texture on top of the broader surfaces.

The resulting columns have a distinct language of form unlike anything created by traditional processes. They exhibit highly specific local conditions as well as an overall coherency and continuity. Their ornament is in continuous flow, yet it consists of very distinct local formations. The complexity of the columns contrasts with the simplicity of the their generative process and the their initial input.

FABRICATION

How can one materialize these forms, i.e. "get them out of the computer"? 3D printers are unable to fabricate objects at such a large scale and at a resolution sufficient to reproduce the column's surface detail. The shear number of 16 million faces exceeds the capabilities of 3D printing software.

Fabrication of the column prototype instead involved writing a program to slice the output geometry into 2700 individual layers. Each layer was cut out of 1mm cardboard sheets using laser cutters, and these are stacked around a common core to produce a 2.7 meter-high prototype. Due to the column's surface features, the lasers travelled a cutting path exceeding 19 kilometers in length. Despite being partially hollow on the inside, a single prototype weighs an astonishing 650 kg. Further prototypes are currently being constructed using ABS plastic and other composites.

Materials: Greyboard, 1mm laser-cut sheet (2700 total), wood core
Dimensions: 40-70cm diameter, 270cm height, 650 kg weight

BIOGRAPHY

Michael Hansmeyer is an architect and programmer who explores the use of algorithms and computation to generate architectural form. He is currently based in the CAAD group at ETH's architecture department in Zurich. He holds an MBA degree from Insead Fontainebleau as well as a Master of Architecture degree from Columbia University. He previously worked with McKinsey & Company, J.P. Morgan, and at Herzog & de Meuron architects.

1-2-3: FOREST OF COLUMNS
        Initial sketches showing many variants (i.e. permutations) of columns that
        were generated using a uniform process, yet with slightly varying process
        parameters. The columns thus appear to belong to one 'family'.

4-5-6: COLUMN PROTOTYPES - ZOOMED IN
        Further developments of the columns, showing three different zoom levels
        of a single image. The zoomed images reveal the nearly infinite level of
        detail that the subdivision process can generate. The further one zooms
        in, the more additional layers of ornament one discovers.

7-8-9: FABRICATION
        Photos of column segments made of stacked layers of cardboard. Image 7 is
        of the outside of the column, while images 8 and 9 show the negative,
        i.e. the cardboard sheets that the column was cut out of.

10-11-12: FABRICATED COLUMN
        The final constructed column made of 2700 sheets of 1mm laser-cut
        cardboard, standing 2.7 meters high. This prototype has been exhibited
        at the Self-Structure exhibition in Paris, Smallspace gallery Berlin,
        as well as the TED Global conference in Edinburgh. It is currently
        exhibited at the Swiss Federal Institute of Technology (ETH) in Zurich.

13-14-15-16-17: HEXAHEDRON STUDIES

18-19: DOME STUDIES

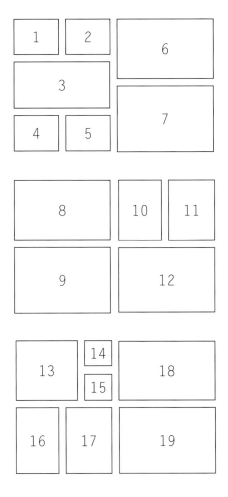

DEPTH

BENJAMIN BALL

BALL NOGUES STUDIO

GASTON NOGUES

feathered edge

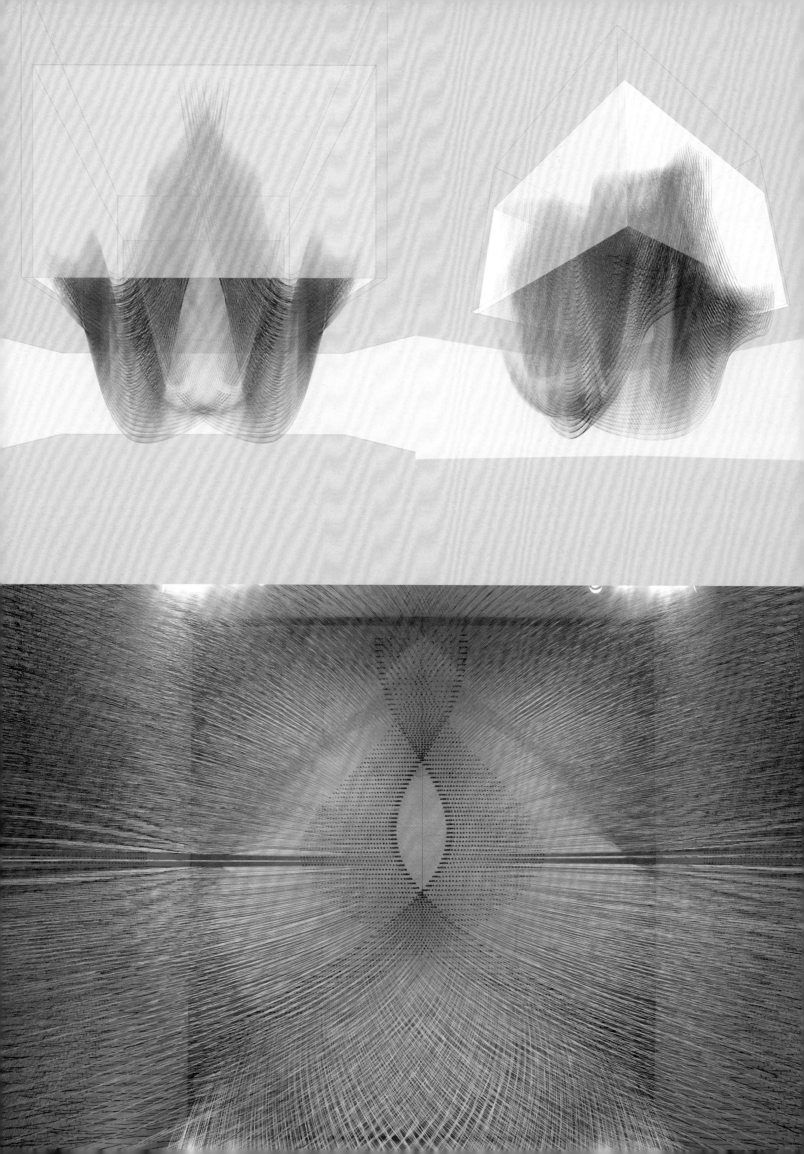

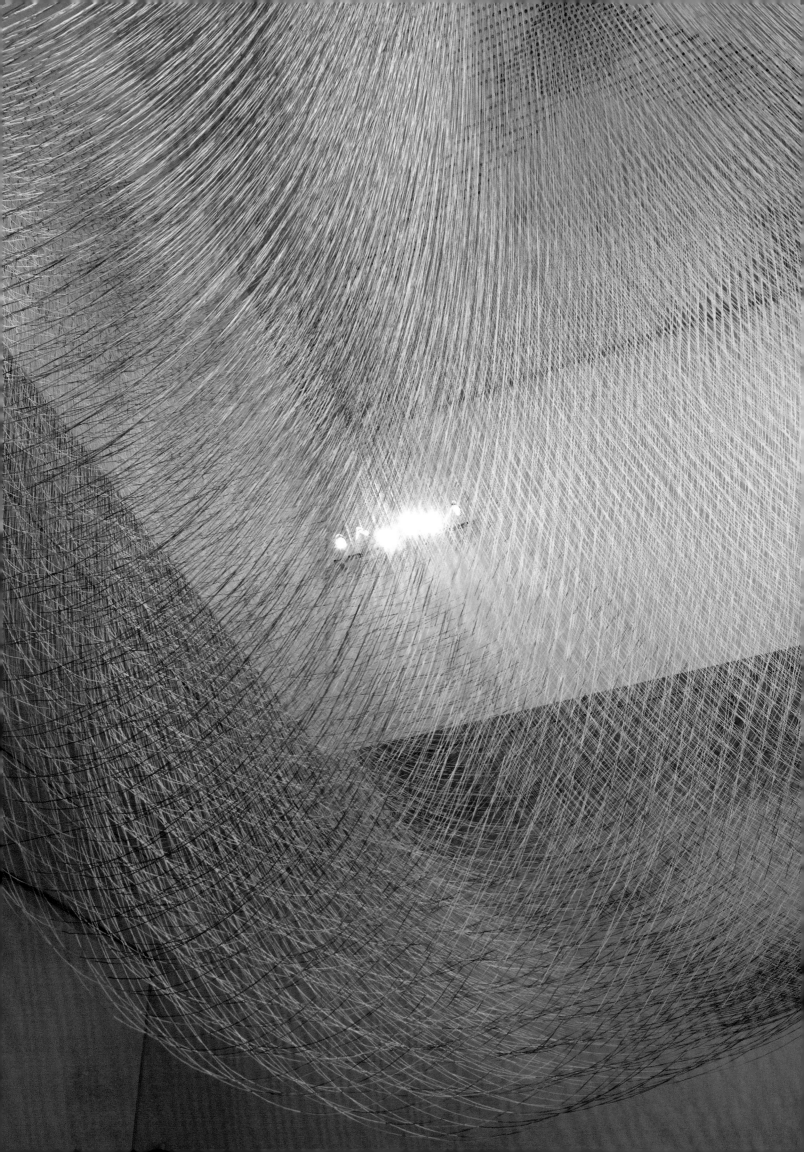

FEATHERED EDGE

BALL NOGUES STUDIO:
BENJAMIN BALL,
GASTON NOGUES

The Museum of Contemporary Art in Los Angeles commissioned *Feathered Edge*. The project explores the convergence of digital technology and craft. It is one in a series of installations curated by Brooke Hodge and Alma Ruiz. Integrating complex digital computation, mechanization, and printing with traditional handcrafted production techniques, *Feathered Edge* explores our desire to alter a space with fluid architectural forms that require a minimal use of material while utilizing a new proprietary technique that yields the effect of three dimensional spatial constructs "printed" to resemble objects hovering in space.

Feathered Edge is comprised of 3604 individual lengths of twine, totaling 21 miles, that were dyed, cut, and then suspended from mesh scrims installed on the walls and ceiling of the gallery. With the aid of the "Insta-llator 1 with the Variable-Information Atomizing Module," a machine designed and manufactured by Ball-Nogues Studio especially for this installation, the strings were precisely saturated with solvent-based inks, created by a chemist for the project, using four digitally controlled airbrushes and then cut to varying lengths. Using specialized parametric software developed with a software programmer, we generated a map that was printed onto the scrim to establish the proper locations and lengths of the twine in the space. Each piece was attached to the mesh scrim, and then knotted by hand in a technique similar to that used to make latch-hook rugs. The weight of the string creates a complex system of overlapping catenary curves on which cyan, magenta, yellow, and black segments were "printed" to yield the effect of ghostly three-dimensional objects. Sometimes the objects are visible, at other times they blur to resemble a fluid-like vapor that floats and hovers in the gallery space.

The software used to develop the parameters of the resulting ephemeral spatial condition can yield nearly infinite possible design configurations. While the environment is defined by the string formations and printed "objects," it is also constructed from the negative space found within the array of catenaries, which allows sight to extend into and throughout the spatial structure. The space is activated by people, movement, and light, creating a continually changing experience.

Computers are great at quickly analyzing large amounts of information, then generating data used for fabrication, but they can't yet produce fully realized works of architecture. At best they can produce highly accurate components and spatial mappings or systems; this is where handcraft comes in. We use our hands and our knowledge of material as a filter for the digital possibilities and to achieve the final "built" environment; in effect, we use the prowess of the computer to push the limits of the hand.

Feathered Edge is the third in a series of projects we refer to as "Suspensions." Unseen Current (2008), exhibited at Extension Gallery for Architecture, Chicago, featured 2,500 suspended string catenaries, and Echoes Converge, exhibited at the Venice Biennale in 2008 used string to create intricate patterns inspired by the baroque ceilings of the city's buildings. These softly structural, open-air spaces encouraged social interaction, enveloping rather than obstructing viewers.

TEAM

Principals in Charge: Benjamin Ball, Gaston Nogues
Project Management: Andrew Lyon
Project Team: Chris Ball, Tatiana Barhar, Seda Brown, Patricia Burns, Paul Clemente, Sergio d'Almeida, Jesse Duclos, Matt Harmon, Karlie Harstad, Ayodh Kamath, Jonathan Kitchens, Andrew Lyon, Lina Park, Tim Peeters, Sarah Riedmann, Joem Elias Sanez, Geoff Sedillo, Norma Silva, Caroline Smogorzewski, Beverly Tang, Blaze Zewnicki, Sasha Zubieta

BIOGRAPHY

Ball-Nogues Studio is an integrated design and fabrication practice operating in a territory between architecture, art, and industrial design, led by Benjamin Ball and Gaston Nogues. Their work is informed by the exploration of craft. Essential to each project is the "design" of the production process itself, with the aim of creating environments that enhance sensation, generate spectacle and invite physical engagement.

The Studio has exhibited at major institutions, including the Museum of Contemporary Art, Los Angeles; the Museum of Modern Art, New York; the Guggenheim Museum; PS1; the Los Angeles County Museum of Art; the Venice Biennale; the Hong Kong | Shenzhen Biennale; and the Beijing Biennale. They have received numerous honors including three American Institute of Architects Design Awards, United States Artists Target Fellowships and a grant from the Graham Foundation for Advanced Studies in the Fine Arts. In 2007, the Studio was the winner of the Museum of Modern Art PS1 Young Architects Program Competition and recently, their work became part of the permanent collections of both MoMA and LACMA. In 2011, they were one of the Architectural League of New York's Emerging Voices. Benjamin and Gaston have taught in the graduate architecture programs at SCI-Arc, UCLA, and USC. Their work has appeared in a variety of publications including The New York Times, Los Angeles Times, The Guardian, Architectural Record, Artforum, Icon, Log, Architectural Digest, Mark and Sculpture.

The Studio is currently working on permanent public commissions for Los Angeles World Airports; the City of West Hollywood; Portland State University; Houston's Buffalo Bayou, and Nashville Music City Center.

1 INSTALLATION. PHOTO: BENNY CHAN
2 INSTALLATION RENDERING
3 INSTALLATION RENDERING
4 INSTALLATION. PHOTO: BENNY CHAN
5 INSTALLATION. PHOTO: BENNY CHAN
5 INSTALLATION. PHOTO: BENNY CHAN

DEPTH

GRAMAZIO
KOHLER

RAFFAELLO
D'ANDREA

flight assembled architecture

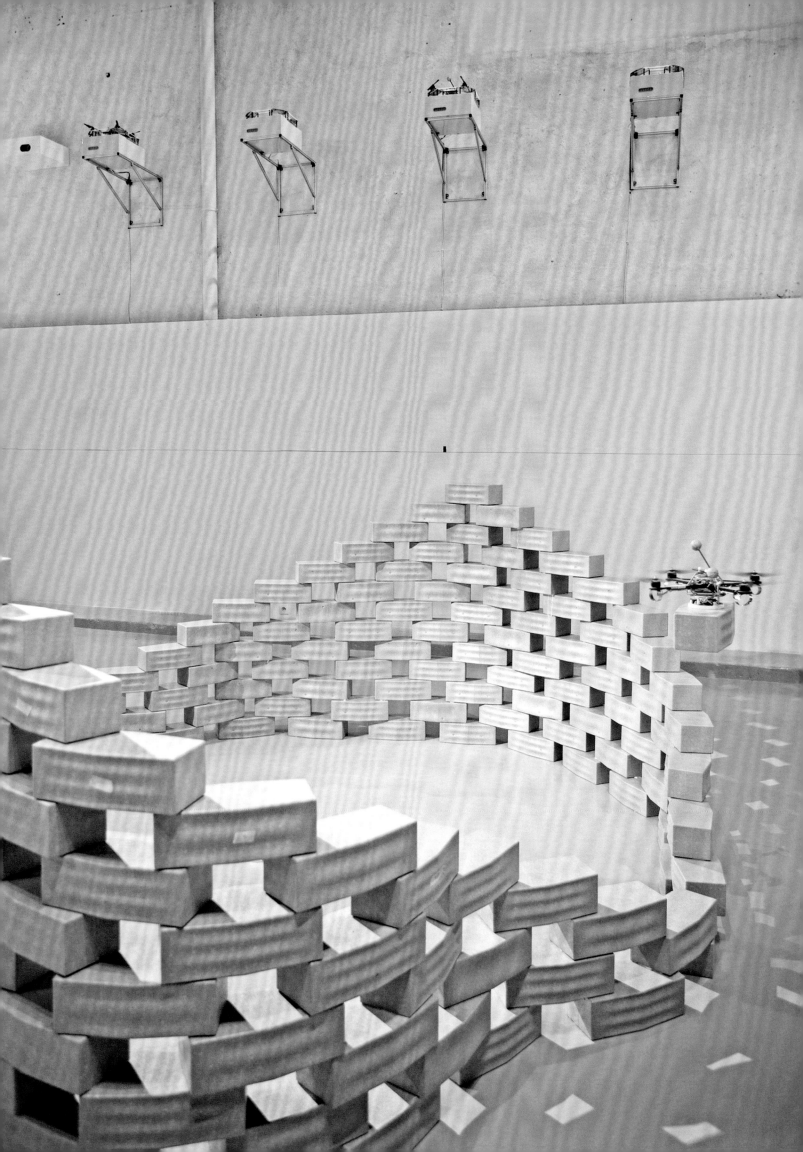

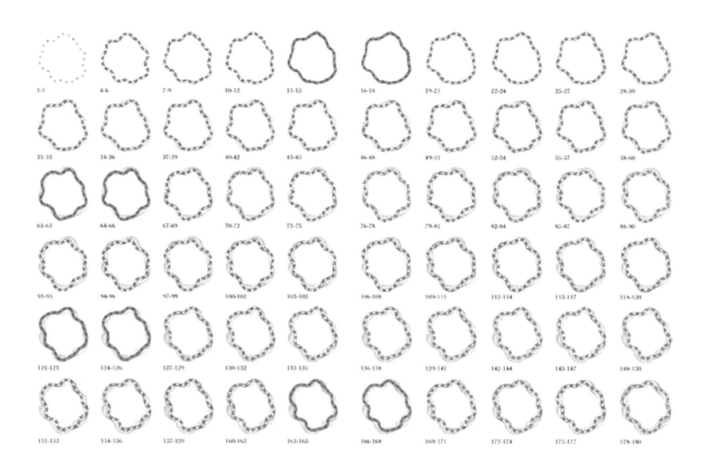

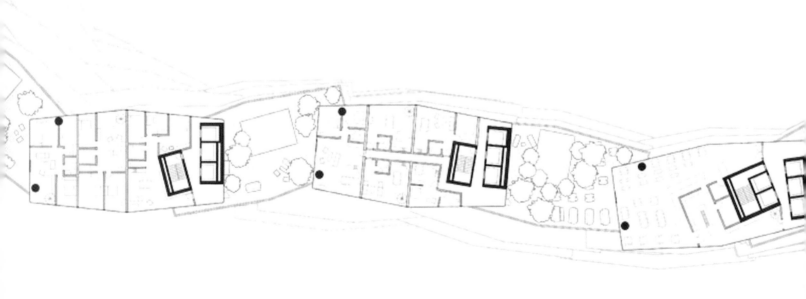

5m

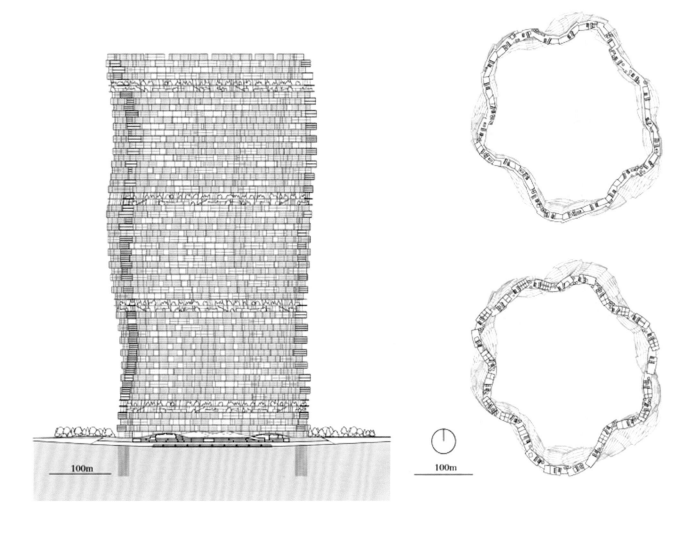

100m

100m

FLIGHT ASSEMBLED ARCHITECTURE

FRAC CENTRE ORLÉANS

Flight Assembled Architecture is the first architectural installation assembled by flying robots, free from the touch of human hands. The installation is an expression of a rigorous architectural design by Gramazio & Kohler and a visionary robotic system by Raffaello D'Andrea.

Flight Assembled Architecture consists of over 1.500 modules, which are placed by a multitude of quadrotor helicopters, collaborating according to mathematical algorithms that translate digital design data to the behavior of the flying machines. In this way, the flying vehicles, together, extend themselves as "living" architectural machines and complete the composition from their dynamic formation of movement and building performance. Within the build, an architectural vision of a 600m high "vertical village" for 30'000 inhabitants unfolds as model in 1:100 scale. This newly founded village is located in the rural area of Meuse, taking advantage of an existing TGV connection that brings its inhabitants to Paris in less than one hour. It is from this quest of an "ideal" self-sustaining habitat that the authors pursue a radical new way of thinking and materializing verticality in architecture.

CREDITS

Gramazio & Kohler and Raffaello D`Andrea in cooperation with ETH Zurich

COLLABORATORS

Andrea Kondziela (project lead), Sarah Bridges, Tim Burton, Thomas Cadalbert, Dr. Ralph Bärtschi, Peter Heckeroth, Marion Ott, Tanja Pereira, Dominik Weber, Dr. Jan Willmann

SELECTED EXPERTS

Wind Tunnel Testing: Chair of Building Physics, Prof. Jan Carmeliet, ETH Zurich and Empa
Structural Engineering: Dr. Lüchinger + Meyer Bauingenieure AG
Façade Engineering: Dr. Lüchinger + Meyer Bauingenieure AG
Energy Consulting: Amstein + Walthert AG

BIOGRAPHY

Gramazio & Kohler is Fabio Gramazio and Matthias Kohler. Our projects combine the physis of built architecture with digital logics. Therefore, we do not design architecture solely by drawing, but conceive spatial relationships and contextual behaviour through programming. In doing so, we use the potentials of the computer and of digital fabrication complementary to traditional design, construction and building methods. The sensual quality of this design culture manifests itself in the novel expression of a Digital Materiality.

1 INSTALLATION ASSEMBLY PROCESS
2 COMPLETED INSTALLATION WALL
3 CONSTRUCTION FLYING ROBOT IN MIDAIR
4 ALMOST COMPLETED INSTALLATION
5 PLAN
6 POTENTIAL FURNISHED PLAN
7 SECTION AND PLANS
8 STRUCTURE DIAGRAM

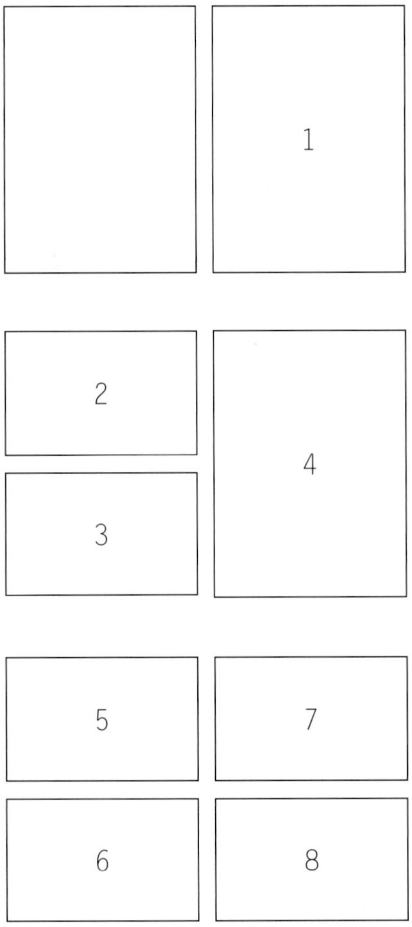

1

2

3

4

5

7

6

8

EVOLO 06
DEPTH
GRAMAZIO KOHLER + RAFFAELLO D'ANDREA
FLIGHT ASSEMBLED
85

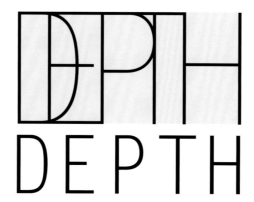

DEPTH

LISA
IWAMOTO

IWAMOTO
SCOTT
ARCHITEC-
TURE

CRAIG
SCOTT

busan opera house, edgar street towers

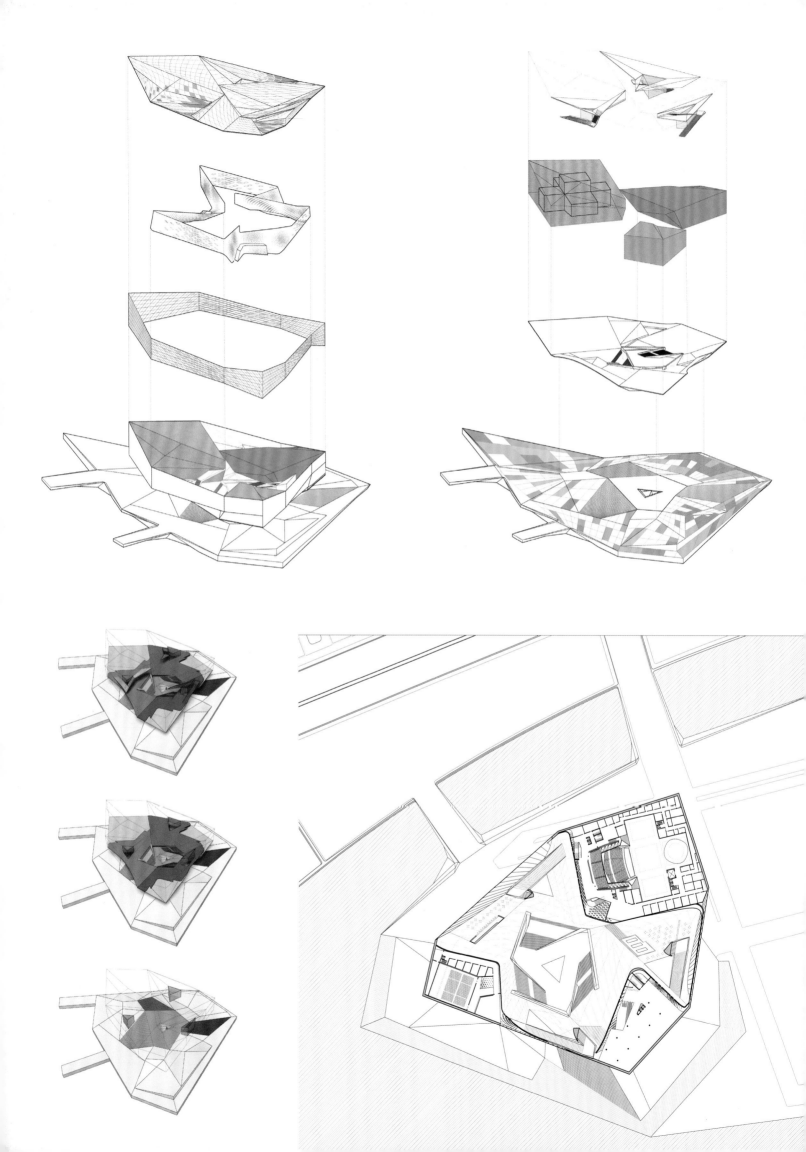

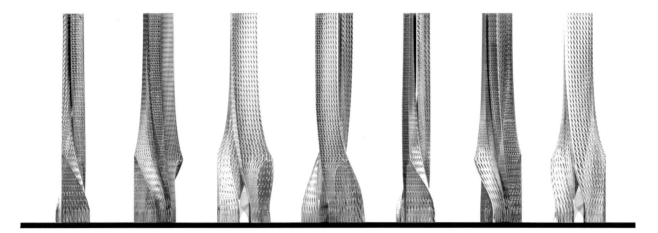

Twisting SkyVoid
from Edgar Street to sky

Fiberoptic Daylight Mesh
w/ glazing wireframe & atrium

Infra-Structure
cores as interior structure

Programmatic Zoning
Floorplates and sky lobbies

Structural Skin
modulated exoskeleton

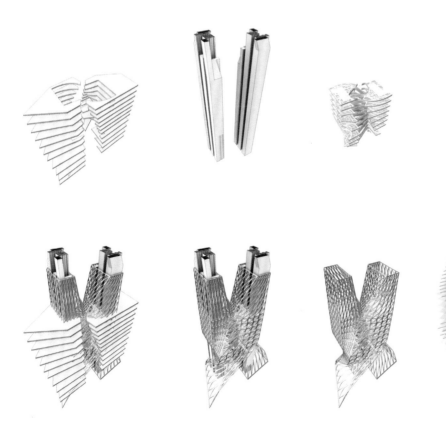

IWAMOTOSCOTT ARCHITECTURE
BUSAN / EDGAR

IWAMOTOSCOTT ARCHITECTURE

The work of IwamotoScott Architecture (ISAR) proceeds along three trajectories: digital fabrication installations, speculative projects, and building-scale architectural design. Each trajectory is involved in an exploration of digital architecture. Where this is most clearly in evidence is in the digital fabrication and speculative work; yet there is crossover between all project types. As a whole, ISAR's body of work forms a consistent line of investigation of the material, spatial, and formal properties of architecture – investigation facilitated greatly by the digital and computational potentials of architecture.

An area in which ISAR aims to make significant contribution is in the exploration of transitive relationships of surface, material and fabrication technique across building scales. For example, Voussoir Cloud, LightFold, Jellyfish House, Busan Opera House and Edgar Street Towers though operating differently and at vastly different scales, each explore adaptable skins through the networked formation of cells. Jellyfish House develops the idea of a systematized collection of modules as a precisely defined geometric and parametric array. Edgar Street Towers is a refined, site-specific development of the digital techniques employed in Jellyfish House. One Kearny employs a similar system as Edgar Street Tower's modulated skin, but adapts it for a functioning luminous ceiling. Busan yet again employs a similar logic of modulated structural skin in the development of its envelope. Together these projects foreground the performative nature of skin and its inherent reciprocity with the environment and user.

Similarly, a continuing fascination of ISAR's is in the quality of form and space created from captured ephemeral conditions and negative space. HydroNet and RestBox for instance, channel movement of water or people through carved voids within the overall context to define the resulting spatial formation. Here again, parallels can be drawn among ISAR's different projects. Both Edgar Street Towers and Busan Opera House take cues from such earlier projects as ORDOS Villa 043 or PS House, which employ negative space making strategies to experientially fold together building and site. These works also resonate with projects completed much earlier like Fog House, 2:1 House, and mOcean. The spatial exploration of Edgar Street Towers and Busan Opera House is largely driven by computational design processes - for instance, the scripted massing of the Tower which ultimately defined its negative space condition, or the complex relationship between the Opera House's layered interiority and its site-inflected modulated envelope. The design thinking and processes behind these large scale works follow along lines of inquiry found in much more modestly-scaled built projects such as Obscura Digital Headquarters or One Kearny. For example, the employment of geometrically streamlined construction methods to create dynamic surfaces such as those seen in ISAR's speculative unbuilt work.

In the end, it is not these particular correlations but the multiple convergences of them that forms the larger research agenda for the work - one that aims at creating a synthetic whole from multiple, sometimes competing concerns. This interest is evidenced through all of ISAR's design work, where there is a search for a digital architecture that conveys a meaningful confluence of form, material, construction, and site in both built and unbuilt work.

BUSAN OPERA HOUSE: TRIFOLD MADANG

Trifold Madang, IwamotoScott's entry in the Busan Opera House design competition, addresses the sponsors' aim to create a new icon in the redevelopment of the North Port area, establishing an international gateway and fostering maritime tourism for the new Maritime Culture District. The design for BOH: Trifold Madang dramatizes the experience of going to the opera while creating a striking sculptural form at the water's edge which maximizes connections between the city and the water.

The building mass is lifted above the surrounding site, supported on three large programmed pedestals. The space of the site flows beneath the building and up onto a landscaped podium that culminates in a mound at the Opera House's center. This center space evokes the history of Korean Opera, which was originally performed in outdoor courtyards (or madang). The Opera House's form and public sequence stems from this Public Madang, where a trio of internal Spiraling Stairs pinwheel around the main space and orchestrate vertical movement within the building.

Approaching the Opera House from the surroundings of the new Maritime Cultural District, visitors ascend one of three exterior Grand Stairs. These meet at the Public Madang at the center of the building. A large central triangular skylight anchors this space. The Grand Stairs face outward toward the site's main directions of orientation and view.

From the Public Madang, visitors continue up the three Spiraling Stairs that each wrap around a prismatic glass-enclosed garden light-well, feeding directly into the Main Lobby, and offering a dynamic spatial sequence and clear sense of orientation for the Opera House. A wood liner in the form of a continuous ribbon defines the perimeter of the Main Lobby's circulation loop. This ribbon is perforated to transmit both filtered daylight from the outer building skin and artificial lighting integrated within the liner's depth.

A Concourse-Exhibition level is housed within the Podium and accommodates the building's accessible entrances, as well as the building's service and loading facilities. The Concourse level also connects to additional auxiliary facilities along the podium's southern and western edges. These include Shopping and Restaurant zones, which orient out to a promenade along the water's edge.

The three Spiraling Stairs ultimately arrive at the Opera House's Rooftop Garden, where a terrain of sloping planes echoes the mountain range to the north while offering panoramic views of Busan and the port beyond.

The main Opera House Theater audience is accommodated in two main seating tiers, defined as a continuous wood surface that splits and folds to form two balconies and open box seats to the sides. Lining the Opera House Theater, a series of acoustically tuned ceiling, wall and balustrade panels are integrated together as a continuous multifaceted wood veneered surface. These planes make an enveloping interior that, like the Main Lobby's perimeter ribbon, reflects and reinterprets the formal character and dynamism of Busan's surrounding mountainous geography.

The Opera House's envelope is comprised of a diagrid structural skin system whose outermost layer is an array of parametrically modulated iridescent metal panels that adjust to varying environmental conditions, light and view.

IWAMOTOSCOTT PRINCIPALS IN CHARGE

Lisa Iwamoto / Craig Scott

PROJECT TEAM

Sean Canty, Jeremy Jih, Paul Cattaneo, Mazyar Kahali, Ryan Golenberg

EDGAR STREET TOWERS. GREENWICH SOUTH, LOWER MANHATTAN

Edgar Street Towers was produced by IwamotoScott for the Greenwich South design study led by Architecture Research Office, Beyer Blinder Belle Architects & Planners and OPEN. Contributing architects, artists and designers included Coen + Partners, DeWitt Godfrey, IwamotoScott Architecture, Jorge Colmbo, Lewis.Tsura-maki.Lewis Architects, Morphosis, Rafael Lozano-Hemmer, Transolar Climate Engineering and WORKac.

Inspired by earlier visionary projects for Manhattan that proposed new hybrids of architecture, infrastructure and public space, Edgar Street Towers responds to its immediate site context while establishing a strong relationship to the larger urban form of Manhattan. The towers' design seeks to reinstate Edgar Street as an east-west public way, reconnecting Greenwich and Washington streets. The space of this passageway through the building twists upwards, rising through the body of the towers, pinching at the mid level to allow for larger floorplates, and culminating at a rooftop sky lobby and civic space. Air rights from surrounding parcels and the Brooklyn Battery Tunnel allow the tower to reach its 1300' height. At the towers' crown, the 'skyvoid' space aligns with the primary Manhattan street grid to the north, directly on axis with 5th Avenue.

Edgar Street Towers' programmatic mixture serves the local neighborhood while enhancing the public realm of lower Manhattan. The scale and mix of uses aims to reflect the grandness of vision and diversity of architectural experiences found for example in the premier civic, cultural and commercial landmarks organized along 5th Avenue to the north. This programmatic mixture is envisioned to include spaces for living, working, art, performance, retail and a branch public library. The program is organized by the towers' central branching atrium, enhanced by daylight channeled from above via an integrated light-transmitting fiber-optic array. In addition, the atrium deploys bio-filtration terrariums occupying hollow spaces within the floors, thus acting as the building's lungs to provide clean air to its occupants. By night, the light-flow is reversed, whereby the fiber-optic array is lit from integrated solar-charged battery packs.

On a macro scale, Edgar Street Towers takes advantage of the visibility and prominence offered by its site, where its dynamic form acts as a civic landmark and beacon for those coming to and leaving the city.

IWAMOTOSCOTT PRINCIPALS

Lisa Iwamoto / Craig Scott

IWAMOTOSCOTT PROJECT TEAM

Ryan Golenberg, Stephanie Lin, John Kim, Blake Altshuler

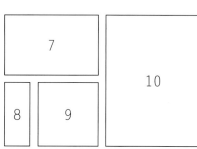

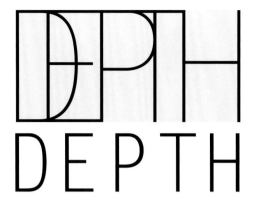

DEPTH

DIGITAL
[SUB]
STANCE

ichnos.03

swarm materiality

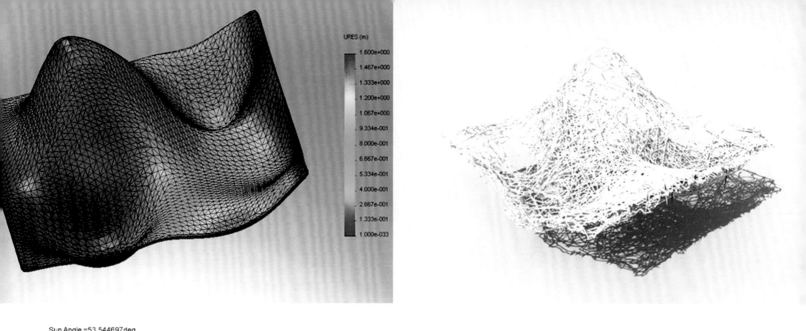

URES (m)

1.600e+000	
1.467e+000	
1.333e+000	
1.200e+000	
1.067e+000	
9.334e-001	
8.000e-001	
6.667e-001	
5.334e-001	
4.000e-001	
2.667e-001	
1.333e-001	
1.000e-033	

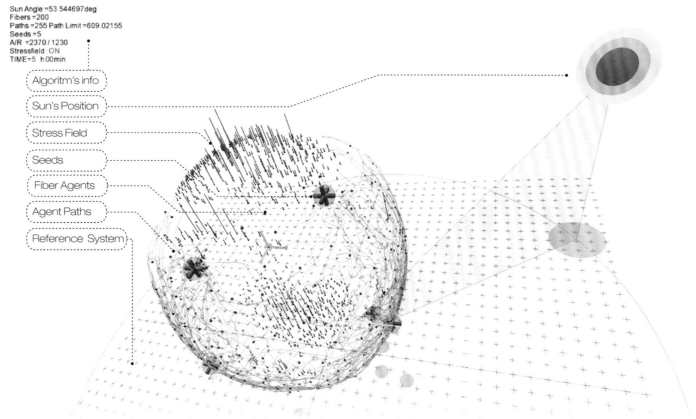

Sun Angle =53.544697deg
Fibers =200
Paths =255 Path Limit =609.02155
Seeds =5
A/R =2370 / 1230
Stressfield : ON
TIME=5 :h:00min

- Algoritm's info
- Sun's Position
- Stress Field
- Seeds
- Fiber Agents
- Agent Paths
- Reference System

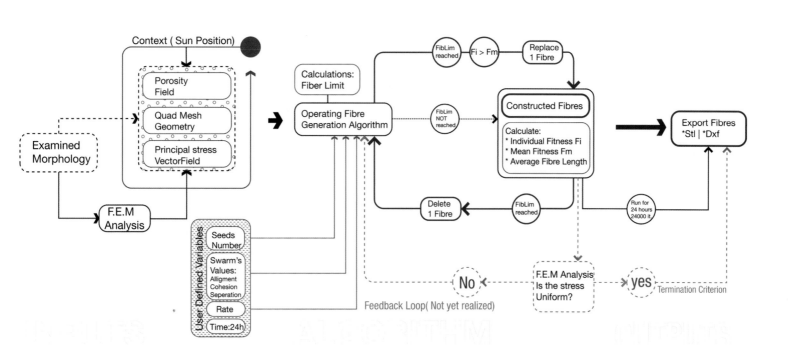

Context (Sun Position)

Examined Morphology → F.E.M Analysis

Porosity Field
Quad Mesh Geometry
Principal stress VectorField

Calculations: Fiber Limit

Operating Fibre Generation Algorithm

FibLim reached — Fi > Fm — Replace 1 Fibre

FibLim NOT reached

Constructed Fibres
Calculate:
* Individual Fitness Fi
* Mean Fitness Fm
* Average Fibre Length

FibLim reached — Delete 1 Fibre

Export Fibres *Stl | *Dxf

Run for 24 hours 24000 it.

User Defined Variables:
Seeds Number
Swarm's Values: Alligment Cohesion Seperation
Rate
Time:24h

No ← F.E.M Analysis Is the stress Uniform? → yes Termination Criterion

Feedback Loop(Not yet realized)

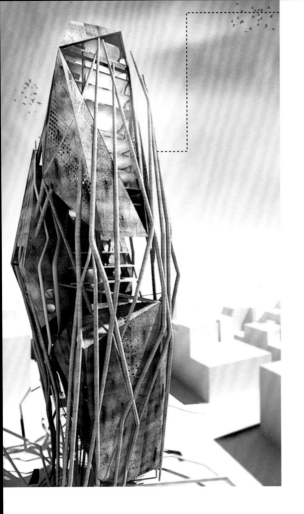

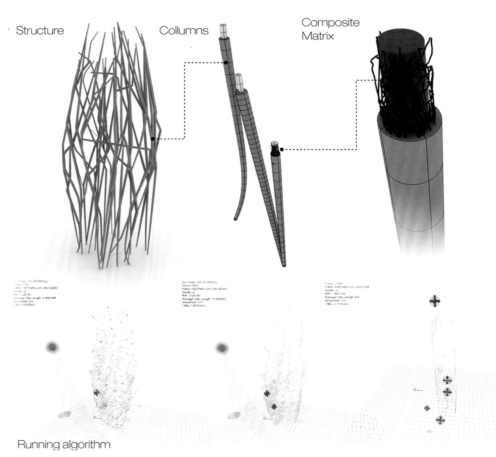

Structure

Columns

Composite Matrix

Running algorithm

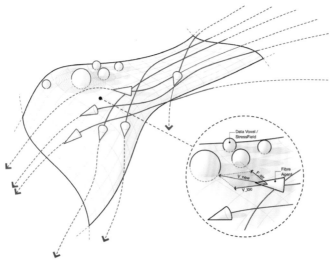

Data Voxel / StressField

Fibre Agent

V_new

F_attr

V_loc

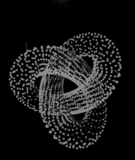

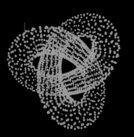

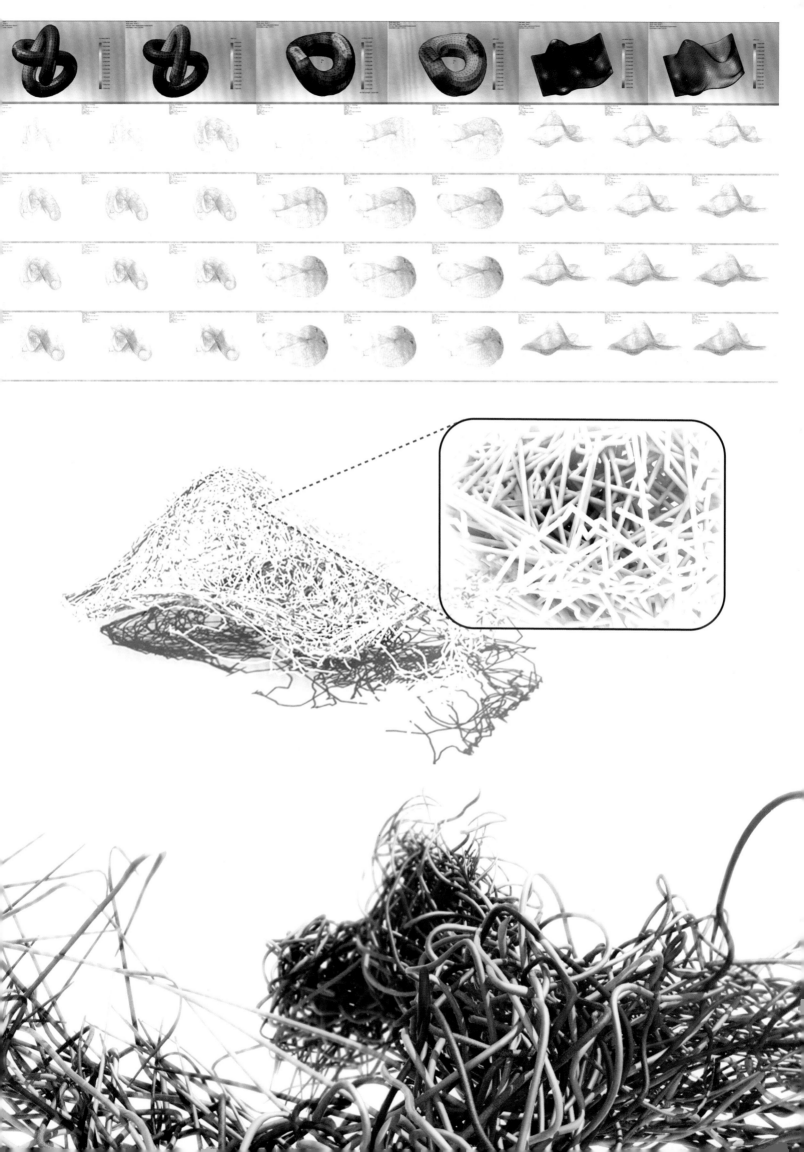

SWARM MATERIALITY

A MULTI-AGENT APPROACH
TO STRESS DRIVEN
MATERIAL ORGANIZATION

DIGITAL [SUB]STANCE

Swarm Materiality is an ongoing research, within the software development context, which is set out to introduce and explore a computational tool, thus a methodological framework, for simulating stress driven material growth and organization by employing a multi-agent system based in swarm intelligence algorithms. The fibrous intrinsic characteristics of this dynamic performative system, following the agents' trails, operate by adapting to certain stimuli while exchanging information in a reciprocal manner with the environment's spatial qualities, fulfilling multiple tasks and consequently converging in local optimal scenarios. Structural information in combination to morphological and topological data become, along with the multi-agent system's characteristics, the driving forces in a bottom-up approach where data flows and components are self-organized into design outputs. This investigation underlies the intention for the material system to be perceived as design itself.

The proposed algorithm, developed in the java-based programming language Processing, is explored via testing on different design cases, offering a coherent understanding on how the various elements perform and a critical evaluation of the system's capacity to produce an acceptable, within the "state-of-the-art" context, solution to material growth optimization and creative form-finding.

The structure of the algorithm is expressed as a linear process constantly resulting to emergent outputs. This input to output procedure introduces a set of dynamically defined routines, both in terms of design-production, but also in relation to the optimization of the results. The fiber-generating algorithm performs on a logic that exploits the multi-agent system's characteristics. Each agent member of the swarm population navigates on the UV surface domain of the examined case study, interacting simultaneously with other members of the population while informed by the adaptation mechanisms. From the total number of fibers generated in the algorithmic process only a few are converted into material design, due to the evaluation routine that replaces fibers with fittest ones. The system is assessed through testing on ten different geometrical configurations, such as spherical cubes, knots and teapots, in addition to variations by altering its user defined, agent or contextual, parameters.

An implementation in a large-scale conceptual project consisting of a multi-story building development is examined by the application of the generative process in a recursive fashion throughout the design. The overall morphology of the building was analysed by the algorithm providing the structural elements of the design, which were then re-designed by the algorithm in the micro-scale level.

Swarm materiality diverges from the other accessible methodologies principally in regard to the implementation of the multi-agent fibre mechanism, and its inherent capability to evaluate multiple design scenarios. This process is primarily defined in natural systems that initially grow the material and then optimize it by re-deposition. The intrinsic incapacity of the system to provide global optima, similar to other optimization methods such as Genetic Algorithms can be addressed as an advantage in terms of design pluralism.

1 Fiber teapot
2 Rendered stills of the teapot geometry at various iterations of the algorithm
3 Rendered still of the algorithm
4 Finite Element Analysis on a free form surface and its fibrous implementation.
5 Explanatory snapshot of the performing algorithm.
6 Schematic overview of the algorithm: Inputs to outputs.
7 Architectural design case study displaying a recursive implementation of the presented algorithm.
8 Schematic diagram of the stress adapting fiber-generating agents.
9 Different porosity levels according to the sun's position
10 Database of three examined geometries
11 Detail on the fiber configuration and distribution
12 Non-geometry depended rendered fiber paths

1	4
2	5
3	6

7	10
8	11
9	12

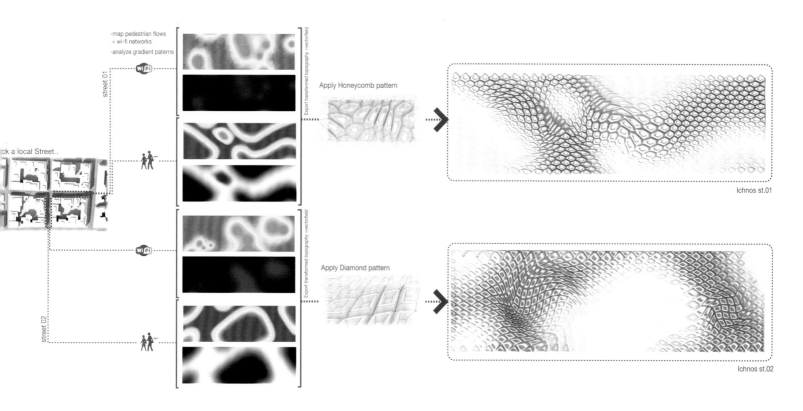

-map pedestrian flows
+ wi-fi networks
-analyze gradient paterns

ck a local Street..

street 01

street 02

Export transformed topography +vectorfield

Export transformed topography +vectorfield

Apply Honeycomb pattern

Apply Diamond pattern

Ichnos st.01

Ichnos st.02

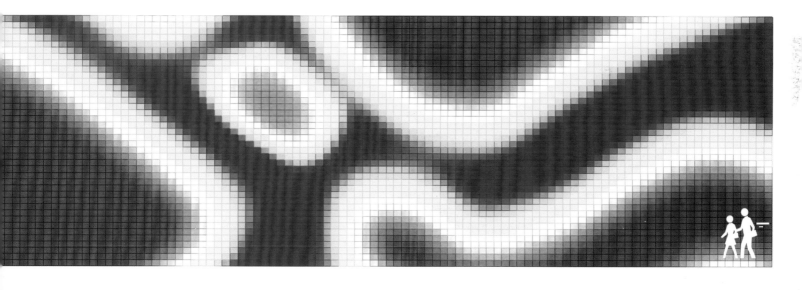

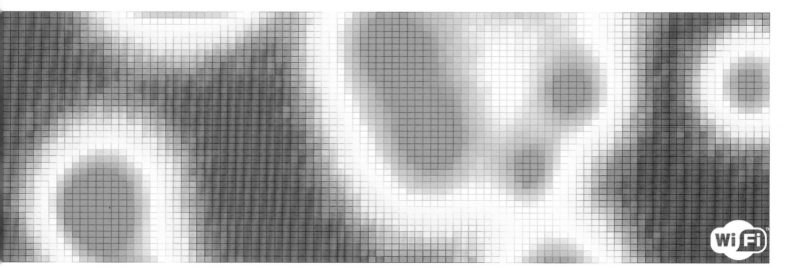

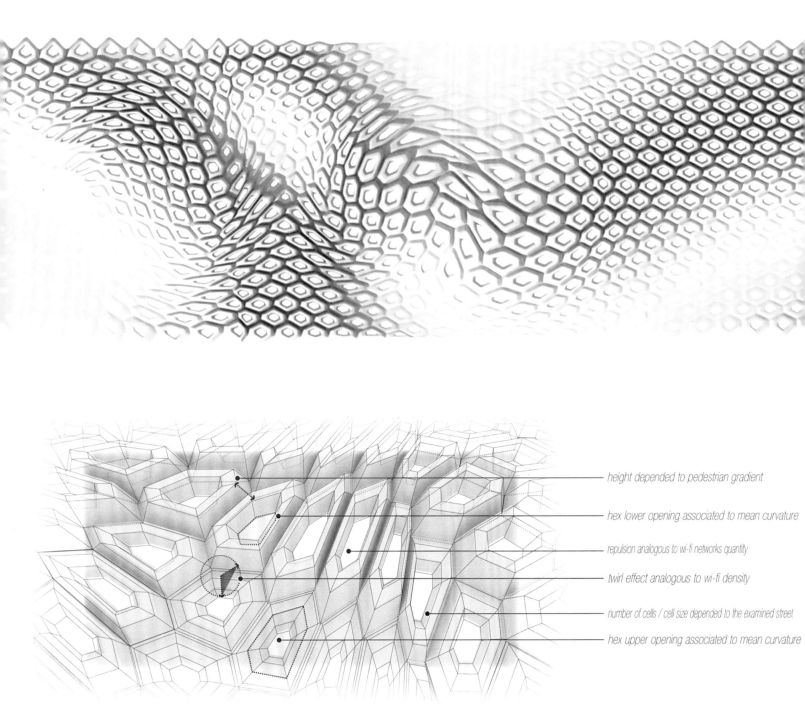

height depended to pedestrian gradient

hex lower opening associated to mean curvature

repulsion analogous to wi-fi networks quantity

twirl effect analogous to wi-fi density

number of cells / cell size depended to the examined street

hex upper opening associated to mean curvature

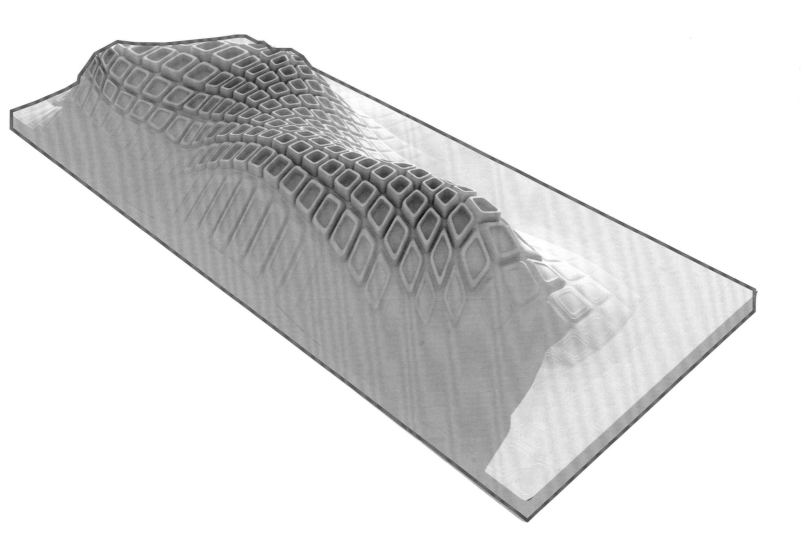

ICHNOS .03

DATA-INFORMED
GENERATIVE ORNAMENTS

DIGITAL [SUB]STANCE

Ichnos .03 is part of the ongoing exploration of "Ichnos" series which commenced as a morphology experimentation and advanced to a multi-platform interactive investigation on the translation of intangible data flows, to design elements and materialized rapid prototyped ornaments. "Ichnos", in modern and ancient Greek, is the trail or the footprint, thus this project is drawing inspiration in theoretical terms from the ethereal trails that human activity deposits, physically or digitally, throughout the day. It consists of a computational process, which attempts to represent and articulate those traces into a perceptible output.

Ichnos .03 is growing within the software development framework; in order to provide an automated hierarchically structured methodology for the translation of data to formal illustration. Until this stage of development, two types of data have been accumulated and mapped. The first one is the density of the pedestrian flows within a certain contextual environment, such as typical Athenian road. The second recorded data set is the quantity and range of Wi-Fi networks in the same area. The tracking and enumeration of these data is achieved through the Arduino platform in a combination of physical computing elements such as proximity sensors and webcams and coding in Processing environment for the translation of data to gradient color maps. Those maps can either be instant recordings, illustrating the data flow in a certain time of the day, or addressing an average or the totality of data throughout a predefined time period.

The collected data are transferred via Udp protocol into Grasshopper3d, where the topological and geometrical transformation takes place. Custom coded C# routines operate simultaneously on the two gradient maps. The first one defines the topography of the outputted geometry by assigning greater surface curvatures where gradient color difference of the pedestrian flow map is larger. In contrast, the Wi-Fi map attracts repulses or rotates the operating topological vector-field in relation to the density of the gradient colors.

Ichnos .03 can be described as a bottom-up approach where a certain set of rules outputs dynamically defined morphological configurations. The initial geometrical tessellation pattern by which the algorithm operates is user defined. However the results are always emergent due to the dynamic nature of the collected data. Even if the Wi-Fi networks remain constantly the same, the amount of pedestrians and certain routes gets greatly differentiated throughout the day. This project focuses in particular on the live feed and on site transformation of the invisible information to morphological experiments.

Ichnos .03 can be considered as a spatial representation methodology. The geometrical outcome can be utilized as a kind of informative ornament. This ornament narrates the story of an area through the informative qualities of human interaction both on physical and digital level. This story can be read just by touching the surface of the ornament, hence feeling the differentiation of intangible data in a physical form.

The exported geometry is fabricated through rapid prototyping methods, like CNC routing, in materials that vary from cherry-wood to corian sheets.

DIGITAL [SUB]STANCE

Digital [Sub]stance is an interdisciplinary practice, founded in 2010 by Marios Tsiliakos, set out to promote a synergetic approach between Architecture, Design and Computation. The practice, based in Athens and London, is engaged in a diversity of projects, both on commercial and architectural research terms, which involve the implementation of digital techniques and innovative computational methodologies.

The research intentions and goals of Digital [Sub]stance lie within the software development context. More specifically, great part of the firm's research is focused on Data-Informed Design and Multi-Performative Systems, as Generative initiatives, in addition to the exploration of the computational processes that can support the depiction of Material as Design itself. Ongoing development involves the employment of multi-agent methodologies into investigating material growth and organization, providing both morphogenetic and analytical tools. Collective behavior and physics as morphogenetic input is another notion of great significance. Hence the large amount of design possibilities explored by physics simulations and particle systems, both as individual research schemes, for instance spatial form finding, and as parts of a greater topic, such as infrastructure design. Experimentation with interactive routines via physical computing and optimization - evaluation implementations on non-linear morphologies may summarize the practice's research range, which is realized primarily through coding in the Processing environment. Part of this research will be presented in this year's international computer aided design conferences.

Digital [Sub]stance offers consulting services to architectural practices in relation to complex geometrical or evaluative design scenarios. These services may vary from façade studies and morphological modifications for multistory buildings, to sustainable design solutions and cost-efficient proposals via optimization routines. Current projects involve sustainable façade studies for international competitions and experimental yacht design. Digital [Sub]stance is also cooperating with a rapid prototyping firm into developing a generative process for creating, client input-based, digitally fabricated objects. Those objects may range from small ornaments and home apparatus, to perforated wall boundaries and sculptures.

Being a enthusiastic supporter of the contemporary "open-source" spirit, Digital [Sub]stance offers online a wide range of digital design tools, both in code or pre-designed in other associative modeling platforms. The practice is also organizing computational design workshops and holds private tutorials on generative methodologies, offering an introduction to the world of Digital Architecture

PAGE 104 + PAGE 105

PAGE 106 + PAGE 107

1 CNC ROUTED ICHNOS ORNAMENT / DETAIL
2 CORIAN CNC ROUTED ICHNOS ORNAMENT / DETAIL
3 SCHEMATIC DIAGRAM OF THE GENERATIVE PROCESS
4 COLOR GRADIENTS AS EXPORTED FROM THE PROCESSING ALGORITHM
5 CORIAN CNC ROUTED ICHNOS ORNAMENT
6 AN ICHNOS CASE
7 ANALYSIS ON THE ATTRIBUTES OF THE APPLIED PATTERN
8 CONCEPTUAL RENDERING OF A FICTIONAL IMPLEMENTATION OF THE ORNAMENT
   ON THE ACTUAL STUDIED STREET
9 AN ICHNOS CASE

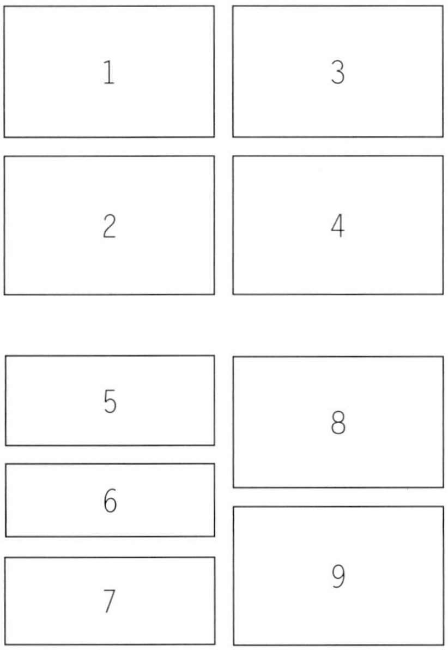

DEPTH

DORIS
SUNG

DOSU
STUDIO

armored corset
bloom
building components for the market

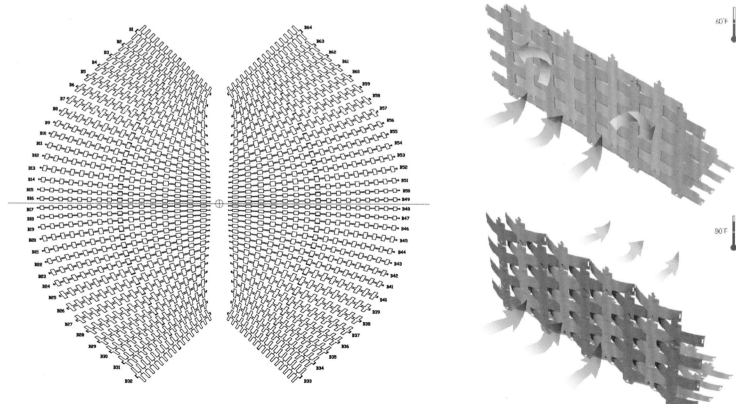

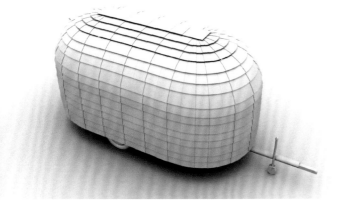

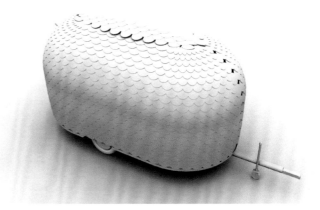

CLOSED SKIN

CLOSED SKIN

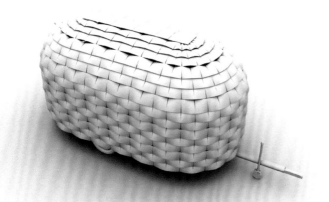

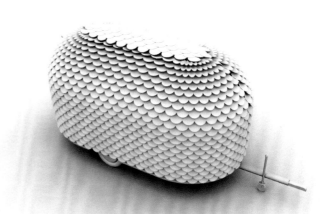

OPENED SKIN

OPENED SKIN

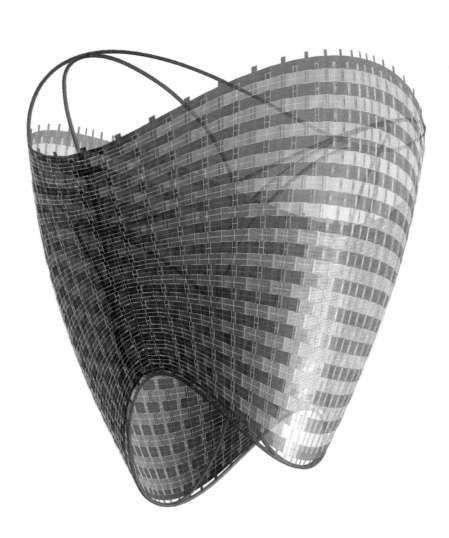

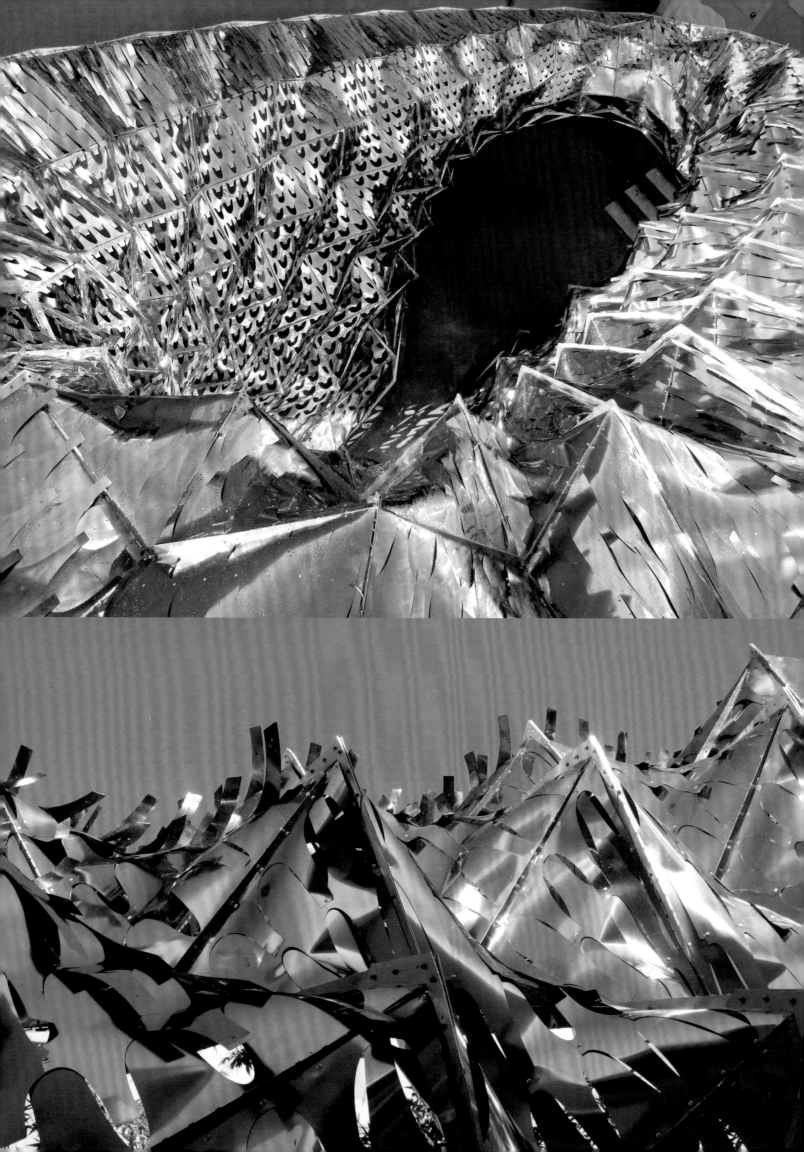

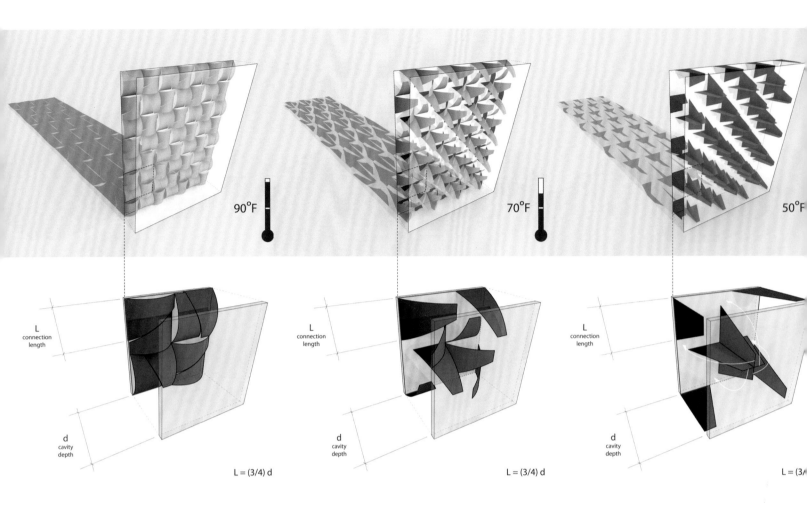

90°F

70°F

50°F

L
connection
length

d
cavity
depth

L
connection
length

d
cavity
depth

L
connection
length

d
cavity
depth

L = (3/4) d

L = (3/4) d

L = (3/

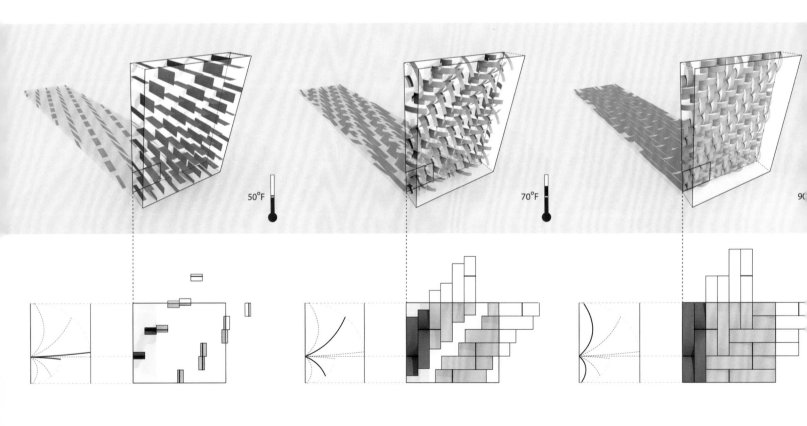

50°F

70°F

9(

DIGITAL ARCHITECTURE
AT DOSU STUDIO

DORIS SUNG

ARMORED CORSET

Commonly used in the form of small strips, this first proof-of-concept prototype considers the application of thermobimetals in architecture by multiplying the capacity of its character into a two-dimensional surface, a skin for a building. The intent is to develop a skin that as the outside (or inside) temperature rises, each individual metal tile will curve and the pores of the skin will physically open, allowing the building to ventilate automatically. To investigate the capacity of this material in this application, various tile shapes and forms were tested and modeled digitally in Catia and ParaCloud. The final selected tile was a simple, but digitally pliable, cross-shape. The dynamic shape of the overall structure allowed each tile to change parametrically, where no two tiles are identical. Depending on the length of the arms of the cross, the tiles will curve horizontally or vertically. The overall form will shrink when heated and will offset the fine-tuned balance of the structure, rocking it to maximize its shade. For this project, complex digital technology is matched with new fabrication techniques such as laser cutting, 3-d milling and rapid prototyping.

BLOOM

A sun-tracking instrument indexing time and temperature, "Bloom" stitches together material experimentation, structural innovation, and computational form/pattern-making into an environmentally responsive installation. The form's responsive surface is made primarily out of 14,000 smart thermobimetal tiles, where no two pieces are alike. Each individual piece automatically curls a specified amount when the outdoor ambient temperature rises above 70°F or when the sun penetrates the surface. The result is a highly differentiated skin system that can smartly shade or ventilate specific areas under the canopy without additional power. For demonstrative purposes, peak performance of the surface is designed for Spring Equinox 2012.

Challenging the traditional presumption that building skins are static and inanimate, the project examines the replacement of this convention with one that posits the prosthetic layer between man and his environment as a responsive and active skin. In order to heighten the sensitivity of the skin, the overall form is oriented towards the sun's arc to maximize solar exposure and away from the shade, much like the growth of plants and flowers. Combined with the sun-facing, freestanding geometry, the reliance on powerful software to generate parametric patterns is inevitable and exemplary. With today's digital technology and driving interest in sustainable design, this simple material can transcend its currently limited role as a mechanical actuating device to a dynamic building surface material, while expanding the discourse of performative architecture on many levels.

1. Material Demonstration

The main goal of this installation is to demonstrate the efficacy of thermobimetal as an exterior building surface with two functions. The first involves the bimetal's potential as a sun-shading device that dynamically increases the amount of shade as the outdoor temperature rises. The size, shape and orientation of the tiles of the tiles are positioned strategically to perform optimally to the relative angle of the sun by use of advanced modeling software. Reliance on digital modeling and physical panel testing prior to final installation is necessary to ensure top performance. The second function for the bimetal is to ventilate unwanted hot air. By optimizing the contortion of individual bimetal tiles, any captured heat would trigger the surface tiles to curl and passively ventilate the space below. In both cases, numerous laser-cutting patterns, solar diagrams, computer analyses and material prototypes were studied, analyzed and tested until the final parameters of the tile cross-shape was set.

2. Structural Testing

Composed of 414 hyperbolic paraboloid-shaped stacked panels, the self-supporting structure challenges the capability of the materials to perform as a shell. The panels combine a double-ruled surface of bimetal tiles with an interlocking, folded aluminum frame system. Like the undulation of the surface, the frame, by nature of its folds, is designed to appear on the inner or outer surface at the same cadence of the peaks and valleys. The final monocoque form, lightweight and flexible, is dependent on the overall geometry and combination of materials to provide comprehensive stability. In some areas of "Bloom", the hypar panels are made stiffer by increasing the number of riveted connections, while, in other areas, the panels are deeper to increase structural capability. The intentionally twisted panel shapes aid in the performance of the structure and challenge the digital and fabrication capabilities of parametric design.

3. Digital Trials

Finally, the use of complex digital tools continues to challenge the process of design and bring it to new levels in fabrication. Original intentions of using CATIA (Computer Aided Three-dimensional Interactive Application) are set aside early due to the unnecessary size and complexity of the digital models. Instead, Rhinoscript and Grasshopper provide a more streamlined and efficient process. The ability to interface with other softwares like Ecotect and other structural analysis tools confirm the selection. With very few mistakes in the final fabrication files, the use of digital software proves to be an amazingly useful tool in computer-aided manufacturing.

The impact of 'Bloom' on the design profession, construction industry, academia and general public is a paradigm shift to emergent technologies: It proposes a sustainable, passive method of reducing reliance on artificial climate control systems and, ultimately, waste of valuable energy; It exhibits an innovative structural strategy that values distributed structural stresses and reduces infrastructural needs; And, it demonstrates the power of digital technologies in the design, analysis, and fabrication of complex tessellated surfaces.

BUILDING COMPONENTS FOR THE MARKET: WINDOW SHUTTER SYSTEMS AND BREEZING BLOCKS

DOSU Studio Architecture is in the process of developing building components for the market that incorporate thermobimetal as a dynamic surface. The products are clearly dependent and derivative the available software and fabrication tools. For sun-shading purposes, thermobimetal is especially useful in window assembly systems. The metal can be lasercut and assembled in a matrix of individual parameterized pieces that can operate like an organic shutter system. The variable mat is sandwiched between two panes of glass as part of a double-glazed window panel system. When the sun penetrates the exterior surface of glass and heats the interior cavity, the bimetal will curl and constrict light from passing. Depending on the brightness of the day, the bimetal shutter system can be calibrated to completely blackout the interior space, if necessary. Applied to a large sun-facing surface, this panel system can help reduce heat-gain, reduce the need for artificial air-conditioning, and conserve energy. Without the need for manual controls or power, this product can operate tirelessly, effortlessly and endlessly.

For self-ventilating purposes, the thermobimetal can perform as a valve system to a network of trachea. DOSU is developing 3-d printed concreted blocks that can stack and allow air to travel through the wall when the temperature escalates on the interior or on the exterior. During the winter months, the valves closes and locks a gap of air in the center cavity, adding another layer of insulating value to wall system. No longer limited by the necessity to manufacture at a mass-produced level, computers and software aid in the development of the concrete form, the preparation of the fabrication files, and the testing of the system for operation. Without those tools, it would be impossible to design and build the prototypes the way that we do.

DOSU STUDIO / DORIS SUNG

The criticism that digital architecture is unrealistic, un-constructible and incomprehensible is not applicable to the work in my office because the purpose of my research is not to make virtual architecture, but rather to make physical prototypes. The mere fact that the work must be built 1:1 preempts commentary and explains the necessity of the computer to be used as an indispensible tool. Additionally, because materiality, gravity, structure, assembly processes and performativity determine the success of the outcome, no single computer program can sufficiently provide all the services needed. Instead, multiple programs are used as means to "cross reference" the development of the design from modeling, programming, simulation and fabrication. The process is fundamentally scientific in nature and performance-driven, but the results are far from looking like engineering diagrams. Clearly, the Vitruvian element of delight is seamlessly integrated in the decision-making process along the way, making the products dynamic, aesthetic appealing and, commonly mistaken as willful. It is where technology meets art.

The use of digital tools in both the Armored Corset and Bloom are invaluable in the performance of the surfaces, the stability of the structure, the facility of fabrication and the ease of assembly. These same aspects are being further tested and developed in ongoing projects in the office. In a double-glazed window panel system, the bimetal infill is designed to curl and block the sun as the cavity heats up. The infill pattern will be parameterized to react to different angles of the sun, the performance will be analyzed and tested through various software; and, the fabrication will be facilitated by nested files for laser cutting. There is also a Breezing Block system that allows a CMU-like block to breathe and ventilate when the interior or exterior heats up. In addition to the previously mentioned tools, other software testing airflow and movement will help in determining shape and form.

1 ARMORED CORSET FRONT VIEW
2 ARMORED CORSET SKIN DETAIL
3 ARMORED CORSET PERSPECTIVE
4 ARMORED CORSET LASER CUTTING SHEET
5 ARMORED CORSET SKIN ANALYSIS
6 ARMORED CORSET AIRSTREAM TEST 1
7 ARMORED CORSET AIRSTREAM TEST 2
8 ARMORED CORSET CATIA DIAGRAM
9 BLOOM SKIN DETAIL
10 BLOOM SKIN REACTING TO TEMPERATURE
11 BLOOM INSTALLATION IN SILVERLAKE, CA
12 WINDOW SHUTTER SYSTEM DIAGRAM 1
13 WINDOW SHUTTER SYSTEM DIAGRAM 2

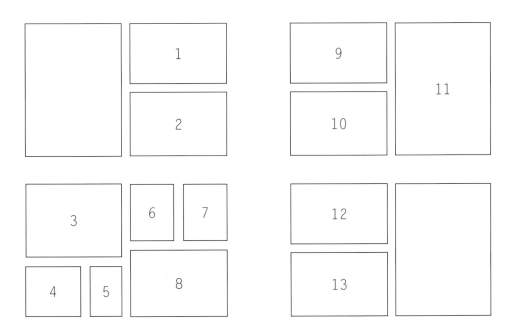

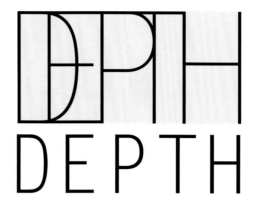

DEPTH

KAS
OOSTERHUIS

ONL

ILONA
LÈNRD

al nasser group headquarters

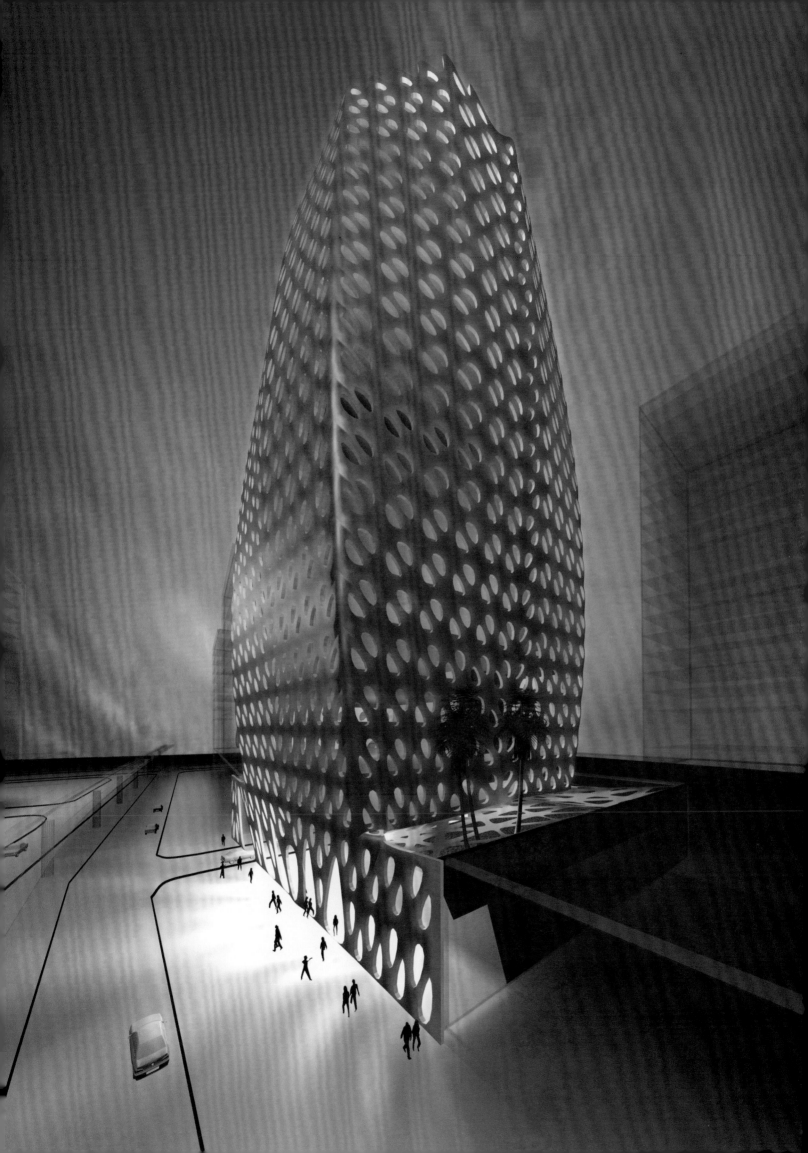

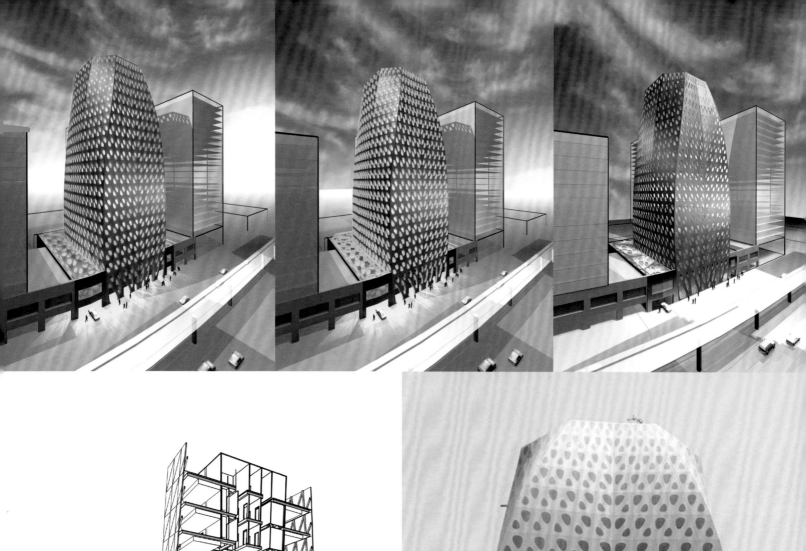
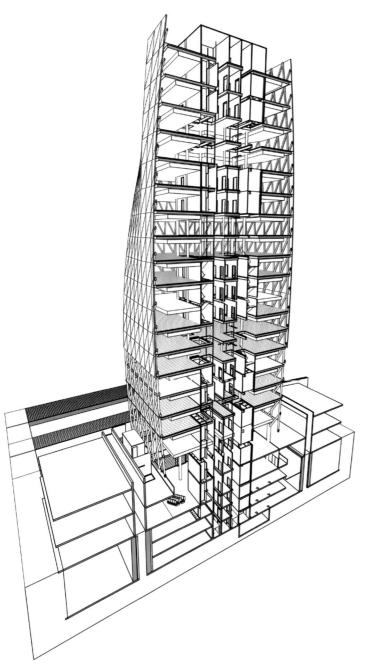

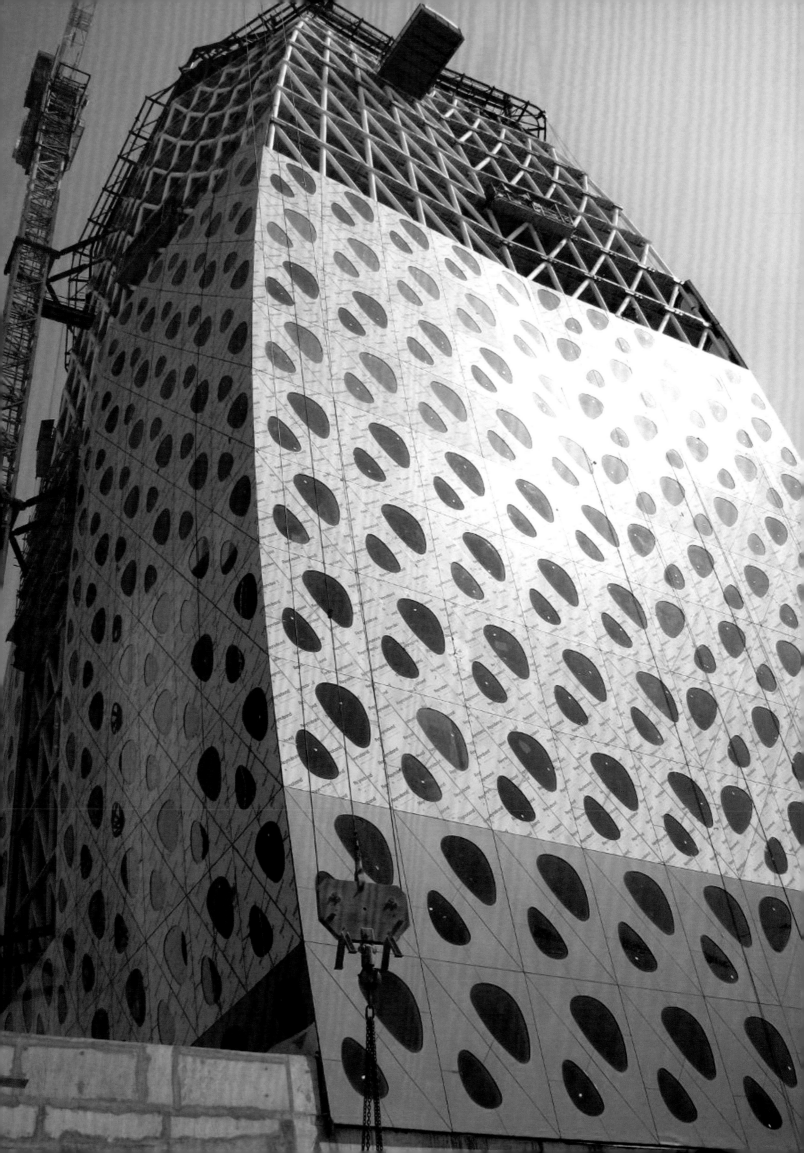

AL NASSER GROUP HEADQUARTERS

NON STANDARD STEEL
STRUCTURE HIGH RISE
IN ABU DHABI, UAE

ONL

After winning the design competition for the Al Nasser Group headquarters in the Capital Centre Development close to the Abu Dhabi National Exhibition Centre (ADNEC) ONL's bold design for high rise office tower on top of a 10m podium has been approved for building by the Master Planners RMJM from Dubai. The Development and Project Manager Northcroft Middle East have scheduled completion for early 2010 for the future user and Client the Al Nasser Group.

The building is designed along the automotive principles of kinetic styling. Gently curved upward moving lines describe the dynamic contours of the tower. Due to the smooth transformation of the shape in vertical direction all floors are unique and vary in dimensions. Earlier realized non standard and kinetic designs of ONL are the Cockpit and the Acoustic Barrier along the A2 highway in Utrecht, The Netherlands.

The tower is among the first towers in Abu Dhabi to use steel for both the core and a structural facade. The majority of existing towers in Abu Dhabi are currently constructed in concrete. The non standard design approach of ONL allows the efficient file to factory production process which facilitates the customization of all steel, aluminum and glass building components of the facade to have unique dimensions and shapes.

The aluminum skin of the Al Nasser Headquarters tower is being developed in collaboration with a Dutch shipbuilders Centraalstaal. The smooth aluminum skin is comnposed of a seaworthy alloy, with a soft copper coating brilliance. LED lights in the windows frames will give the building an intriguing evening glow.

ARCHITECT

ONL [Oosterhuis_LÈn rd] Bv, Rotterdam

CLIENT

Al Nasser Investments, Abu Dhabi UAE

PROJECT ARCHITECTS

Kas Oosterhuis, Ilona LÈn rd, Gijs Joosen

DEVELOPMENT AND PROJECT MANAGERS

Northcroft Middle East, Abu Dhabi UAE

LOCATION

ADNEC Capital Centre Development, Abu Dhabi UAE

COMPLETION

2012

SIZE

26.000 m2 GFA

BUDGET

Undisclosed

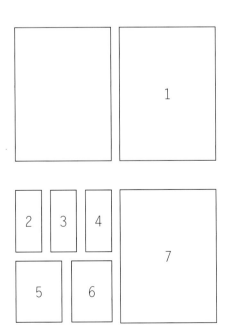

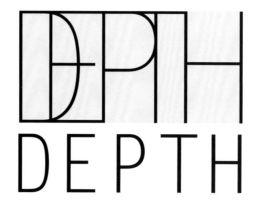

DEPTH

MARK
GOULTHORPE

DECOI
/ MIT

digital praxis
hyposurface
one main office renovation

DIGITAL PRAXIS

DECOI / MIT

dECOi Architects has continued to operate as a dispersed network of technical partners, re-formatted for the particular needs of each project, which are typically pressing to define new potentials of design, form and fabrication. The communication potential of digital systems, and the common protocols they offer, remain a prime driver towards new modes of collaborative praxis with mathematicians, programmers, etc.

We invested a great deal of time developing a highly sophisticated parametric model for the Bankside Paramorph (some 350 generative algorithms whispering in a highly constrained internal conspiracy!), and the degree of control it offers entices further experimentation with rule-based generative logics. These alloplastic logics are not at all easy to master intellectually given our autoplastic inheritance and training; but they seem prescient at the threshold of a digital age, intoxicating in their promise of extremely nuanced formal genesis that is imbued with performative attributes.

Of great interest in all our projects, but especially in the Bankside Paramorph, has been to attempt to find material corollaries for the sophisticated formal and structural output of the digital design process. Increasingly we have looked to composites, and successfully tendered the Bankside Paramorph entirely in carbon fibre using boat-building techniques. Here we recognized the highly sophisticated material-process logic of the composites industry, and it remains of great interest to us.

The recent development of a new version of HypoSurface, where we have redesigned not only the drive system (from pneumatic to electrical actuators) but every aspect of its surface and structure to handle the increased performance, has been very engaging as a physical challenge – how to get robust and elegant performance at high speed operation. But it is the origination of the software protocols to drive the system that is most compelling, and in particular the interactive interfaces logic and user interfaces. These are also conceived as highly complex generative rule-based systems, where we are attempting to tease out highly nuanced and complex layering of sonic/movement and light responsiveness.

Most recently, we have been looking to devise a quasi-automated design-to-build housing logic using robotic fabrication of thermoplastic panels. We envisage parametric design logics overlaid by automated scripts that allow stiff lightweight composite panels to be rapidly cut and assembled. This combines new design, material and fabrication logics to suggest entirely new modes of house building, which seem extremely efficient economically, logistically and environmentally. Our goal (in all these projects) is an adequate revision of architectural praxis that adequately realigns it in light of the profound technological paradigm shift occasioned by digital technology.

HYPOSURFACE
A DYNAMICALLY INTERACTIVE ARCHITECTURAL SURFACE,
A NEW MEDIUM FOR THE PLASTIC ARTS

As an evolving experimental prototype, HypoSurface (Aegis) is a literally-dynamic architectural surface, a new medium of dynamic form, where a matrix of computer-controlled actuators deform a large elastic surface at high speed, offering a directly-responsive formal plasticity. As a literally alloplastic architecture (reciprocally linked to people's sound and movement) our central interest has been to understand the cultural affect of such animate form, and to deploy a variety of interactive systems to elicit different modes of audience engagement. The interactive interfaces have been developed as highly sophisticated parametric systems, offering extraordinary nuance and range to the generation of movement and sound, HypoSurface being an extreme example of multi-media digital architecture.

The technical attainment of a now electrical (no longer pneumatic) Hypo3 system has demanded extreme high-speed digital communication (new EtherCAT protocols). The intense research activity that has been brought to bear on it has foregrounded the need

for multi-disciplinary teamwork, but also offers insights into many potential areas of architectural application aside from its current info-tainment potency. These extend from establishing effective base protocols for interactive control systems, to the layered intensities of emerging aesthetic aptitude of a digital socius, to the real-time multi-device logicistics of sophisticated environmental control systems.

ALLOPLASTIC FORM

The interactive capacity of HypoSurface offers an immediate plastic reciprocity of form with people that seem to breach the static, autoplastic history of architectural form. Such reciprocal modification of self and environment suggests an alloplastic modality, an entirely changed psychic state of heightened yet uncertain environmental connectivity. This implies an unstable and evolving aesthetic, where active input provokes ever-modifying output, setting off chain-reactions akin to a metonymic triggering of association; clearly at odds with the metaphoric, representative semantics of more static media. The experiments we have done with the interactive protocols then look to probe this alloplastic potential, and our initial assessment of the affectivity of such unstable yet evolving generative systems (sound and movement) confirms it as being far more engaging with people than a direct or uniform causal triggering. One conjectures that such alloplastic reciprocity is a form of trauma, where the essential event is missed in the very intensity of its occurrence, provoking a restless, sensitized cognitive aptitude. What we have learned from the powerfully visceral interactive potential of HypoSurface is that digital technologies invite exploration of such alloplastic desire, and to theories of trauma as a now active cultural trope.

GENERATIVE PARAMETRICS

There are two interactive 'engines' that provide the central nervous system of HypoSurface, each evolving for the various events we have engaged (CeBIT digital show, IMTS robotics show, BIO biotechnology show...) The base control of surface movement relies on a mathematical engine that outputs sequential arrays of real-time data, refreshing every moving actuator continually. This is linked digitally to a sonic 'engine' that outputs sound, either as real-time processed sound or as combinations of pre-recorded sounds. Both these 'engines' can give output to a lighting control system, such that movement, light and sound can be linked effectively, and all three aspects can be triggered by any input signal, most typically sound (via microphone) or movement (via two video cameras), or as a cross-wired synaesthesia where one system triggers the others.

Crucially, these two engines have been conceived as rule- based generative systems, where a variety of parameters can be altered to offer variance in the output, transforming or deforming the affect. The input (typically sound or movement from an audience) may also be analyzed to establish the parametric value of the output, offering a linkage between behavior of people and sonic/plastic register.

TEAM

Mark Goulthorpe, MIT (Architect/Creative Director), Steven Shpiner (Technical Director) consultants Dr Marc Downie, MIT (Interactive Math/Movement System / Programming (OpenendedGroup)), Mikey Fujihara, MIT (User Interface Development/Programming), Prof Paul Steenhuisen (Digital Composer/Sound Interface), Dr Alex Scott, Oxford (Mathematics), Prof Saeid Nahavandi, Deakin (Mechatronics/Control Protocols), Prof Mark Burry (SIAL/ Continued Support)

ONE MAIN OFFICE RENOVATION

The project was for the penthouse offices of an investment group in green building and clean energy technologies (CChange). The design drew from our prior sculpture, In the Shadow of Ledoux, 1993, and the Galerie Miran, 2003, proposing the milling of all elements of the interior from sustainably-forested spruce plywood using numeric command machines: information carves renewable carbon-absorbing resource.

The project essentially comprises two planes - the floor and ceiling, both of which are articulated as continuous surfaces inflected by function. The curvilinearity expresses both the digital genesis and the seamless fabrication logic, with the architect providing actual machining files to the fabricator. As far as possible, the ethos was to replace typical industrial components (such as vents, door handles, etc) with articulate milled timber, offering a radically streamlined protocol for delivery of a highly crafted interior. The intention was to offer a reduced carbon footprint whilst celebrating both a new formal virtuosity and a radical level of detail finesse. Effectively this allows the architect to fully customize all elements of the building, placing material in space with full authorial control (for the first time since industrial components became standard). Other than sprinklers, lights, glass and hinges, the substance of the interior architecture was realized via this unitary material/fabrication logic, with a high degree of prefabrication.

The early sketch design grasped the potential for plastic control of the spatial and detail definition allowable within a fully CAD-CAM environment. The client asked that the work chairs be purchased for liability reasons, but all shelves, desks, benches, storage units, etc were accepted for direct fabrication in plylam via the same method. Ultimately we devised automated algorithms for generating actual milling files, passing from design to fabrication seamlessly and with high tolerances and extremely low percentages of error.

The developed design was nuanced parametrically in celebration of the indifference of the CNC machine to formal complexity. The entire project was nested onto 1200 4ft x 12ft plywood sheets, and milled using a small 3-axis CNC router, which effortlessly carved the ply sections according to our prescribed 'weeping' tool paths. Well over a million linear feet of cut were issued, yet the mechanic process was essentially error-free and highly accurate. Assembly proved relatively straightforward given the accuracy of the milling, and we enjoyed the elegance of the emerging forms.

The project was nuanced down to the smallest detail, such as the ventilation grille for the computer boxes being inflected to provide a handle to open the door; or the milling of custom mathematical surfaces for each office; even the door handles were carved as customized elements, proving cheaper than stainless steel D- handles! We aimed at formal coherence at macro and micro scales, such that an inflection in the ceiling was echoed in the benches and carried down to the sinuous lines of the door handles.

Functional needs such as ventilation grilles and shrouds for the bright LED lights gave a detail finesse to the ceiling; whilst focal elements such as the conference table or directors' desks were plastically formed to permit electrical data outlets in the spine, and were embellished mathematically according to parameters of 'tension' and 'irony'. Quite literally, the material substance of each space was nuanced according to the character and mood of each client during the fabrication period.

TEAM

dECOi: Mark Goulthorpe, Raphael Crespin (Project Architect),
        Gabe Cira, Matt Trimble (Scripting), Priyanka Shah
MIT: Kaustuv de Biswas
Mathematics: Prof Alex Scott (Oxford University)
Consultants: Helen Heitman (Gensler Associates)
General Contractor: Paul Jacobson (Tricore)
Millwork Contractor: Shawn Keller (CWKeller)
Client: CChange Investments / Zero+

HYPOSURFACE
1 HYPOSURFACE IN ACTION
2 HYPOSURFACE WRITING WORDS
3 HYPOSURFACE DETAIL
4 HYPOSURFACE INTERACTING WITH USERS

ONE MAIN
5 ONE MAIN HALLWAY
6 ONE MAIN LOBBY
7 ONE MAIN OFFICES
8 ONE MAIN OFFICES
9 ONE MAIN COMMON AREA

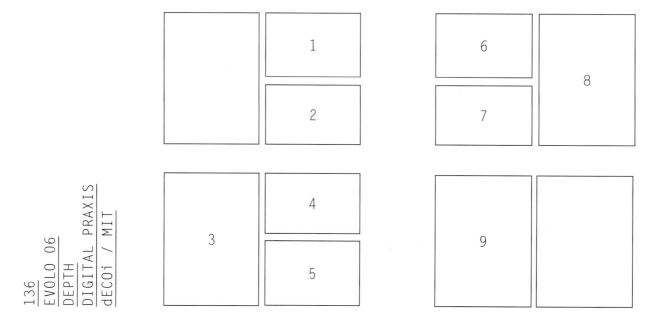

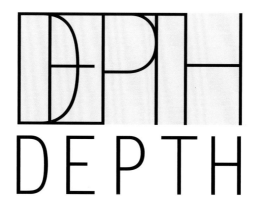

DEPTH

ANDREW
KUDLESS

MATSYS

chrysalis, p_wall

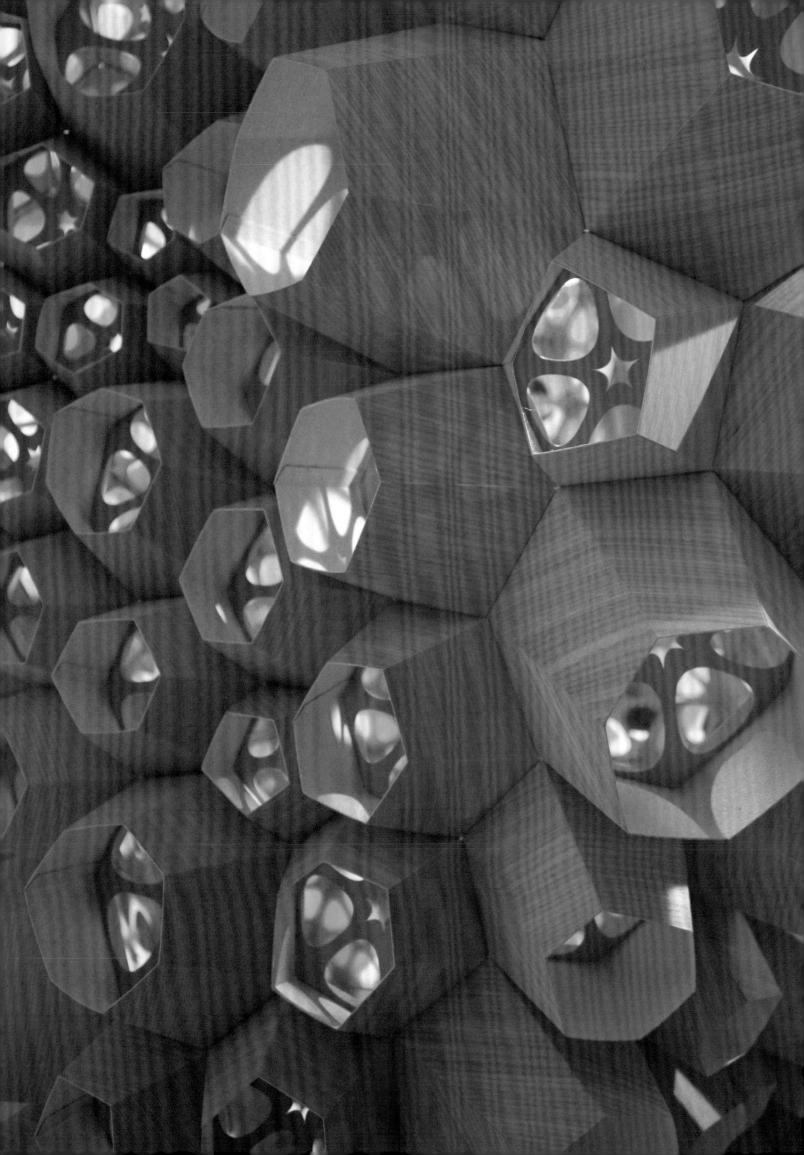

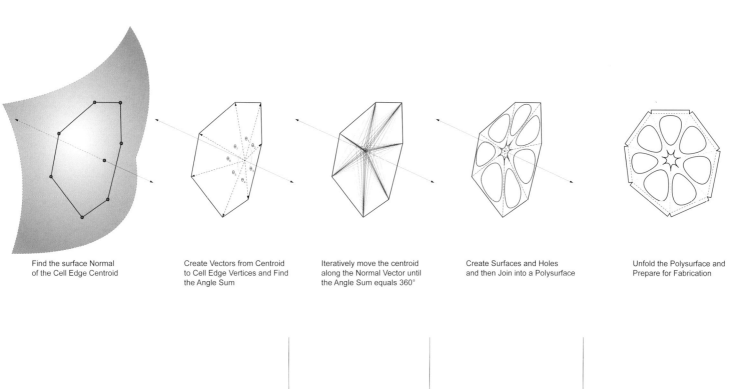

Find the surface Normal
of the Cell Edge Centroid

Create Vectors from Centroid
to Cell Edge Vertices and Find
the Angle Sum

Iteratively move the centroid
along the Normal Vector until
the Angle Sum equals 360°

Create Surfaces and Holes
and then Join into a Polysurface

Unfold the Polysurface and
Prepare for Fabrication

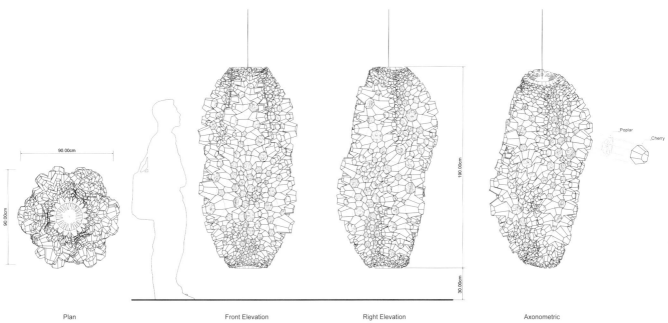

Plan

Front Elevation

Right Elevation

Axonometric

90.00cm

90.00cm

190.00cm

30.00cm

Poplar

Cherry

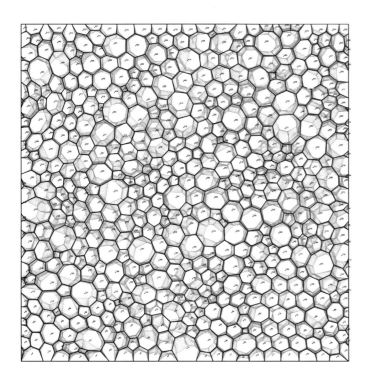

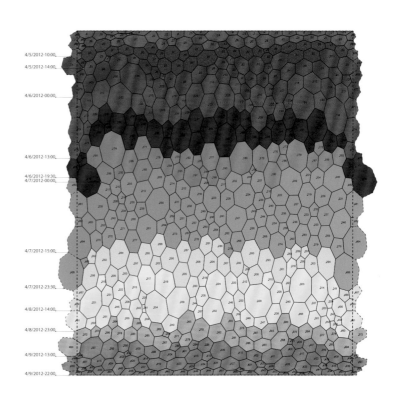

4/5/2012-10:00,
4/5/2012-14:00,
4/6/2012-00:00,
4/6/2012-13:00,
4/6/2012-19:30,
4/7/2012-00:00,
4/7/2012-15:00,
4/7/2012-23:30,
4/8/2012-14:00,
4/8/2012-23:00,
4/9/2012-13:00,
4/9/2012-22:00,

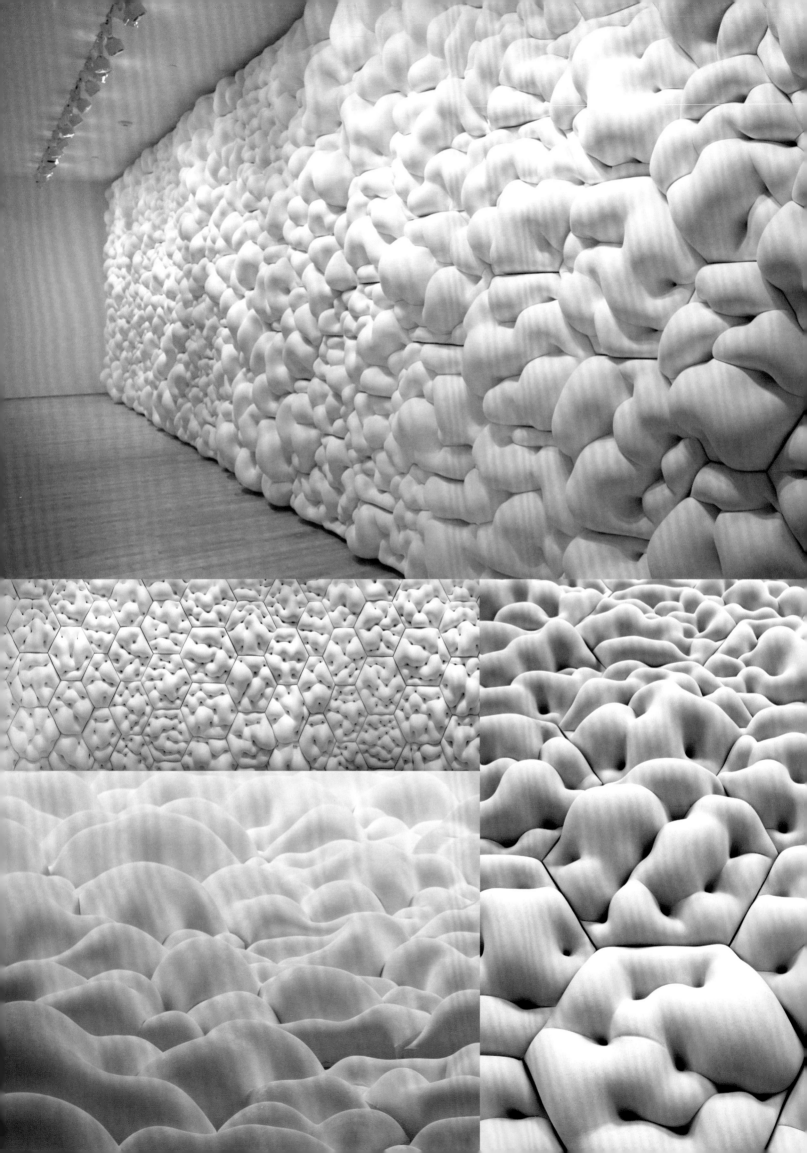

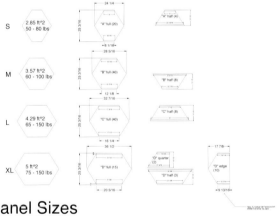

4 Panel Sizes

150 Panels   area: 546 ft^2

avg.: 100 lbs

S	2.85 ft^2 / 50 - 80 lbs	"A" full (20), "A" half (4)
M	3.57 ft^2 / 60 - 100 lbs	"B" full (40), "B" half (8)
L	4.29 ft^2 / 65 - 150 lbs	"C" full (40), "C" half (8)
XL	5 ft^2 / 75 - 150 lbs	"D" full (15), "D" quarter (2), "D" half (3), "D" edge (10)

MATSYS
ANDREW KUDLESS

MATSYS is a design studio exploring the emergent and integral relationships between form, growth, and behavior in material systems. The studio works at all scales and pursues a practice that blends art, design, architecture, and engineering. Our methods of research focus on the tension between digital morphogenesis and physical form-finding, knowing that each domain contributes essential information to the design process. In the pursuit of innovative syntheses of geometry, material, and performance, we build our custom digital tools in the form of parametric models and scripts. Craftsmanship, in both digital and physical forms, is the core of our research and practice. This interest in craft, combined with a fascination with the emergence of structure, form, and intelligence in the natural world, drive us to create objects, spaces, and landscapes that are complex, playful, and a bit uncanny.

MATSYS was founded in 2004 by Andrew Kudless, a San Francisco designer and educator. In addition to being the principle designer at MATSYS, Andrew is an assistant professor at the California College of the Arts and has taught at the Architectural Association, Yale University and The Ohio State University where he was the Howard E. LeFevre Fellow for Emerging Practitioners. He has a Master of Arts in Emergent Technologies and Design from the Architectural Association and a Master of Architecture from Tulane University. The work of MATSYS can be found in the permanent collections of the San Francisco Museum of Modern Art and the Centre Pompidou.

CHRYSALIS (III)

Over the last 8 years our research has returned again and again to the morphology of cellular systems. As D'Arcy Thompson noted in his seminal volume On Growth and Form, cellular systems exist somewhere on the border between living and non-living matter. From sea foam to our own material bodies, cellular system are pervasive in natural material systems as well as many industrially produced materials.

In designing Chrysalis (III), we were inspired by an interest in the way that certain barnacles populate surfaces along the coast. The close packing of the barnacles blurs the distinction between individual organism and a nearly geologic swarm that encases boat hulls, rocks, and almost anything with a certain intertidal zone. These living mats of cellular bodies spread across the host surface to form what we liked to call a cocoon or chrysalis, concealing a new organism within. The ocean rock, once inert, is transformed through its cellular occupation into something new, unknown, and hidden within the chrysalis.

Working with this idea, a cellular spring network was distributed across a host digital surface. The springs were released and the cells were allowed to relax on the surface, producing an even, yet non-uniform and topologically distinct, cellular network. Each of these cells was populated with a barnacle-like truncated and faceted cone. The interior of each cell was populated with a structural plate that keeps the cell rigid.

The relaxed cellular geometry produced two interesting qualities in regards to fabrication. By relaxing the spring network, acute angles are reduced in the cells, making them easier to cut, nest, and join together. In addition, since each cell has more than three sides, the interior plate will always be non-planar as it conforms to the host surface. Although this is problematic for fabricating it out of flat sheet material, this non-planarity was used to stiffen the plates. An iterative search algorithm was used to find a non-planar surface that could still be approximated by an unfolded plate without any interior seams.

The final piece is composed of 500 cells, each made from 2 laser-cut parts. The inner plates are cut from poplar micro-veneer while the outer cones are cut from cherry micro-veneer. After cutting, pieces were hand-assembled into the final form based on a precise numbering system as each cell is unique and only fits in one position.

TEAM

Andrew Kudless (design), Jason Vereschak (cutting) and Emily Kirwan (prototyping), Maciej Fiszer (for the lending of assembly space in Paris), and the Pompidou Centre Industrial Prospectives Department (Valerie Guillaume, Hélène Ducate, Dominique Kalabane, and Marguerite Reverchon)

P_WALL

SFMOMA Architecture and Design Curator Henry Urbach commissioned P_Wall (2009) for the exhibition Sensate: Bodies and Design. The wall, part of a series started with P_Wall (2006), is an evolution of the earlier work exploring the self-organization of material under force. Using nylon fabric and wooden dowels as form-work, the weight of the liquid plaster slurry causes the fabric to sag, expand, and wrinkle. Although the outer frame of the panel and the wood dowel constraints are fixed, everything happening between the dowels and the frame is free to move around and find a balance between the mass of the plaster and the elasticity of the fabric.

The constraint positions are located through the use of a digital script that attempts to recreate an image through a series of points, similar to a stipple drawing technique. However, the maximum distance between any two neighboring points in the script is informed by the limits found through material testing. If the points are too far apart, the system fails under the overloading of the fabric. If the points are too close together, the system fails as the fabric is over-constrained and cannot flex to accept the plaster load that results in cross-sections that are too thin and weak. The image that was used in the script is a simple sine wave moving up and down which resulted in the wall tiles undulated from floor to ceiling in the finished piece. These large spatial undulations create coves and overhangs in the wall that can be seen and experienced as one moves along the wall.

From the exhibition text written by Henry Urbach:
Andrew Kudless's P_Wall, commissioned by SFMOMA for this exhibition and its permanent collection, marks a radical reinvention of the gallery wall. Typically smooth, firm, regular and, by convention, "neutral," the gallery wall has shed its secondary status to become a protagonist in the space it lines. Made of one hundred fifty cast plaster tiles — individually formed by pouring plaster over nylon stretched atop wooden dowels — the new wall possesses an unmistakable corporeal quality. Bulges and crevices; love handles and cleavage; folds, pockmarks, and creases: these are among the characteristics of human skin that come to the fore. Contemporary in its effort to capture dynamic forces in static form, P_Wall nonetheless has its origins in the experiments of earlier, 20th century architects including Antoní Gaudí and Miguel Fisác, both of whom investigated the potential of cast material to yield unique, sensual and, at times, bizarre shapes. P_Wall replaces the modern gallery wall with an unwieldy skin that can only approximate the fleshy enclosure that we, as human beings, inhabit throughout the course of our lives.

TEAM

Andrew Kudless (design and fabrication lead) Chad Carpenter (design and prototyping assistant), Dino Rossi (formwork carpenter), Dan Robb (fabrication assistant), Frances Lee, Dorothy Leigh Bell, Janiva Ellis, Ripon DeLeon, Ryan Chandler, Ben Golder, Colleen Paz (fabrication crew)

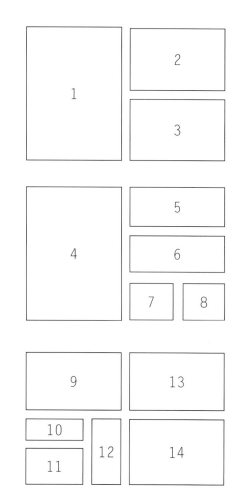

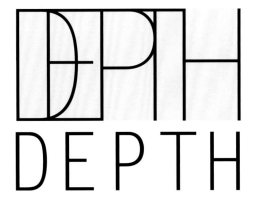

DEPTH

BRANDON
CLIFFORD

MATTER
DESIGN

WESLEY
MCGEE

periscope foam tower, la voute de lefevre

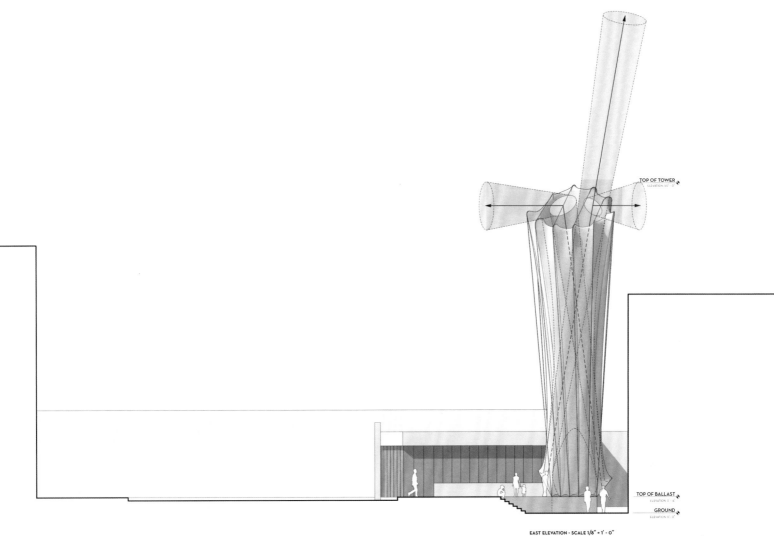

EAST ELEVATION - SCALE 1/8" = 1'- 0"

TOP OF TOWER
ELEVATION 50' - 0"

TOP OF BALLAST
ELEVATION 3' - 6"

GROUND
ELEVATION 0' - 0"

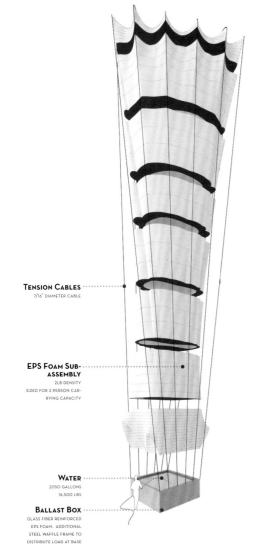

Tension Cables
7/16" DIAMETER CABLE

EPS Foam Sub-
assembly
2LB DENSITY
SIZED FOR 2 PERSON CAR-
RYING CAPACITY

Water
2050 GALLONS
16,500 LBS

Ballast Box
GLASS FIBER REINFORCED
EPS FOAM. ADDITIONAL
STEEL WAFFLE FRAME TO
DISTRIBUTE LOAD AT BASE

ASSEMBLY DIAGRAM

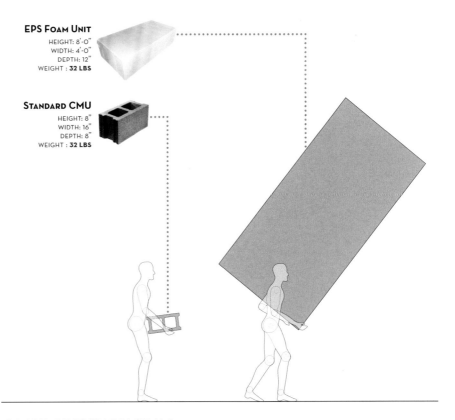

EPS Foam Unit
HEIGHT: 8'-0"
WIDTH: 4'-0"
DEPTH: 12"
WEIGHT : **32 LBS**

Standard CMU
HEIGHT: 8"
WIDTH: 16"
DEPTH: 8"
WEIGHT : **32 LBS**

SCALE OF UNIT DIAGRAM
SCALE : 1/2" = 1'-0"

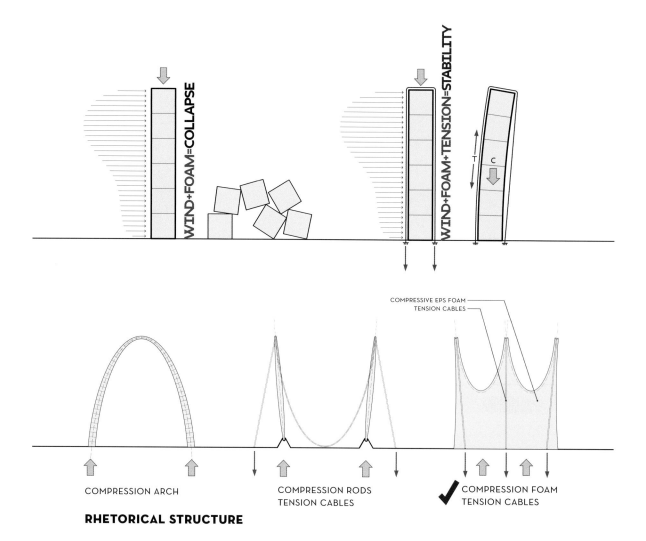

COMPRESSIVE EPS FOAM
TENSION CABLES

WIND+FOAM=COLLAPSE

WIND+FOAM+TENSION=STABILITY

COMPRESSION ARCH

COMPRESSION RODS
TENSION CABLES

✓ COMPRESSION FOAM
TENSION CABLES

RHETORICAL STRUCTURE

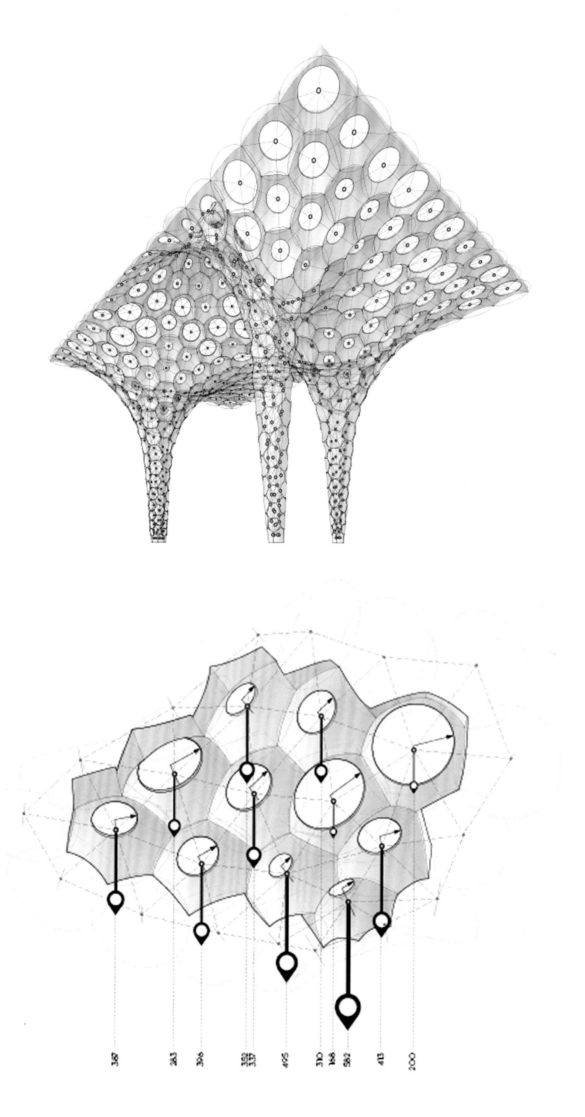

MATTER DESIGN

BRANDON CLIFFORD,
WESLEY MCGEE

In order to understand Matter Design, one needs to understand the unlikely partnership that constitutes the practice. Matter Design is a collaboration between Brandon Clifford and Wesley McGee. While both are academics (Clifford teaches at MIT and McGee at the University of Michigan), Clifford has bachelors and masters degrees in architecture while McGee has a bachelors in mechanical engineering and a masters in industrial design. For clarity, lets say McGee is proficient in making, with a respect for design, while Clifford is the inverse. What they both have in common is a dedication to digital design. This partnership forced the pair to envision the practice as a marriage between drawing and making.

Matter Design revolts against the idea that the role of the architect should be relegated to producing representations of architectural intent, while the contractor maintains control of the means and methods of making. This is a revolt against the standard practice of the architect, but is also situated in a field of digital design that bounds in the fantasies of renderings and gravity-less designs. Matter Design is truly digital but they are grounded in the realities of materials, loads, and physicality — topics that don't immediately exist in the digital.

Matter Design's goal is to develop means and methods of making in reciprocity with the architectural intent. This process does not propose the architect become contractor, but rather that the architect partners with the contractor. They has found that this process of working leads to innovation that emerges through resolving problems from both ends of this spectrum meeting in the middle with a solution. This is a result of their dichotomous partnership, but it is also their hope for the future of the profession (as it ironically existed in the past).

Many of the projects begin with a vague idea that is the result of a long-winded conversation that drift from ideas, through limitations, budget constraints, back to fantasies, and ultimately to a suggestion (most typically a joke) — "What if we built a giant tower out of foam that looked like fabric?" This serious joke is then either laughed upon or more typically validated by the other partner with a historical reference — "Well actually that is precisely how the Inca detailed their walls" (joke from Periscope and validation from La Voûte de LeFevre). At this point the project exists as the vague idea and both are set off with respective tasks. Clifford finds a way of drawing the design informed by the method of making agreed upon, and most typically amplifying the joke that the legitimate reference emerged from. McGee tends to design and build the custom tool, as well as the code that translates the drawing into an action of construction. As the project moves forward, shared information pulls both of these tasks together to a merged solution.

PERISCOPE FOAM TOWER

Periscope is the winning entry in the 10Up! National Architecture Competition: an experiment derived from Matter Design's obsession ongoing pre-occupation with volume.

The 10Up! competition brief called for entries that could be constructed by a two-person team, working with a five thousand dollar budget for a ten foot square plot, and less than twenty-four hours for installation. Mounted in only six hours, Periscope is not only a beacon for the Modern Atlanta Event, but is also a product of contemporary digital fabrication culture in that the means and methods of fabrication were developed in parallel to the design, namely custom robotic fabrication tools. The regulations did not stipulate a height restriction and most entries assumed the ten-foot cube volume. Periscope, at fifty feet tall, was more ambitious.

From a distance, the observer confronts the sheer magnitude of the figure. The tower appears as tensile fabric stretched vertically by impossibly thin compression rods. This initial confusion is productive: it pulls the observer in for closer inspection to reveal Periscope's logic of rough stereotomic construction. Two portholes at ground level invite the spectator to peer up the 'skirt' and through the body of the tower. Persicope resists an initial reading of its form as a surface membrane. Where the eye once read tensile fabric there is now solid compressive foam. The compressive rods are actually tensile cables.

This rhetorical inversion is both a commentary on the contemporary practice of surface operation (as opposed to volume) as well as a vehicle to pull spectators in — ultimately to the Modern Atlanta Event. The tower was fabricated using a custom built, seven-axis robot controlled hotwire cutter at the University of Michigan's Taubman College of Architecture and Urban Planning. Over 500 custom foam units are carved from stock blocks of EPS (expanded polystyrene) foam assembled into three-foot tall sub-assemblies. Each sub-assembly was designed to be light enough for two people to easily carry. Fourteen sub-assemblies stack to construct the fifty-foot tall figure held down with tension cables to the ballast base. This ballast weighs approximately 16,500 lbs to resist the overturning forces of the design wind.

Most contemporary digital fabrication techniques are developed and informed by relatively sheet materials. We at Matter Design translated the developed surface technique into a digitized process as a way of embracing the somewhat lost practice of stereotomy. The developed surface was a method for customizing stone carving through the minimal means of a sweeping line that can be flattened or from a three-dimensional geometry into a two-dimensional drawing otherwise known as a trait. By extracting this principle, it is possible to conceive of this hypothetical line as a physical and CNC (computer numerically controlled) device — a custom robot controlled four foot long hot-wire. This converging of past techniques with contemporary materials and methods informed reciprocity between drawing and making.

Stereotomic construction is inherently a compression-based system as its material is stone — a very heavy material. Foam on the other hand is without significant self-weight. Ironically the impetus to engage the process of stereotomy conflicts with the prompt for a temporary installation. In designing this tower, tension is required, but the research agenda is not limited to lightweight materials; further applications of these methods with materials of self-weight will re-empower contemporary architecture with the old and now new tool — volume.

DESIGN TEAM

Matter Design: Brandon Clifford \ Wesley McGee
In collaboration with Supermanoeuvre \ Dave Pigram

STRUCTURAL

Simpson Gumpertz&Heger: Matthew Johnson

BUILD TEAM

Matter Design: Brandon Clifford \ Wesley McGee \ Johanna Lobdell \ Deniz McGee \ Kris Walters \ Maciej Kaczynski

RIGGING

Boutte Tree: TiersonBoutte

FABRICATION

University of Michigan Taubman College of Architecture and Urban Planning

LA VOÛTE DE LEFEVRE

We are truly conflicted. We are pre-occupied with computational design and digital fabrication — commonly assumed to be rapid, fashionable, and surfacial, though simultaneously pre-occupied with volume — thick, heavy, ancient, and permanent. We also maintain an emphasis on speculation, and yet our dedication to reality resists this claim. We intend to innovate and transform the future of architecture, yet we look to history in order to do so. Somewhere in this milieu of confusion and confliction is the kernel that defines us.

Marc Jarzombek recently suggested one could determine how well a society is doing by their ability to precisely carve stone. We like his metric for its simplicity, but also for its assumption that we must not be doing so well today. So much of the discussion surrounding digital design has focused on the surface. We are not immune. Much of our previous research has dealt with the economically friendly sheet material, while maintaining a common thread of a dedication to volume. This dedication originally manifested in volumetric occupation through bending from 2d to 3d. More recently this desire has formalized into stereotomic (the art of cutting solids, most typically stone) research with such projects as Periscope: Foam Tower and Temporal Tenancy. These projects mined the past knowledge of stereotomy as a way to robotically carve foam for temporary installations. The irony of these projects is they apply knowledge from heavy stone construction to light temporary projects that require tensile cables to stand. While the irony exists, these exercises in carving solids could also be applied to materials with significant mass as a way to re-engage the thick, heavy, and permanent compression-only architecture of the past.

La Voûte de LeFevre is the result of a call for help. This call is simple. It asks architects to cut it out with the addiction to the thin. It begs for an intervention, which came in the form of a one-year fellowship dedicated to experimenting with this request. This year was a form of re-hab. "You will build a heavy, permanent, and volumetric architecture. You will learn from this process and report back to us."

When posited the task of building a full-scale project with heavy and volumetric process, two obstacles emerged — assurance and ambition. How can we guarantee a vault with significant mass will stand, and how can we build a project of such volumetric scale on budget and schedule? The answers existed in these two words — computation and fabrication.

The vault is computed with a solver-based model that elicits a compression-only structure, from a non-ideal geometry. The model requires a fixed geometry as input, and opens apertures in order to vary the weight of each unit. This dynamic system reconfigures he weight of the units based on a volumetric calculation. If unit A contains twice the volume of unit B, then unit A weights twice as much. It requires that the material of the project be consistent, and solid (hollow does not work). The computed result produces a project that will stand 'forever' as there is zero tension in the system precisely because of the weight and volume of the project, and not in spite of it.

The vault is produced with Baltic Birch plywood. The plywood is sourced in three quarter inch thick sheets awaiting the 'thickening'. Each custom unit is dissected and sliced into these thicknesses, cut from the sheets, and then physically re-constituted into a rough volumetric form of their final geometry. These roughs are indexed onto a full sheet and glued, vacuum pressed, and re-placed onto the CNC (computer numerically controlled) router.

On the topic of ambition, this project is produced on a 5-axis Onsrud router. The carving bits are larger than life. The tool-paths utilized are dedicated to removing the most material with the least effort. These tool-paths are called swarfs. Instead of requiring the end of the bit to do the work, this path uses the edge of the bit to remove much more material. Because this method traces the geometry with a line as opposed to point, it requires the units be constituted of ruled surfaces. This requirement results in the conical-boolean geometry. As these units transition down to the column (below the calculation as the columns contain only vertical thrust vectors) the rhetoric of the units continue as if to say the weight is increasing.

The purpose of this research is not to revert to this 'antiquated' architecture. It is intended to re-engage in a problem unfamiliar to our contemporary culture. This unfamiliar terrain produces a new monster. An architecture that is somehow ancient yet contemporary, heavy yet light, familiar yet alien.

PROJECT TEAM

Jake Haggmark \ Maciej Kaczynski \ Aaron Willette
Build Team: Edgar Ascaño \ Kristy Balliet \ Katherine Bennette \ Beth Blostein \ Jenna Bolino \ Chris Carbone \ Tim Cousino \ Anthony Gagliardi \ Brian Koehler \ Darwin Menjivar \ Paul Miller \ Tony Nguyen \ Bart Overly \ Aaron Powers \ Steve Sarver \ Katy Viccellio \ Sean Zielinski

ACKNOWLEDGEMENTS

Project funding by the Howard E. LeFevre '29 Emerging Practitioner Fellowship \ Fabrication support by the University of Michigan TCAUP FABLab \ Nesting Software provided by TDM Solutions

PERISCOPE

1 PERISCOPE
2 PERISCOPE EAST ELEVATION
3 PERISCOPE EXPLODED AXON
4 PERISCOPE SCALE OF UNIT
5 PERISCOPE STRUCTURAL DIAGRAMS
6 PERISCOPE
7 PERISCOPE

LA VOÛTE DE LEFEVRE

8 LA VOÛTE DE LEFEVRE UNDER THE STRUCTURE
9 LA VOÛTE DE LEFEVRE UNASSEMBLED PIECES
10 LA VOÛTE DE LEFEVRE CONNECTIONS DIAGRAM
11 LA VOÛTE DE LEFEVRE UNIT DIAGRAM
12 LA VOÛTE DE LEFEVRE ELEVATION
13 LA VOÛTE DE LEFEVRE INSIDE DETAIL
14 LA VOÛTE DE LEFEVRE UNASSEMBLED PIECES
15 LA VOÛTE DE LEFEVRE PERSPECTIVE

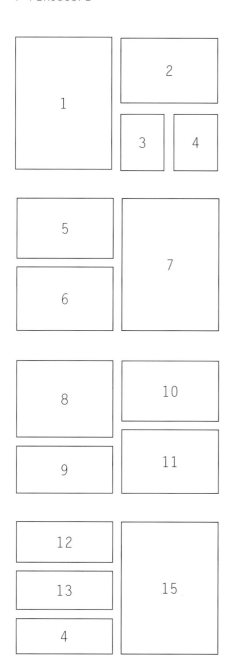

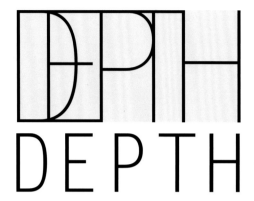

DEPTH

PHILIP BEESLEY

the hylozoic series

THE HYLOZOIC SERIES
PHILIP BEESLEY

The immersive environments of Philip Beesley's Hylozoic Series explore a new generation of responsive spaces, inviting viewers to raise fundamental questions about how architecture might behave in the future. Might future buildings begin to 'know' and 'care' about us? Might they start, in very primitive ways, to become alive?

Responding to the movement of visitors, ripples of vibration, glowing light, and whispering sound move throughout the immersive layers of these spaces. Floating overhead, hundreds of thousands of custom-made components spread out into diffuse, translucent clouds. Hylozoic environments can sense and interact with viewers and contain chemical systems that act like a primitive metabolism, processing and exchanging material with the environment. Floating overhead, many hundreds of thousands of custom-made components spread out into diffuse, translucent clouds. The structural cores are delicate transparent meshworks of acrylic and silicone, that form vaulted canopies and groves of basket-like columns. These are clothed with dense clusters of feathered filter clusters and interconnected chains of glass vesicles. A primitive chemical metabolism is housed within the massed vessels. 'Protocells' within this system show the early stages of self-generating growth, exchanging chemicals that can help to renew surrounding spaces.

These environments use a steadily evolving family of custom-made lightweight components made by digital fabrication. Hundreds of thousands of custom-made interlinking components make up the mechanisms and structural layers. Fine-grained interactive control systems use nested arrays of microprocessors that are integrated within the meshwork.

Recent projects undertaken by Beesley's Toronto studio illustrate how specialized ideas are guiding the immersive qualities of the Hylozoic environment. Initial phases of the Hylozoic Series concentrated on the textile-like qualities of a specialized diagonally-oriented corrugated meshwork that could span and curve, making highly flexible architectural canopies and column structures. Digital fabrication within the studio has supported many generations of refinement of these textile structures. By fitting mechanisms within the flexible surfaces, early generations of the environments gained kinetic functions, flexing and shifting in response to the presence of visitors. Distributed computation systems for controlling these responsive functions were originally based on open-source 'Arduino' microprocessors. Custom-built processors are now being integrated, using shift registers that allow very simple components to handle large volumes of varying signals. Arrays of specialized glassware are now being developed to provide labyrinthine fluid circulation and filtering functions. These circulation systems have been recently developed by combining the expertise of specialized craftspeople with three-dimensional printed prototypes from the studio. Filtering systems employ this glasswork to support the artificial-life chemical interactions integrated within the most recent generations of the Hylozoic environments.

HYLOZOIC VEIL
THE LEONARDO, SALT LAKE CITY, UTAH, 2011
PHILIP BEESELY

Hylozoic Veil opened alongside the official opening of The Leonardo, a museum dedicated to exploring the intersections between technology, science, art, and the humanities. The sculpture integrates large portions of the Hylozoic Ground installation developed for the 2010 Venice Biennale for Architecture. It occupies the three-storey space of the Tanner Atrium, which provides central orientation for the varying levels of the building. Visitors enter the museum and encounter a soaring volume with multiple cloud-like sculpture layers suspended within the lower levels. Banks of escalators invite visitors to move upward through these floating layers, reaching intricately detailed upper sections that contain horizontal expanses of kinetic filters and densely massed glass vessels containing protocells. Hyperbolic vaulted canopies composed of corrugated diagrid acrylic meshwork stretch horizontally to enclose the second level of the sculpture. These structures are densely encrusted with glasswork chains and hovering fronds of acrylic and mylar. Viewers can continue upward through this level to the upper floor of the atrium, reaching an auditorium and a lounge with soaring views of the desert.

HYLOZOIC SERIES: SIBYL

18TH BIENNALE OF SYDNEY. COCKATOO ISLAND, SYDNEY,AUSTRALIA, 2012

Sibyl is installed within a massive basilica-like hall of stone and metal truss-work lying within a historic ship-building complex on Cockatoo Island within the harbour of Sydney. The space of the sculpture intersects a high, central passage and reaches back into a recess that provides a shelter of darkness and quiet. Rivers of delicate hexagonal skeleton filters reach high overhead and spiral down to surround an intimate room that lies within the centre.

Groves of meshwork columns frame the darkened inner end of this space. Scented wicks and glands attract visitors close to the lower details of these columns, detailed with delicate glass spines that glow in response to approaching visitors. Shivering patterns of vibration and rustling sound move upward when individual clusters are stimulated by viewers. Reaching outward toward a public entry oriented to the central hall are layers of undulating seaweed-like filter clusters, housing protocell flasks. Touch-sensitive whiskers are fitted to each filter cluster, inviting viewers to gently stimulate the growth within the flasks. At the uppermost levels, lying just below the roof trusses that enclose the space, clusters of gauze bladders open and close in rolling, tide-like motions, responding to the larger movements of viewers below.

The space was used as a prison and reformatory prior to its industrial use. The fragile detailing contrasts the primal qualities of the surroundings.

PHILIP BEESLEY

Philip Beesley is a professor in the School of Architecture at the University of Waterloo. A practitioner of architecture and digital media art, he was educated in visual art at Queen's University, in technology at Humber College, and in architecture at the University of Toronto.

Dedicated to expanding the role for the arts integrated within architecture, Beesley has worked in sculpture, next-generation digital media and cross-disciplinary experimental visual art for the past three decades. He has focused on public buildings accompanied by field-oriented sculpture and landscape installations, exhibition and stage design. His experimental projects in the past several years have increasingly worked with immersive digitally fabricated lightweight "textile" structures, while the most recent generations of his work feature interactive kinetic systems that use dense arrays of microprocessors, sensors and actuator systems. These environments pursue distributed emotional consciousness and combine synthetic and near-living systems.

Beesley`s work was selected to represent Canada at the 2010 Venice Biennale for Architecture, and he has been recognized by the Prix de Rome in Architecture, VIDA 11.0, FEIDAD, two Governor General's Awards, and as a Katerva finalist.

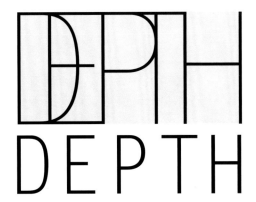

DEPTH

MAGNUS
LARSSON

ORDINARY

ALEX
KAISER

dune - f2f

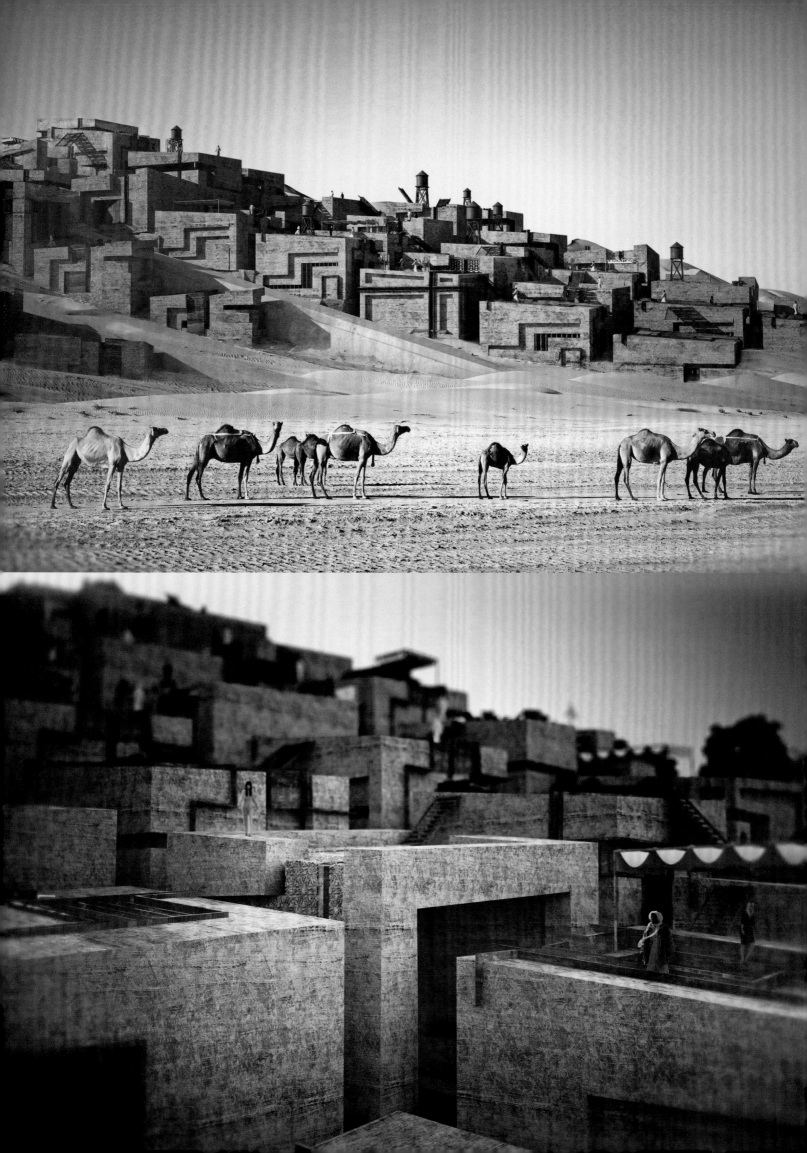

ORDINARY

MAGNUS LARSSON
AND ALEX KAISER

During our first years of architecture studies in Oxford, the hottest topic on the curriculum was called Digital Culture. A decade later, that title has become an impossible tautology. We live in a digital society, in a digital era, in which culture is per definition digital, and where anything analogue is an interesting deviation from the norm. At least since the prescient predictions of Marshall McLuhan, and in even more obvious ways when writers such as Douglas Coupland begun their investigations into the digitalization of human culture, it has become clear that the ones and zeros we invented are now physically re-wiring our brains. We are not just producing and consuming more digital culture, we are becoming the digital beings inhabiting that digital culture.

This explosive development has affected architecture (as it has affected almost all areas) in ways that are simply irreversible. We have crossed the Rubicon, and there are no analogue rides going back. We were once taught that architects make drawings of buildings rather than the buildings themselves. This is no longer true. Architects make digital buildings, using digital tools and digital materials, and then communicate those buildings digitally to a digital society. From initial communication via preliminary sketch through to simulations, experimentation, design, dissemination, and everything in between, we are working within a digital tradition that was still largely inconceivable at the time we chose our profession. As anyone who has read Mario Carpa's 2011 essay The Alphabet and the Algorithm will tell you, the world's current modes of architectural production constitute an unparalleled break with the consolidated categories that ruled architecture for the past five centuries. Once architecture entered the digital sphere, the way the discipline is taught, practiced, managed, and regulated has irrevocably changed.

One of Carpa's theses is that our use of digital technologies brings us closer to the building industry as we knew it in Medieval times. Digital manufacturing tools close the divide between architect and builder, remove the distinction between designing and making, provides architects with new building blocks and possibilities: codes, scripts, algorithms. If architecture is per definition a consilient practice, then digital architecture is where we are able to fully explore the possibilities of other disciplines. The architect is no longer a mere draughtsman, but also a matte painter, an animation expert, a concept artist, a visual effects specialist, a film director, a computer programmer, a simulations supervisor, and a hundred other things.

We are interested in exploring this Medieval-tinged consilience and see how it might turn us into more interesting human beings capable of designing more interesting buildings and cities. We are decidedly unconcerned with architecture that needs to redundantly communicate its digitalness. In our material investigations, we are already mixing digitally controlled processes with analogue ones, such as the natural growth of materials across 3d-printed substrates. Knowing that the model is the building, we recently invested in a CNC router, with which we aim to close the gap between modelling and making even further.

Ordinary is a London-based design studio founded in 2011 by long-time collaborators Magnus Larsson and Alex Kaiser. Currently primarily investigating strategies for how material research combined with radically speculative experimentation might move architecture beyond biomimicry as well as mere sustainability, the studio initiates and creates projects, lectures widely on the international stage, and has been extensively published in both popular and academic press.

DUNE

Dune was first presented at TED Global in July 2009, having already reached an architetural audience through an enthusiastic review on BLDGBLOG, where Geoff Manaugh called it "a kind of bio-architectural test-landscape".

The scheme seeks to investigate an adaptive way of living with desertification through the engineered solidification of existing sand dunes. The initial project called for a a 6,000km-long habitable wall to be created through microbial lithification of sand dunes in the Sahara desert. The resulting sandstone building, literally spanning the African continent from east to west, would offer a green wall against the future spread of the desert.

Dune is an architectural speculation aimed at creating a network of solidified sand dunes in the desert – a proposition that suggests a manipulation of the ground through methods that perhaps brings to mind images of what Manaugh called "rogue basement chemists of the future". The selective solidification of a sand dune into a building volume using bacteria is indeed a novel building technology and a groundbreaking material strategy. Furthermore, the scheme advocates a radical shift in structural thinking, away from existing construction methods and material palettes, towards the localised cementation of granular materials using the bacterium, Bacillus pasteurii.

The idea is to use this biocementation strategy to create a very narrow and very long pan-African city with the capacity to mitigate against the shifting sands of Sahara. The images presented here show an urban nodal point within the sandstone network – a city within the city.

Buildings made from a material such as rammed earth – which when properly constructed can outlast those of traditional timber-frame construction – need ten or 20 times less energy to build than concrete or brick ones. Still, in actual, non-vernacular practice we remain largely stuck with the usual material suspects: concrete, glass, metals, brick, stone, and (since fairly recently) wood.

Any serious attempt to move away from this material palette will be met with suspicion or worse from an industry comfortably making its living off of today's equilibrium rather than spearheading tomorrow's research and development.

Contemporary architectural discourse largely investigates the nature of architecture; we are currently more interested in the architecture of nature. Not the observation of nature's forms so much as the constructional and material possibilities of the processes producing those forms. This is what we mean by going beyond biomimicry.

Dry areas cover more than one-third of the earth's land surface, and upward of a billion people live in arid or semiarid environments, coexisting with the shifting sands, sometimes struggling to get by in the wake of increasingly harsh conditions. The spatial pockets of Dune would help retain scarce water and mineral resources necessary to turn the scheme into a micro-environmental support structure capable of assisting the formation of the Great Green Wall for the Sahara and Sahel Initiative (GGWSSI). The final outcome is a habitable anti-desertification structure made from the desert itself, a sand-stopping device made out of sand, dunes turned into a city.

F2F

The world population has experienced continuous growth since 1350. According to current projections the planet will support between 7.5 and 10.5 billion people by 2050. This is a good thing.

Not only does this mean there will be more intelligence in the world, more beautiful innovation, more valuable human capital, more education, more culture, more heartbreaking works of staggering genius. There will also be more of us living in larger and larger cities. Emotional and intellectual playgrounds built on complexity and diversity, cities are humanity's most successful invention for delivering prosperity and progress.

The young and the poor don't go to the countryside to make their fortunes. They go to cities. This migration towards metropolitan cores intensifies the urban experience but not, crucially, the heedless burning of fossil fuels. New York City is a model of environmental responsibility. Unfortunately, the city is often too slow to adapt and adopt its new inhabitants, which leads to sprawl. The horisontal skyscraper F2F challenges this through a radical interpretation of Superstudio's 1969 Continuous Monument: a massive grid building that negotiates the boundary between city and suburb.

Harvard economist Edward Glaeser argues that where land is scarce, density becomes vital. Cities that cannot build out must build up. The resulting conurbations should be pinnacle achievements in the history of the world. And yet the resulting urban centres, based on capitalist doctrines of hyper-density, are too often, in the words of Rem Koolhaas, well on their way to "a grotesque saturation point of total extrusion".

With F2F, we offer an alternative to these grotesque extrusions. A radical redefinition of the closely-stacked logic of contemporary urban typologies, this skyscraper is based on the notion of low-density mass housing. This reasoning acknowledges the need for vertical extrusions while arguing that many downfalls of the contemporary metropolitan condition, in particular in a non-western context – overcrowding, environmental stress, social inequalities, lack of light and air, food security, diseases – could be overcome through the controlled use of spatial redundancy.

By using a stacking paradigm within a massive grid structure made from cross-laminated timber, within which we position prefabricated timber units, we achieve compression in the time and effort it takes to construct the building. And by shifting those units across the length of the skyscraper, we create de facto redundant spaces;

bodies without organs; volumes without walls and floors; strategic perforations in the city fabric.

This internal logic is based on a programmatic reconsideration of what it means (or should mean) to live in a skyscraper – smaller contained interior spaces are matched by exterior spaces that offer framed views of the street- or landscape below, with vertical volumes acting as supporting storage capacities; the raised and fluid grid allow for chance meetings in the sky; at pavement or field level, the ground is given back to the people; from its plug-in living units, F2F offers the public astonishing views of the inner circuits of the great computer for human interactions that is the metropolis.

PAGE 172 + PAGE 173

PAGE 174 + PAGE 175

PAGE 176 + PAGE 177

PAGE 178 + PAGE 179

DUNE
1 DUNE AERIAL VIEW
2 DUNE AERIAL VIEW DETAIL
3 DUNE STREETS
4 DUNE VIEW FROM DESERT
5 DUNE PERSPECTIVE
6 DUNE VIEW AT NIGHT
7 DUNE AERIAL VIEW AT NIGHT

F2F
1 F2F AERIAL VIEW
2 F2F DETAIL CLUSTER OF BUILDINGS
3 F2F ELEVATED STRUCTURES
4 F2F ELEVATED STRUCTURE OVER FILED
5 F2F ELEVATED STRUCTURE OVER EXISTING CITY
6 F2F ELEVATED STRUCTURE OVER LAKE
7 F2F ELEVATION

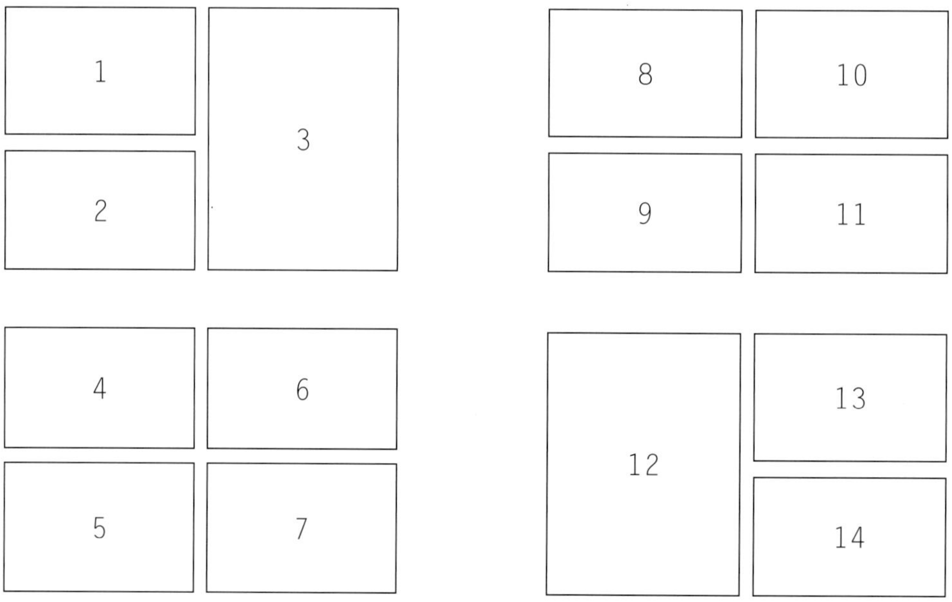

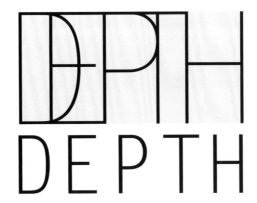

DEPTH

IAIN
MAXWELL

SUPERMA-
NOEUVRE

DAVID
PIGRAM

city breeder
urban computations
the clouds of venice

GROWTH TYPES
VISIBLE WHEN "BREED NEW CITY" MODE HAS BEEN CHOSEN.
SELECT FROM A LIST OF PRELOADED GROWTH PATTERNS.

PRELOADED CITIES
VISIBLE WHEN "ALTER EXISTING CITY" MODE HAS BEEN CHOSEN.
SELECT FROM A LIST OF PRELOADED WORLD CITIES.

DRAW / EDIT TOOLS
SELECT A TOOL AND THEN EDIT THE CITY WHILE IT IS RUNNING.
ADD AND DELETE STREETS & PLAZAS OR SEED ACTIVITY TYPES.

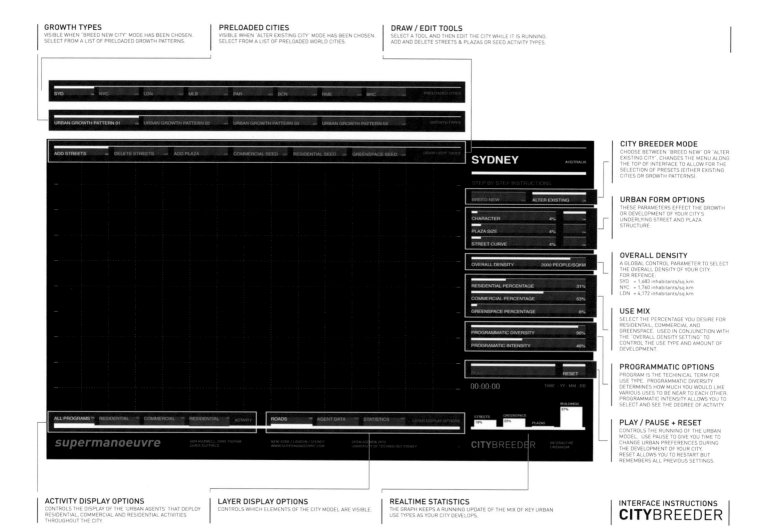

CITY BREEDER MODE
CHOOSE BETWEEN "BREED NEW" OR "ALTER EXISTING CITY". CHANGES THE MENU ALONG THE TOP OF INTERFACE TO ALLOW FOR THE SELECTION OF PRESETS (EITHER EXISTING CITIES OR GROWTH PATTERNS).

URBAN FORM OPTIONS
THESE PARAMETERS EFFECT THE GROWTH OR DEVELOPMENT OF YOUR CITY'S UNDERLYING STREET AND PLAZA STRUCTURE.

OVERALL DENSITY
A GLOBAL CONTROL PARAMETER TO SELECT THE OVERALL DENSITY OF YOUR CITY.
FOR REFENCE:
SYD = 1,683 inhabitants/sq.km
NYC = 1,760 inhabitants/sq.km
LDN = 4,172 inhabitants/sq.km

USE MIX
SELECT THE PERCENTAGE YOU DESIRE FOR RESIDENTAIL, COMMERCIAL AND GREENSPACE. USED IN CONJUNCTION WITH THE "OVERALL DENSITY SETTING" TO CONTROL THE USE TYPE AND AMOUNT OF DEVELOPMENT.

PROGRAMMATIC OPTIONS
PROGRAM IS THE TECHINICAL TERM FOR USE TYPE. PROGRAMMATIC DIVERSITY DETERMINES HOW MUCH YOU WOULD LIKE VARIOUS USES TO BE NEAR TO EACH OTHER. PROGRAMMATIC INTENSITY ALLOWS YOU TO SELECT AND SEE THE DEGREE OF ACTIVITY.

PLAY / PAUSE + RESET
CONTROLS THE RUNNING OF THE URBAN MODEL. USE PAUSE TO GIVE YOU TIME TO CHANGE URBAN PREFERENCES DURING THE DEVELOPMENT OF YOUR CITY.
RESET ALLOWS YOU TO RESTART BUT REMEMBERS ALL PREVIOUS SETTINGS.

ACTIVITY DISPLAY OPTIONS
CONTROLS THE DISPLAY OF THE 'URBAN AGENTS' THAT DEPLOY RESIDENTIAL, COMMERCIAL AND RESIDENTIAL ACTIVITIES THROUGHOUT THE CITY.

LAYER DISPLAY OPTIONS
CONTROLS WHICH ELEMENTS OF THE CITY MODEL ARE VISIBLE.

REALTIME STATISTICS
THE GRAPH KEEPS A RUNNING UPDATE OF THE MIX OF KEY URBAN USE TYPES AS YOUR CITY DEVELOPS.

INTERFACE INSTRUCTIONS
CITYBREEDER

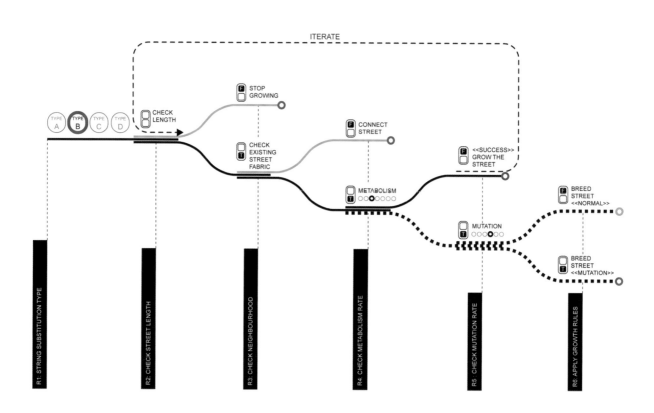

_DIAGRAM: GENERATIVE STREETS: DECISION MAKING FLOW CHART

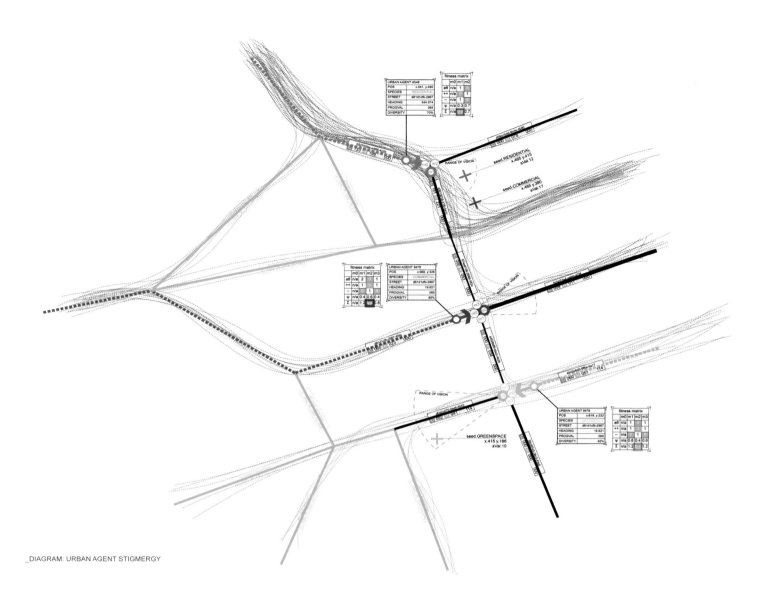

_DIAGRAM: URBAN AGENT STIGMERGY

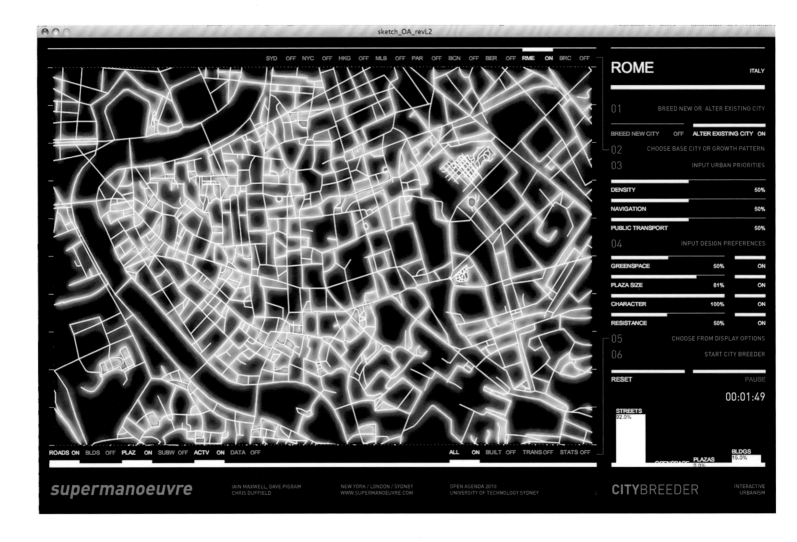

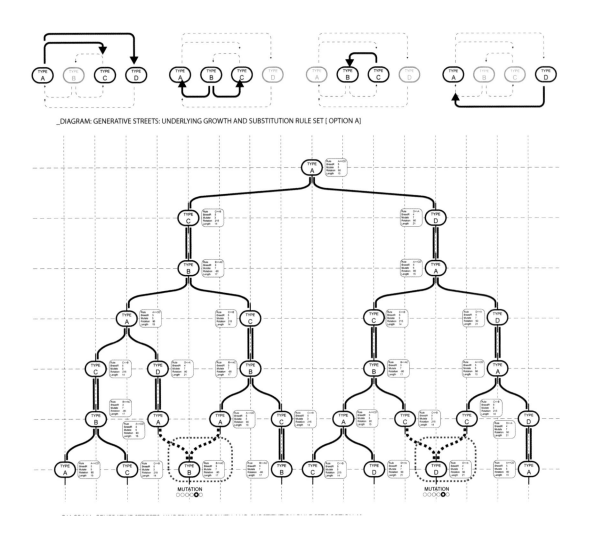

_DIAGRAM: GENERATIVE STREETS: UNDERLYING GROWTH AND SUBSTITUTION RULE SET [OPTION A]

MUTATION

MUTATION

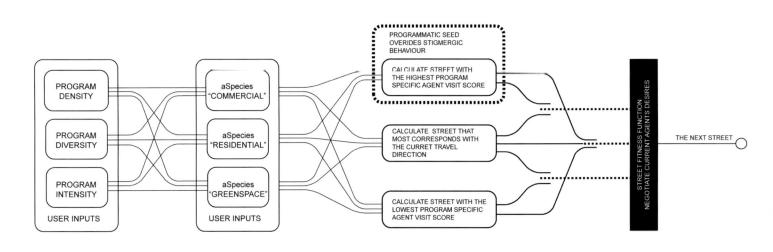

PROGRAM DENSITY	aSpecies "COMMERCIAL"	PROGRAMMATIC SEED OVERIDES STIGMERGIC BEHAVIOUR
PROGRAM DIVERSITY	aSpecies "RESIDENTIAL"	CALCULATE STREET WITH THE HIGHEST PROGRAM SPECIFIC AGENT VISIT SCORE
PROGRAM INTENSITY	aSpecies "GREENSPACE"	CALCULATE STREET THAT MOST CORRESPONDS WITH THE CURRET TRAVEL DIRECTION
USER INPUTS	USER INPUTS	CALCULATE STREET WITH THE LOWEST PROGRAM SPECIFIC AGENT VISIT SCORE

STREET FITNESS FUNCTION
NEGOTIATE CURRENT AGENTS DESIRES

THE NEXT STREET

_DIAGRAM: URBAN AGENT DECISION FLOW CHART

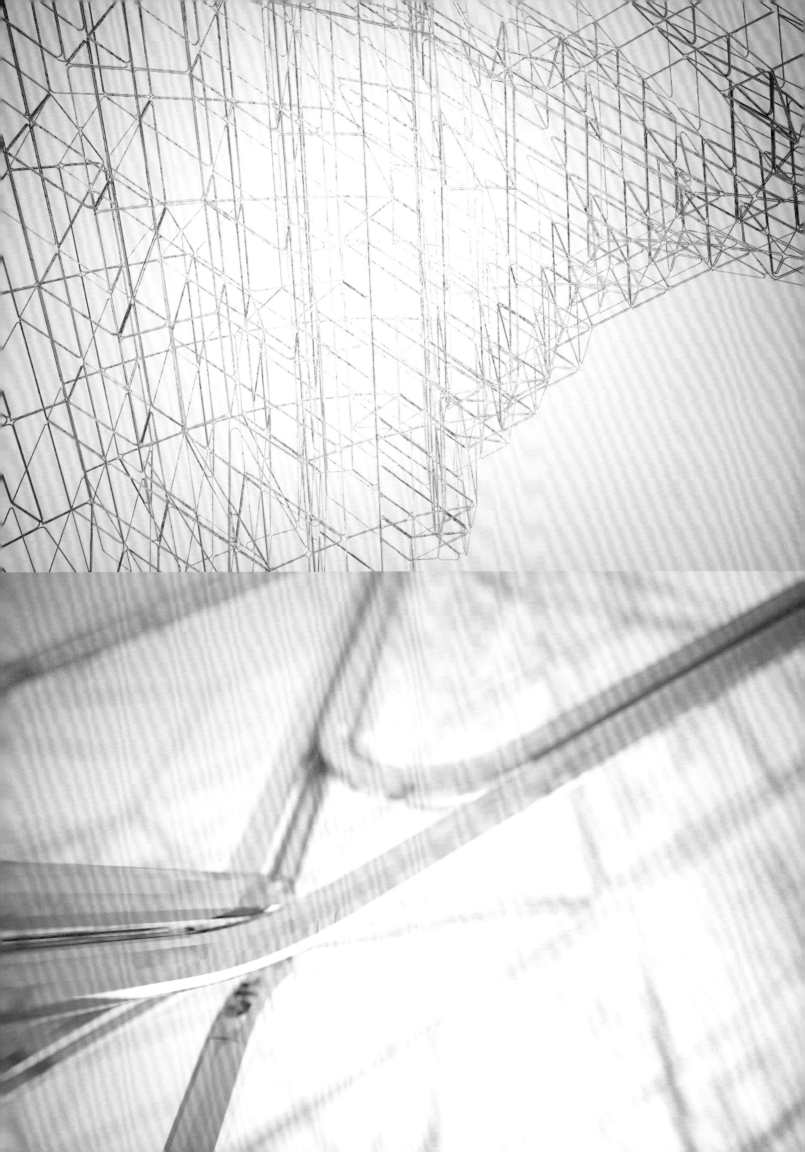

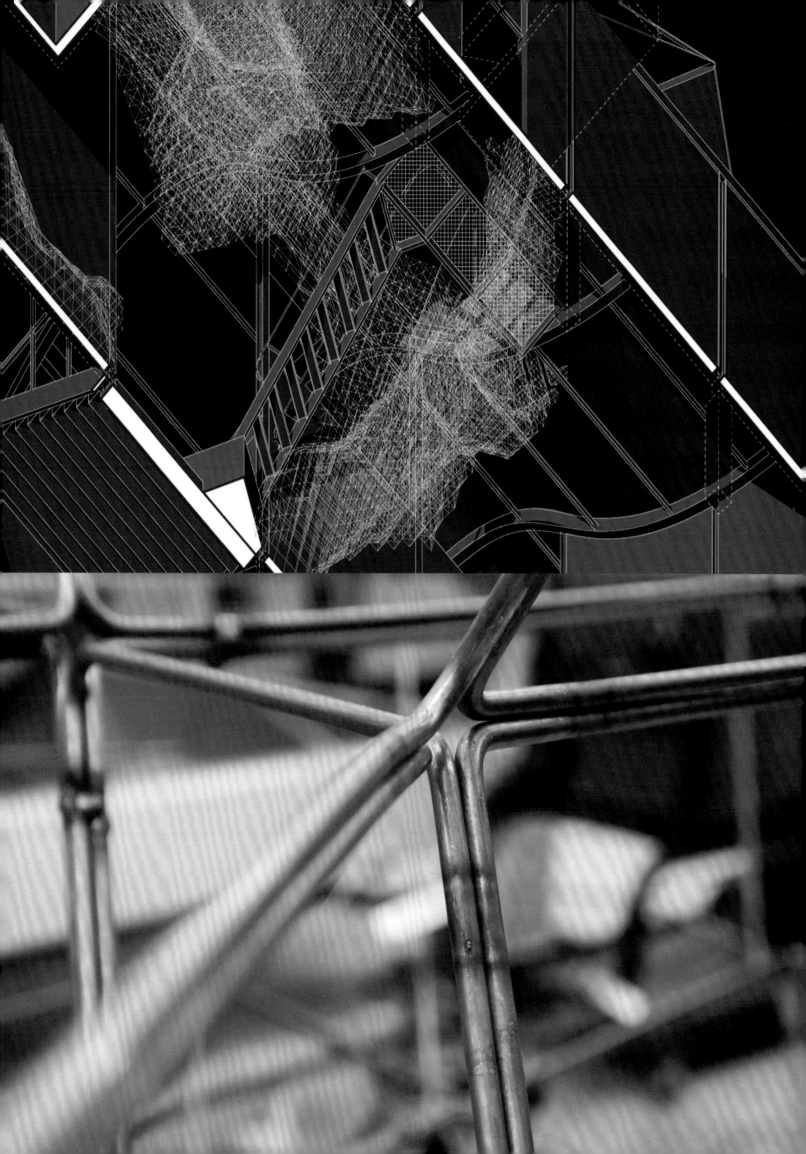

SUPERMANOEUVRE

CITY BREEDER

CityBreeder project is an interactive urban model and a collection of analytical drawings of international cities. The project provides a new and participatory mode of modeling the processes of the city, one that builds upon an understanding of urban form as highly contingent and continuously re-negotiated.

Generative algorithmic design techniques are used to encode specific low-level connective intentions, rules and relationships to produce an emergent condition capable of adaption to its own self-generating body of information: the collective decisions and actions of the model's population. In developing a time-based model that approaches urban creation via the accrual of a very high population of small (simulated) real-time decisions we posit a mobile platform of design that operates in a continuous but minimal way. We believe the city should be allowed to evolve in a largely self-regulating manner, but one monitored and at times micro-adjusted in the pursuit of a diverse and informal sense of dynamic order.

Such models provide a forum for participants to better understand their urban desires and the negotiations necessary to realize them.

TEAM

Design directors: Iain Maxwell (London), David Pigram (New York)
Project team (Sydney): David Vu, Bruna Souto, Lily Thuy Tien Li, William Feuerman, Amy Leenders

URBAN COMPUTATIONS

Cities are cultural artifacts, the emergent outcomes of open and continuous (design) processes enacted through the collective decisions, desires and anxieties of their populations. The prevailing way to envision the future of a city is via the masterplan, which freezes the complex and plural dialogues between the social, cultural and ecological aspirations of the city into a singular vision of urban form. As either a projective vision, or reactionary measure, the viability of the masterplan is continually challenged by the dynamic and complex nature of the urban use patterns that it attempts to direct. Recent technological advances are beginning to offer new modes of urban representation through increasingly real-time mappings of actual urban behavior and events. Through these contemporary techniques we are shedding light not only on the dynamic states, patterns and complexities of the city, but also enabling a critical comparison between the initial intentions and ultimate effects of the masterplan itself. Such techniques also enable broader speculations to be made: could we soon possess the ability to connect in a real-time manner the non-linear study of 'behavior' and 'event' with the very processes of design in order to realize a more open-ended and adaptive form of city planning? Could these techniques also enhance and extend the constituency of a city's inhabitants within urban design processes?

In the 1950s, the Situationists argued that the disciplines of architecture and urban design were systematically destroying the nature of the 'city' through the elimination of spontaneity and citizen participation. Indeed, the Situationists portrayed the design disciplines as the crusaders of institutionalization and not champions of the collective. Their strategy for reorganization was simple: empower the city's inhabitants to decide for themselves what urban conditions and forms of architecture they wanted, and how they wished to appropriate them. In doing so, the city could be radically reconfigured from the bottom-up and the impositions of the state (and the politic of imperialism) disbanded. Political manifesto aside, the work of the Situationists', notably their 'Naked City' project, demonstrates an alternate mode of urban thinking that shifts away from prevailing disciplinary tendencies to describe urbanism as a geometrical act (street, block and zoning patterns), and instead posits the city as the accumulation of events and behaviors.

The contemporary arrival of geographical tagging techniques: the visualization of urban patterns through digitally-tracking the routines and behaviors of a city's inhabitants ranging from their usage of public transport to the origins of their mobile phone calls, tourist snapshots, and contributions to social pages on the internet, are providing a lens through which to consider the 'evidenced' fabric of the city. Such mapping exercises provide insight into the experiences and movements of the city, and allow direct comparison between the intentions of the masterplan and their real-world form. Perhaps not surprisingly, such visualizations frequently highlight a disjuncture between the infrastructure of the city; the geometry of the streets, zoning and planning controls, and the actual emergent patterns of urban life that oscillate in far less obvious ways.

Jane Jacobs has argued, "once one thinks about city processes, it follows that one must think of catalysts of these processes"1. In the case of the city these processes stem from the unpredictable events and behaviors of a city's inhabitants. Jacobs criticizes the reduction of modern cities to simplistic two variable relationships. Ebenezer Howard's Garden City, which dealt exclusively with the allocation of garden houses and employment, and Le Corbuiser's Radial City, which promoted an indexical relationship between population and open-space, exemplify the dangers of idealized monocultures that ignore the complex nature of the city as a rich social body. Jacobs writes, "it takes large quantities of the 'average' to produce the 'unaverage' in cities…[where]…. the 'unaverage' can be physical, as in the case of eye-catchers which are small elements in much larger, more 'average' visual scenes. They can be economic, as in the case of one-of-a-kind stores, or cultural, as in the case of an unusual school or out-of-the-ordinary theatre. They can be social, as in the case of public characters, loitering places, or residents or users who are financially, vocationally, racially or culturally 'unaverage'."2 In this regard, the parameters of the city are elusive and unpredictable because they are played out through the entire heterogeneous population of the city.

"Cities are juxtaposition engines and owe their existence to complex patterns of human contact."3 The correlation of human processes and active design systems was a fundamental occupation of MIT's Architecture Machine Group founded by Nicholas Negroponte in the 1970s. In a seminal experiment entitled Seek (also called Blockworlds), building blocks were located on a regular grid within a glass vitrine, wherein a population of willing citizens, in this instance Mongolian Gerbils, was introduced and allowed to make habitat. In parallel to the appropriation of space being undertaken by the gerbil population, a robotic scanning arm moved forth and back checking and maintaining the alignment of the cubes. The arm did not seek to re-establish any pre-determined global orders, but merely attend too slight anomalies via ongoing and extremely local acts of realignment. In an approach more akin to that of a constant gardener, the robotic arm serves as an exemplar of the potential of a real-time urban planning instrument. One that does not seek total control and radical Hausmann-esque style interventions, but rather acknowledges that all "cities do evolve and, like all species, they reach a form of completion…dynamic segues from large-scale tasks to internal adjustment and renewal, a kind of steady state."4

Giambattista Nolli's plan for Rome radically changed the way in which cities were viewed. Now, digital mapping of urban behavior is radically altering our perception and understanding of the city in use. Such analytical techniques challenge the design disciplines to engage with and model the complex, dynamic and irreducible 'parameters' that shape the city. To 'measure is to know'5, and the geo-mapping of our cities provides an apparatus through which latent urban properties can quantified and masterplans assessed. However maps, regardless of how information-rich, do not offer a generative vehicle through which possible futures of the city can be envisioned. It is critical for designers to transcend the map, and develop interactive models and processes capable of generating the granularity and flow of urban phenomena, with sufficient capacities to negotiate the influence of competing forces, in order to evolve new speculative visions of the city. Such models would provide a forum for participants to better understand their urban desires and the negotiations necessary to realize them.

Supermanoeuvre's CityBreeder project seeks a new and participatory mode of modeling the processes of the city, one that builds upon an understanding of urban form as highly contingent and continuously re-negotiated. Generative algorithmic design techniques are used to encode specific low-level connective intentions, rules and relationships to produce an emergent condition capable of adaption to its own self-generating body of information: the collective decisions and actions of the model's population. In developing a time-based model that approaches urban creation via the accrual of a very high population of small (simulated) real-time decisions we posit a mobile platform of design that operates in a continuous but minimal way. We believe the city should be allowed to evolve in a largely self-regulating manner, but one monitored and at times micro-adjusted in the pursuit of a diverse and informal sense of dynamic order.

1. Jacobs Jane. The Death and Life of Great American Cities. The Modern Library, NY. 1961. p 575
2. Ibid. p 577
3. Sorkin, Michael. Traffic and Democracy. p9
4. Ibid.   p42
5. Lord Kelvin. Paraphrased

THE CLOUDS OF VENICE

Supermanoeuvre is one of six practices selected to represent Australia in the 2012 Venice Architecture Biennale.

Supermanoeuvre's contribution to the exhibition will be a large site-specific installation designed to test the architectural potential of ultra-high population assemblies of unique elements. Here space is defined not by limit conditions (boundaries), but through density gradients (clouds).

An installation of approximately 1000 uniquely bent steel rods has been prefabricated using a custom constructed rod-bender integrated within a robotic workcell at the University of Michigan, Detroit. The design was generated with custom written algorithms that incorporate such variables as steel's modulus of elasticity (causing spring-back) and robotic joint-limitations. The software that directly generates the robotic instruction code has been developed by supermanoeuvre in collaboration with Wes McGee, a researcher at the University of Michigan, as a continuing research project initiated 3 years ago. The project will also integrate LED lights controlled by a network of 'Organic Response' adaptive distributed intelligence lighting sensor nodes. This will be the world's first arts based installation using this patented technology and custom printed circuit boards have been developed by Organic Response Pty. Ltd.'s engineers in collaboration with supermanoeuvre specifically for the project.

No drawing of the project exists! Instead some 5,000 lines of generative code and almost 50,000 lines of file-to-factory robot control code allowed 6,800 unique bends to be applied to over 5,200 linear metres of ¼" diameter mild steel rod. The installation is an exemplar of a novel and highly collaborative trans-continental workflow where design files were generated in Sydney and London while manufacture took place in Ann Arbor, Michigan with final assembly of course taking place in Venice.

TEAM

Design directors: Iain Maxwell + David Pigram (Supermanoeuvre // Sydney // London),
                 Wes McGee (Matter Design // Michigan)
Project team (Michigan): Ben Hagenhofer, Lauren Vasey, Whit Self
Project team (Sydney): Walter Brindle
Project team (London): Tom Lea

CITY BREEDER
1 CITY BREEDER APPLET INTERFACE
2 CITY BREEDER GENERATIVE STREET, DECISION FLOW CHART
3 CITY BREEDER URBAN AGENTS, TRACKING
4 CITY BREEDER SYDNEY URBAN PHEROMONE ACTIVITIES
5 CITY BREEDER ROME URBAN PHEROMONE ACTIVITIES
6 CITY BREEDER LONDON RESIDENTIAL
7 CITY BREEDER SYDNEY COMMERCIAL
8 CITY BREEDER SYDNEY RECREATION PHEROMONE
9 CITY BREEDER GENERATIVE STREET, UNDERLYING LSYSTEM
10 CITY BREEDER URBAN AGENTS, DECISION FLOW CHART

THE CLOUDS OF VENICE
11 THE CLOUDS OF VENICE GENERAL VIEW
12 THE CLOUDS OF VENICE DETAIL
13 THE CLOUDS OF VENICE INTERIOR
14 THE CLOUDS OF VENICE DETAIL
15 THE CLOUDS OF VENICE AXONOMETRIC DIAGRAM
16 THE CLOUDS OF VENICE DETIAl

| 1 | 3 | | 9 | 11 |
| 2 | 4 | | 10 | 12 |

| 5 | 7 | | 13 | 15 |
| 6 | 8 | | 14 | 16 |

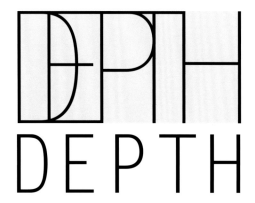

DEPTH

FRANCESCO
BRENTA

ORPROJECT

CHRISTOPH
KLEMMT

RAJAT
SODHI

anisotropia

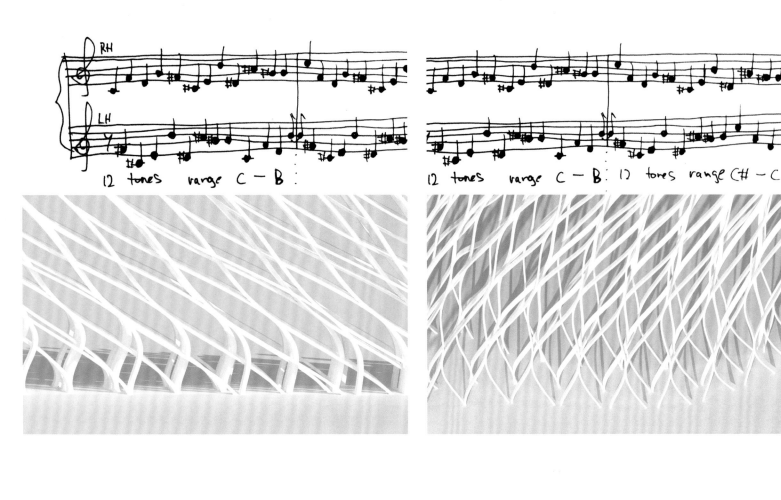

12 tones range C – B
12 tones range C – B
12 tones range C# – C

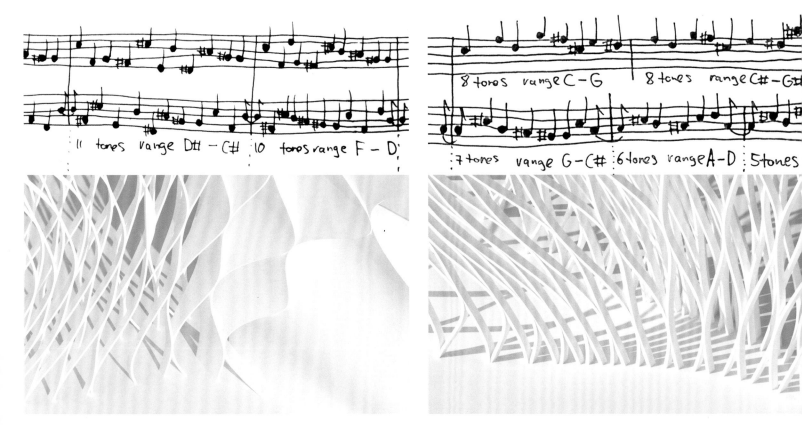

11 tones range D# – C#
10 tones range F – D
8 tones range C – G
8 tones range C# – G#
7 tones range G – C#
6 tones range A – D
5 tones

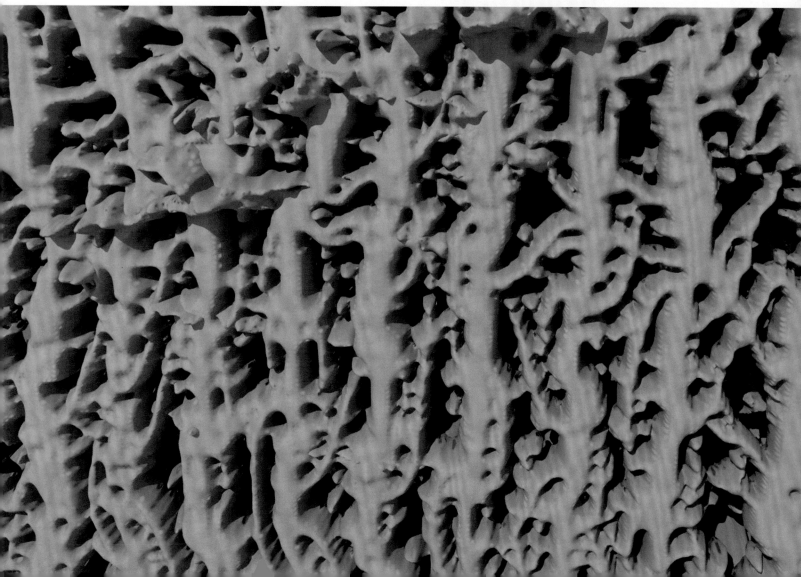

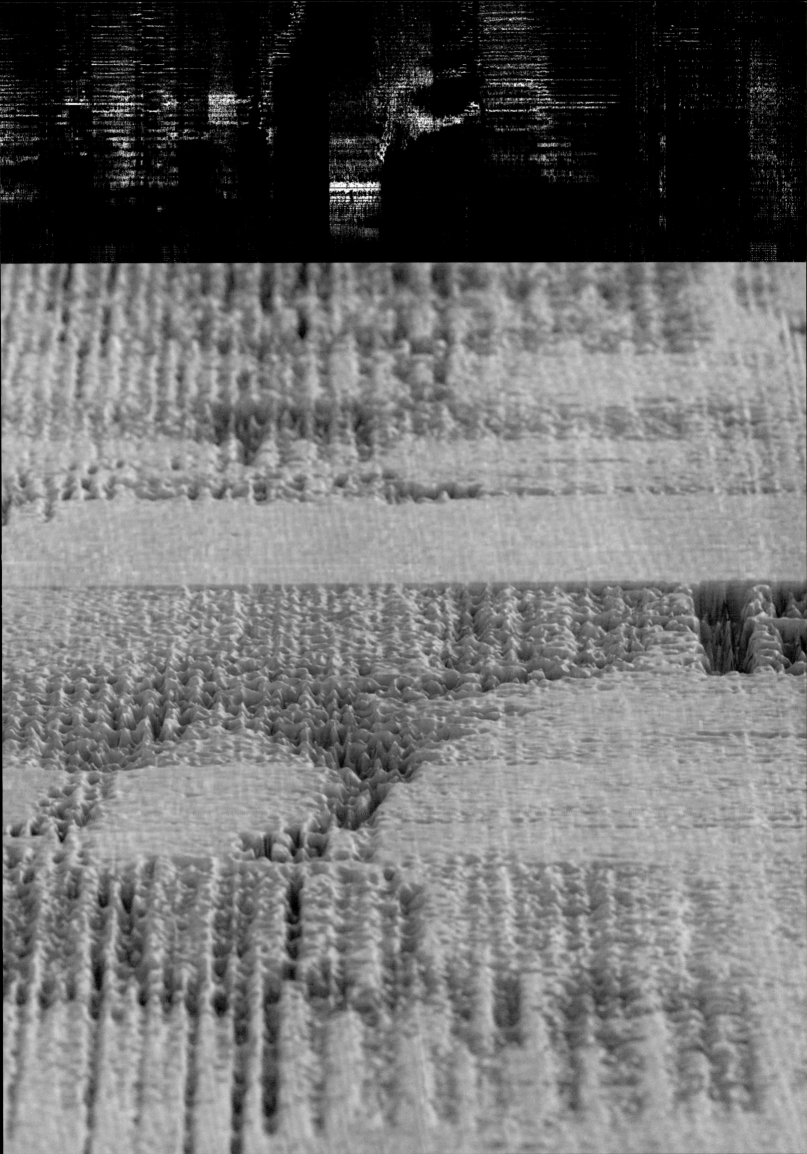

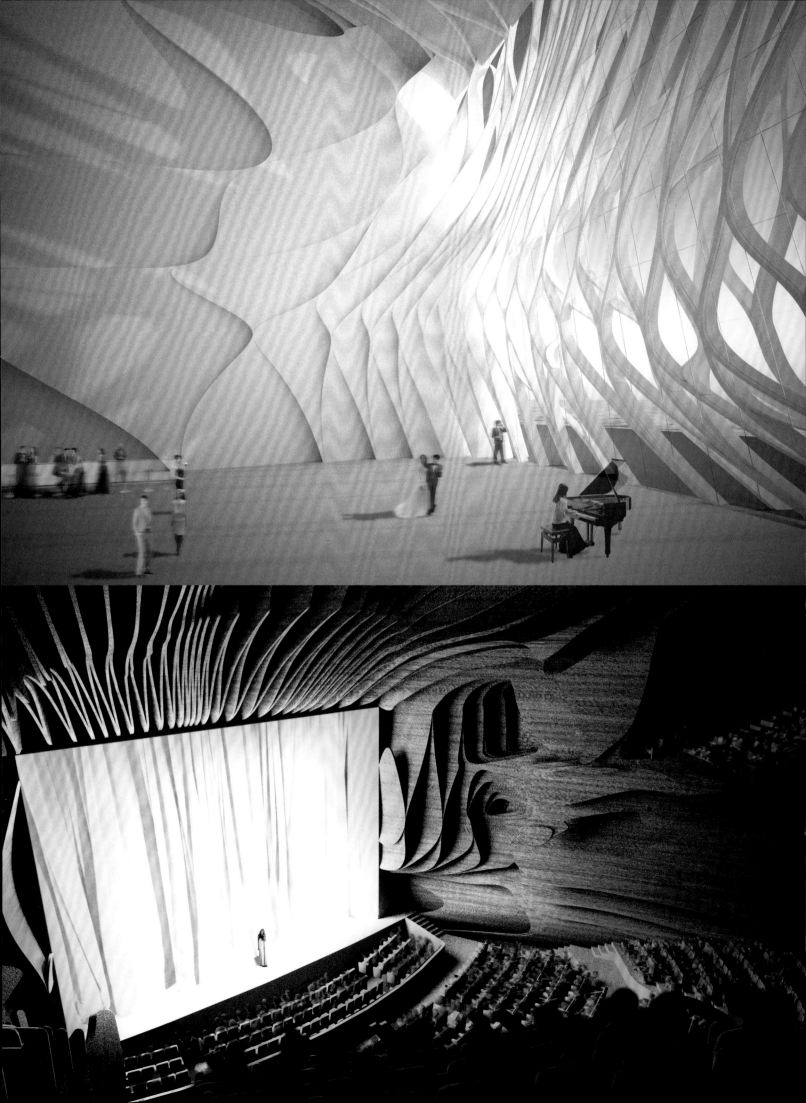

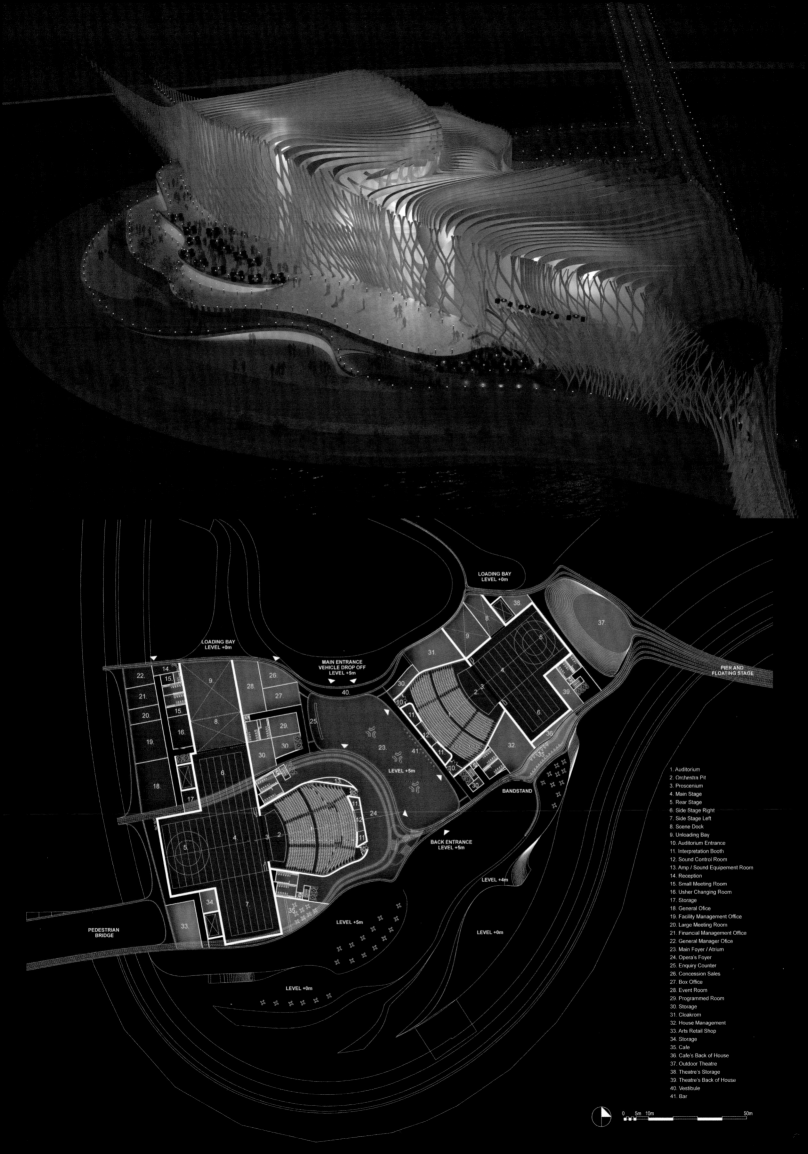

LOADING BAY
LEVEL +0m

LOADING BAY
LEVEL +0m

MAIN ENTRANCE
VEHICLE DROP OFF
LEVEL +5m

PIER AND
FLOATING STAGE

40.

LEVEL +5m

BANDSTAND

BACK ENTRANCE
LEVEL +5m

LEVEL +4m

PEDESTRIAN
BRIDGE

LEVEL +5m

LEVEL +0m

LEVEL +0m

1. Auditorium
2. Orchestra Pit
3. Proscenium
4. Main Stage
5. Rear Stage
6. Side Stage Right
7. Side Stage Left
8. Scene Dock
9. Unloading Bay
10. Auditorium Entrance
11. Interpretation Booth
12. Sound Control Room
13. Amp / Sound Equipement Room
14. Reception
15. Small Meeting Room
16. Usher Changing Room
17. Storage
18. General Ofice
19. Facility Management Office
20. Large Meeting Room
21. Financial Management Office
22. General Manager Ofice
23. Main Foyer / Atrium
24. Opera's Foyer
25. Enquiry Counter
26. Concession Sales
27. Box Office
28. Event Room
29. Programmed Room
30. Storage
31. Cloakrom
32. House Management
33. Arts Retail Shop
34. Storage
35. Cafe
36. Cafe's Back of House
37. Outdoor Theatre
38. Theatre's Storage
39. Theatre's Back of House
40. Vestibule
41. Bar

0   5m 10m   50m

ANISOTROPIA

ORPROJECT

As different as music and architecture are, the two forms of art also share a close relationship, and many composition and design concepts can become applicable to both. This essay explains some of the historical relations between the two disciplines, and how research by architects Orproject explores digital formations and algorithmic aggregations using sound and music. Their research is based on two levels: acoustics, wherein digital analysis of time based sound attributes are translated into spatial material aggregations, and compositional, wherein algorithmic design principles are applied to create both music and architecture.

ARCHITECTURE AND MUSIC

Architecture and music are two very different forms of art: One is the manifestation of physical matter in order to solve practical problems, the other one tries to create emotions and pleasure along a physical absence. Yet still there lies a strong relationships between the two.

EMOTION

At an instinctive level, both physical spaces and music can manage to evoke very similar emotions. Visiting a special place will give a special feeling, where both light and space translate into emotional feelings. This can apply to buildings, to urban spaces or to spaces in nature.

Music is well known to evoke emotions; in fact most of the time we listen to music we use it specifically for that purpose, to make us happy or relaxed. Cinema and advertising employ music to enhance emotions and create drama in a scene.

And sometimes music can evoke the feelings of space, and a space can evoke the feelings of sound or music. Quite famously, Johann Wolfgang von Goethe quoted Novalis when describing architecture as "frozen music".

PROGRAM MUSIC

Opposed to Absolute music, in program music composers used extra-musical narratives to be described through the compositions, and quite often those are relating to spaces and landscapes. A paradigm example for this is the piece Vltava by Bedrich Smetana, also known as The Moldau, in which he tone paints the river of his homeland03.

Another example is the cycle Pictures of an Exhibition by Modest Mussorgsky, in which he musically describes the visit through an exhibition of paintings by Viktor Hartmann. Probably the most famous movement is titled The Bogatyr Gates, which depicts Hatmann's design sketch for new city gates in Kiev. In his musical interpretation Mussorgsky describes the visitor moving through the exhibition space, and by describing the drawing of the city gates he musically describes a building.04

LONTANO BY GYORGY LIGETI

A more contemporary example is the composition Lontano by György Ligeti, which was written in 1967. Notable is already the title, which is Italian and translates as 'distant' or 'from far'. This directly refers to a spatial dimension, to a distance, and to a space, which is situated between the listener and this 'distant'.

The music itself appears as if it is coming from far, slowly approaching until it is all around us. Or as well, it might be the listener who is slowly approaching and getting closer, until he is engulfed by the sound.

When explaining the composition, Ligeti refers to a painting, Die Alexanderschlacht by Albrecht Altdorfer05. It is the image of a battle which we are overlooking from higher up, with the landscape spreading beyond, with a city, grand mountains and the sea, appearing in the distance, covered in mist. And there is a very strong sense of light in this painting, the sun is appearing from far, glittering into the viewer's eye, blinding, drawing the viewer into the image and into the distance.

Referring to this image, the listener of Lontano is the viewer of the painting, and the music is the landscape and the light. We are approaching slowly, our eyes moving through the image and our mind moving through the landscape, hearing the light from the distance and then the battle from near. We are slowly getting closer, getting engulfed, moving further away and then closer again. And finally we distance ourselves and the sound and light fade and disappear.

Like this, listening to Lontano becomes a journey, and Lontano itself becomes the space which the listener is travelling through.

LINGUISTICS

But it is not only the emotional side where music and architecture relate to each other. For such distant disciplines, the vocabulary which we use to describe them is surprisingly similar: Words like 'composition' and 'structure' refer to the very basic ideas of both music and architecture. We refer to the 'colour' of sound when describing an instrument, and we speak of 'rhythms' when describing the repetition of architectural elements.

NOTATION

Also both music and architecture are forms of art which require additional mediums for their transmission and proliferation, other than just the piece itself or a depiction of it: Both are transmitted via a notation, via drawings which are made to describe the sounds or a building to other people, who are then able to create or re-create the intended piece. In musical notation this happens via a symbolization, in architecture via a combination of both diagrammatic depiction and symbolization.

SCRIPT

Already the notation of script takes sound and turns it into a physical product, into a formation of ink on paper, or into carved grooves within a base material. The first step was the development of a symbol: The material formations or abrasions symbolize meanings, which are orally represented by sounds, and their notation becomes a physical manifestation of those sounds in a quasi two-dimensional object.

TIME AND SPACE

Importantly, in a second step the symbols have been placed in an order and they are read in a certain direction. With all writings we start to read at a start point, and following the symbols we move towards the end, usually in a linear manner, or quite often in a broken linear manner as in a text, which is written across several rows and pages.

Like this, time has been translated into space. The spoken sentence unfolds for a specific duration in time, the written symbolization of it unfolds on the paper in space, the time dimension has become a spatial dimension.

MUSICAL NOTATION

Similarly in musical notation, the time dimension gets transformed into a linear or broken linear spatial dimension. One of the most important aspects of music, which gets symbolized in the notation, is the pitch, the base frequency of the sounds which are to be created. In most musical notations, the notation of the pitch happens in a second dimension: Where the time dimension is read in a horizontal manner, the pitch is read vertically. This applies to the notation using modern musical symbols, but it also applies to early western or Asian forms of musical notation.

Also the pitch of a sound is a property which is time-based, it is the duration at which the waveform of a sound is repeated in time. Therefore also the notation of the pitch in the vertical direction is a transformation of time to space.

In gramophone records and CDs, both time and frequency of music are transformed into physical objects, in both cases the time dimension gets transformed into a curved linear space dimension.

ARCHITECTURAL NOTATION

Architecture as opposed to music requires the notation of a building not in order to re-create the piece, but in order to create the original piece, based on the ideas of the architects and engineers. The notation of a building tends to use different mediums at the same time, such as visualization in form of images, models, architectural drawings, which are a combination of often scaled diagrams of the building with descriptive text and dimensions, and written specifications which describe the building.

Especially on a diagrammatic level the notations of both music and architecture can become similar to each other and propose relations between the spaces and the sounds they represent, as for example in the drawings of Yannis Xenakis, who applied the same concepts to both music and architecture.

A FROZEN SOUND

Based on the idea that sound can be translated into space by translating its intangible time-based attributes into tangible spatial dimensions, Orproject started investigations into notating sound in three-dimensional form. Using digital processes, various acoustic attributes of a sound can be analysed and extracted. For the piece "A Frozen Sound", time, melodic range and peak frequencies have been translated into a multi-dimensional spectrogram. The result is as much an object as it is notation, analysis and representation of the sound.

ATMOSPHERES

In a similar way that A Frozen Sound is the transformation of a sound into space, Atmosphères is the translation of a composition. Based on Atmosphères for orchestra by György Ligeti, which is the predecessor to his composition Lontano, the object becomes a three-dimensional transformation of the orchestra piece.

With Atmosphères, a piece of music has been transformed into three-dimensional space, however it has not been transformed into architecture, nor into a possible concept for architecture. An architectural proposal needs to be usable, it needs to answer functional requirements, and the design concept of it needs to fulfill those requirements. Atmosphères is not useful to fulfil these tasks, it remains a form only. As such it may be regarded as fine art, but not as a part of architecture.

DATA REASSIGNMENT

The data which are recorded for digital sound analysis are air pressure values at repetitive moments in time, the sound waves. The mathematical method of extracting the frequency values from those data is called the Fourier Transform. However, precisely defining a frequency requires constant data for a certain length of time, which do not exist if the sound is changing, and as a consequence the outcomes of the Fourier Transform are blurred data. In order to sharpen those data and to extract precise frequency information, a reassignment of the values to their closest peak can be applied. This reassignment requires a time window to be applied, which can be chosen as longer or shorter, and which will enhance the focus on either the harmonics or the impulses of the sound. In a complex harmonic situation it therefore becomes an uncertain kind of Heisenberg situation in which we can choose at which intensity to focus on either the harmonics or the impulses, but we are never able to pinpoint both at the same time.

Regarding the generation of shape based on the analysis of reassigned frequency values, this situation allows us to generate both a horizontal as well as a vertical repetitive system, together with the fluent transition between the two. The harmony-focused analysis of a sound, as a result of its repetitive overtone frequencies, results in repetitive horizontal layers, whereas the impulse analysis results in shifted, repetitive vertical information. The combination of the two lends itself to the use as a structural building system which requires both horizontal floor plates as well as vertical columns or walls between them, and structural connections which transmit the forces between those two.

ASUVATI

This principle has been applied in the design of Asuvati, a mixed-use multi-story complex with two towers connected by a podium. The horizontal floor plates slowly gain in inclination, turn into vertical circulation spaces, and then form the vertical structure and the facade of the building. The analysis of varying time frame sizes has been used to create a continuous monolithic object, which fulfills different structural functions throughout its volume; the originating sound has become a diagram of the building's distribution and density in space.

KLAVIERSTRUCK I

To fulfil architectural functions with a translation of music, Orproject developed the installation Anisotropia based on Klavierstück I, a composition for piano by Orproject director Christoph Klemmt.

Rather than translating the resulting sound of the composition, Orproject has instead translated its composition tools, which became the design tools for Anisotropia.

SHIFTING TONES

Klavierstück I use a twelve tone row, which starts with the lowest key of the piano. After its first cycle the row gets repeated, though shifted up by a halftone. However rather than transposing up every tone by a halftone, only the lowest tone of the row is transposed up by one octave. Like this the row remains the same, but its range has been shifted.

In the next repetition this shift continues, but the range now also gets reduced in its size: The lowest tone gets transposed up by one octave again, and the second lowest tone gets dropped out, so that only the remaining eleven tones of the row are played. Instead of the twelve tones the range now only covers eleven tones, and also its length is reduced accordingly.

The range of the twelve tone row continues to be reduced and shifted upwards until only one tone is left in each repetition of the original row. Then the range grows again, and still moving upwards goes through further modulations: The different voices of the piece are starting to separate, the size of the different parallel ranges starts to diverge and they move around each other. Finally they grow together again, still moving up, their range fading out and they end with the highest key of the piano.

Similar to African Baginda music, audible are only ever the highest tones which form rhythms rather than melody. Piano Piece No.1 is based on a simple row of the twelve tones, but by shifting and translating its range of influence, complex and continuously evolving rhythmic patterns are generated and turned into a floating field of sound.

ANISOTROPIA

Anisotropia becomes the physical manifestation of Klavierstück I, a frozen piece of music. The installation, designed by Xin Wang and Christoph Klemmt of Orproject, is based on strip morphology instead of a twelve tone row, which creates the structure, openings and rhythm within itself, its repetition happening in space instead of time.

STRUCTURE AND LIGHT

Layers of the strips form the wall system, and the shifting and alteration of these patterns creates the formation of complex architectural rhythms which are used to control the light, view and shading properties of the structure. The basic unit of two strips is constructed from parallel bamboo lamella, it creates form in two dimensions and becomes a straight extrusion into the third dimension. A proliferation of the unit happens into those first two dimensions, with a development and modification happening in the same way in which the twelve tone row gets repeated and modified in time. The extrusion in the third dimension allows for a horizontal modification during the development of the wall, which is used in a linear direction similar to the continuous upwards movement of the piano piece. In the piano piece only ever the upper few tones of each twelve tone row are audible and create the floating field of rhythmic transformations. Similarly in the installation, only the peaks of each strip become visible and create a floating field of structure, shadow and light.

CURVED NON-LINEARITY

Anisotropia is the geometric prototype for a façade system, tested along the short length of a straight line. The notation of music along straight lines is useful, however for the creation of architecture a wider range of possibilities can be used for the translation of time to space. Orproject therefore investigated algorithms to describe time-based flow patterns of particles, and translating those into space via their non-linear trajectories. The particle movement evolves in both space and time dimensions, their trajectories become the possible spatial directions for the translation of the time dimension of music.

FLOW

Particular interest was given to flow simulation past deflectors, similar to planets moving around each other, or similar to the flow of particles past electrodes. If there are no deflectors, the flow of an object will be linear straight. However if the object comes within the range of a deflector, which can either attract or repulse the object, its trajectory will be distorted and become curved

and non-linear. The benefit of the simulations lie in the possibility to calculate flows past pre-existing conditions, they become applicable information for the development of architectural space defined by site conditions and architectural requirements.

KINETIKA

The basic movement of a request object can happen in three ways: The movement can originate externally and be assumed linear at the point of entry of the simulation, as it would be the case with particles moving past electrodes. The movement can originate from the deflectors, as in the case of simulations of magnetic fields. Or the movement can be orthogonal to the direction towards the deflectors, as in the movement of planets around a star.

This last type of movement has been visualised in Orproject's Kinetika, which shows a two-dimensional movement around deflectors. The third dimension reflects the velocity of the request point during its movement.

BUSAN OPERA HOUSE

For Orproject's design proposal for Busan Opera House, a directional flow simulation was used to define the extents of the building on the site. The algorithm describes a flow that is influenced and altered by a set of deflectors, which each act according to the magnitude of their attraction and the range of their influence.

The distribution of the programmatic elements on the site is used as the deflector set that guides the flow of the trajectories. The different elements of the building, such as the auditoria, atrium and back of house spaces, have been assigned deflector attributes depending on their requirements, so that the resulting trajectories of the simulation are enclosing the space around them accordingly, forming the base lines for the facades of the building.

Busan Opera House is situated on an artificial island between the sea and the city, and the flow of the simulation originates from the sea. On their way towards the city, the lines flow around the building elements such as the theatre and auditoriums, splitting up and being diverted by the deflectors.

STRUCTURE AND LIGHT

As in the installation Anisotropia, the proposed façade structure becomes the physical manifestation of Klavierstück I, for the building constructed as a strip morphology made from curved steel sections. Several parallel layers of the strips form the façade, and the alteration of its patterns results in the architectural rhythms which have been tested with the installation.

At the start of the façade structure at the sea, its different layers are aligned and appear to be one. Then slowly the layers start to repeat at different intervals, resulting in a shift between them, the alignment breaks up, and a varied field of the façade rhythms begins to emerge.

The façade structure is altered in the length of its repetition, but also the orientation and the depth of the extrusions are manipulated in order to control the view and light, depending on the programmatic requirements on the inside of the building.

The flow of the façade layers is influenced by the programs which they enclose. As an effect of this the layers split up at certain points, and after forming a coherent system with the overlay of its rhythms, the individual layers separate and their individual patterns become visible.

In the musical composition the different voices converge again. For the building, the separate façade layers have been designed to spread out towards the city, forming various landscape elements such as walls and the structure of a bridge, until they slowly fade out and disappear back into the ground.

MUSIC AND ARCHITECTURE

As different as music and architecture are, the two forms of art also have very close relations, and many composition and design concepts can become applicable to both. However the importance lies in finding and using the relevance of their relation, so that both music and architecture can benefit from each other.

1 FROZEN SOUND
2 FROZEN SOUND
3 KLAVIERSTUCK I FAÇADE DETAIL 1
4 KLAVIERSTUCK I FAÇADE DETAIL 2
5 KLAVIERSTUCK I FAÇADE DETAIL 3
6 KLAVIERSTUCK I FAÇADE DETAIL 4
7 ANISOTROPIA
8 ANISOTROPIA
9 ANISOTROPIA
10 ANISOTROPIA
11 ASUVATI
12 ASUVATI
13 ATMOSPHERES
14 ATMOSPHERES
15 BUSAN OPERA HOUSE ATRIUM
16 BUSAN OPERA HOUSE AUDITORIUM
17 BUSAN OPERA HOUSE NIGHT VIEW
18 BUSAN OPERA HOUSE PLAN
19 KINETICA
20 REASSIGNED SPECTROGRAM OF SPEECH

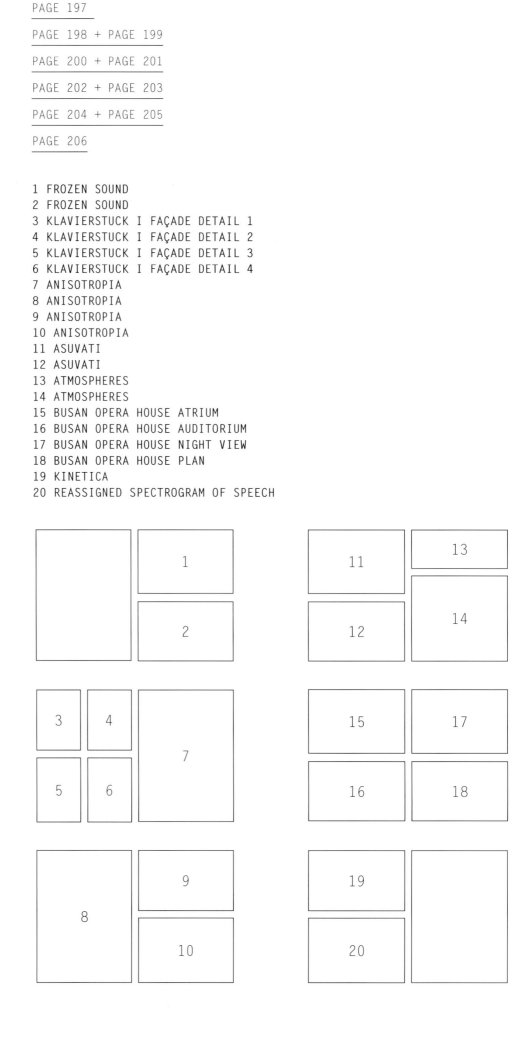

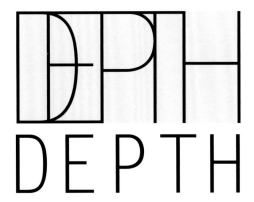

DEPTH

YAN
MENG

URBANUS

XIAODU
LIU

vanke experience center

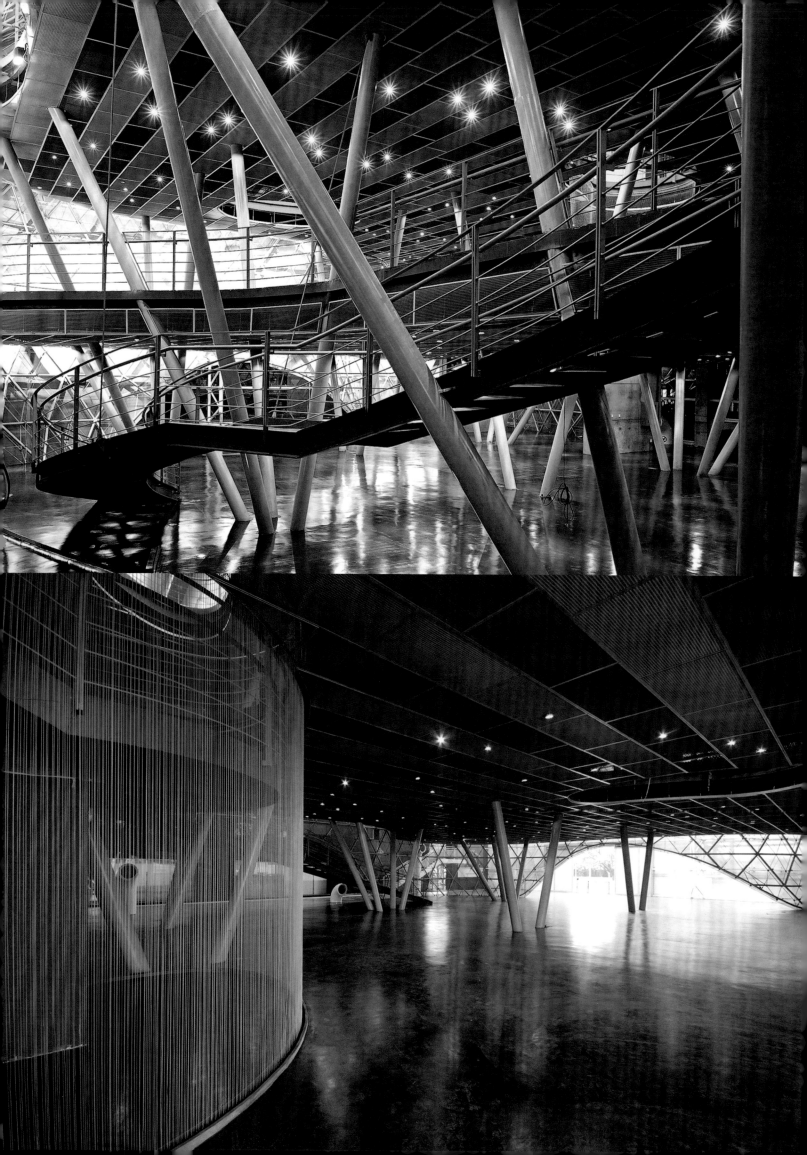

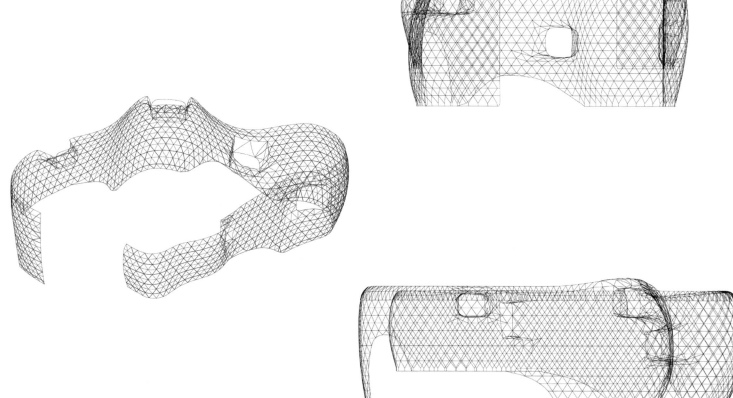

VANKE
EXPERIENCE
CENTER

URBANUS

Vanke Experiment Center (VEC) is located in the east exhibition hall of Vanke Architecture Research center, Futian, Shenzhen. The project asked to create a three-floor exhibition space that incorporates the latest impressive and innovative product designs from the research group, as well as to provide a place to communicate and share the products with their clients. Vanke groups wanted something encouraging and inspiring.

As a point of departure for the design, Urbanus considered that Vanke is a real-estate group, but to study and exhibit architecture their research center needed to be visualized as a place full of live and exciting activities. The challenge was to introduce a concept that can soften the toughness and heaviness of the existing structure. Urbanus stated the new design should be a more organic and self-structured single element while leaving the existing building untouched. Keen to leave the existing interior open and free, the designers inserted a fluent three-dimensional cocoon made of aluminum.

The design respects and engages the existing exhibition hall in a dialogue that lifts it to a higher plane of excellence without compromising its integrity.

TEAM

Urbanus partners in charge: Yan Meng, Xiaodu Liu. Project architect: Dan Deng, Jiang Tu

PAGE 214 + PAGE 215

PAGE 216 + PAGE 217

1 VANKE EXPERIMENT CENTER STAIRS AND BRIDGES
2 VANKE EXPERIMENT CENTER UNDER BELLY
3 VANKE EXPERIMENT CENTER MAIN ENTRANCE
4 VANKE EXPERIMENT CENTER SECOND FLOOR ENTRANCE
5 VANKE EXPERIMENT CENTER STRUCTURE
6 VANKE EXPERIMENT CENTER SKIN
7 VANKE EXPERIMENT CENTER ELEVATIONS

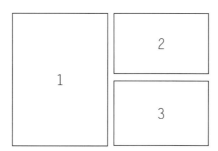

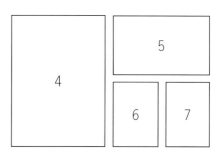

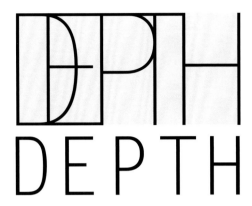

DEPTH

KATHY
VELIKOV
GEOFFREY
THUN
RVTR
+
MTTR
MGMT
BENJAMIN
RICE

nervous ether: shiver of bodies

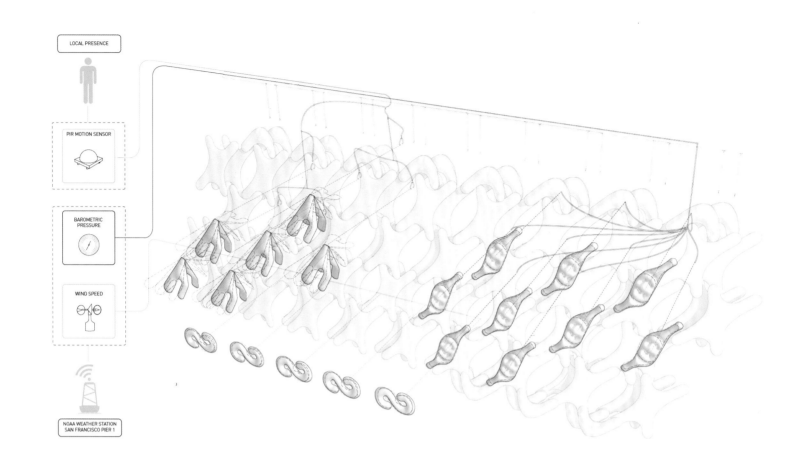

LOCAL PRESENCE

PIR MOTION SENSOR

BAROMETRIC PRESSURE

WIND SPEED

NOAA WEATHER STATION
SAN FRANCISCO PIER 1

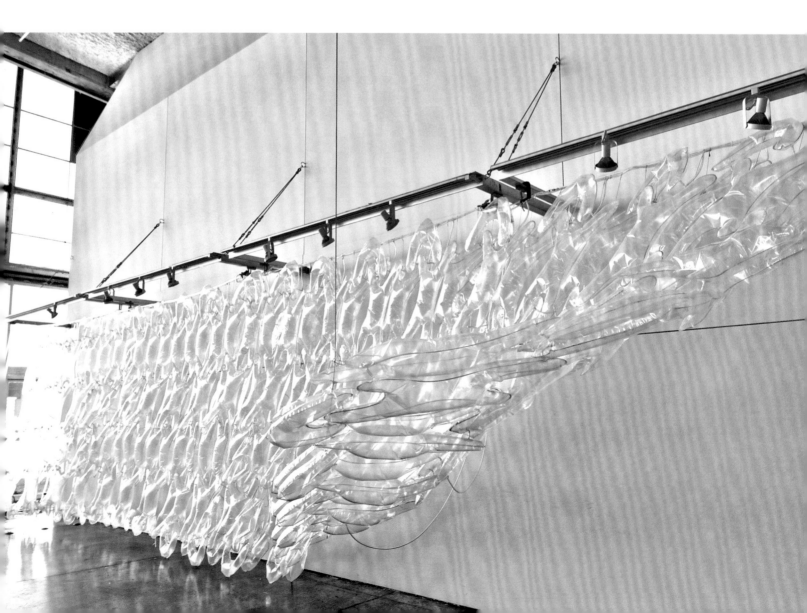

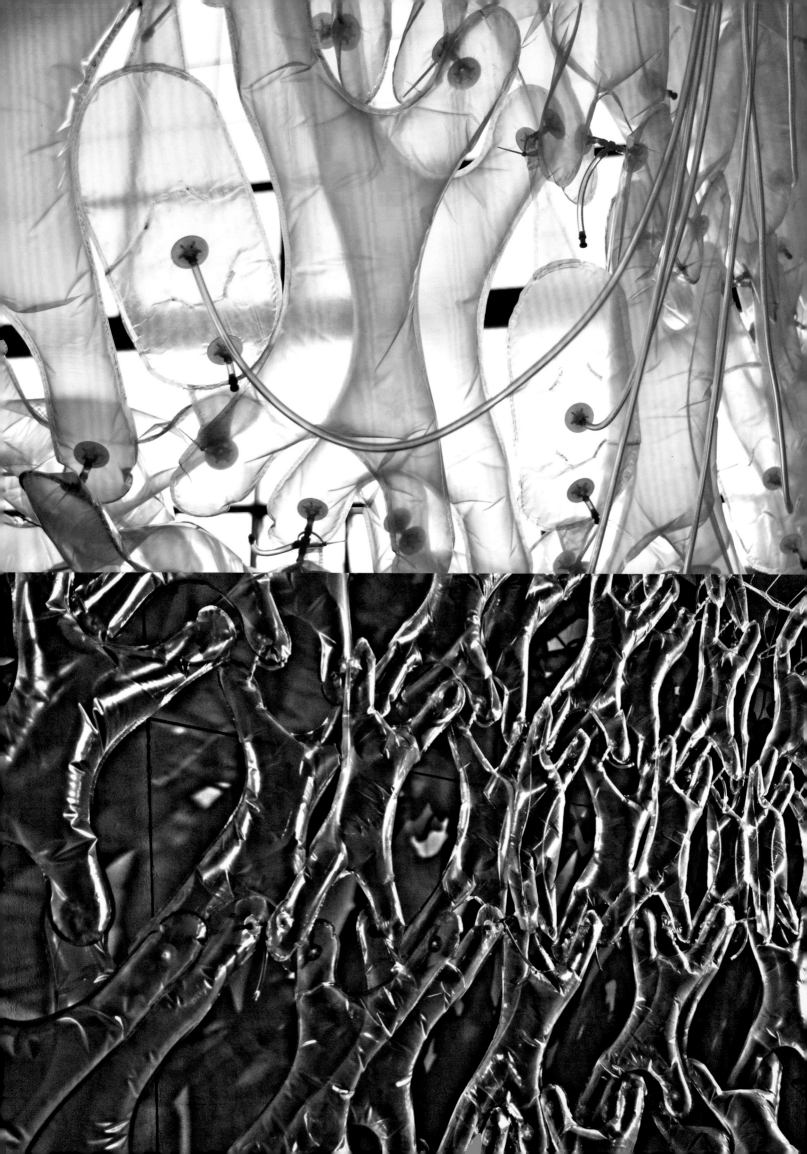

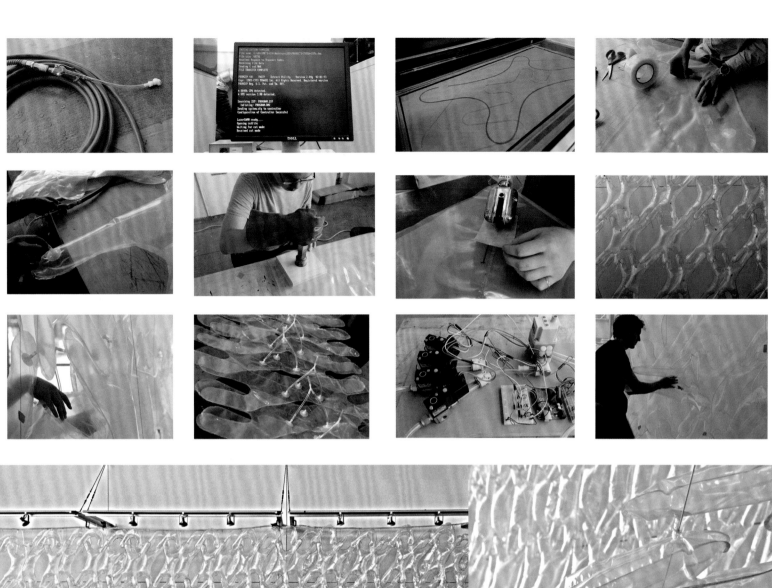

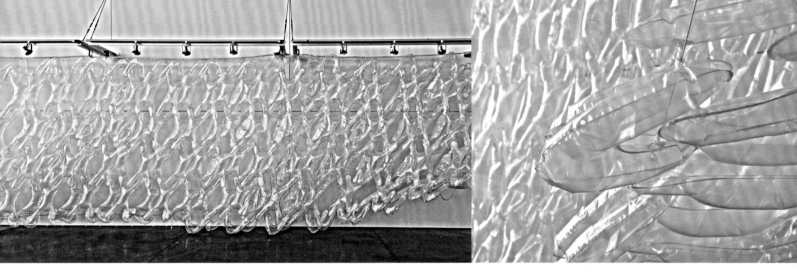

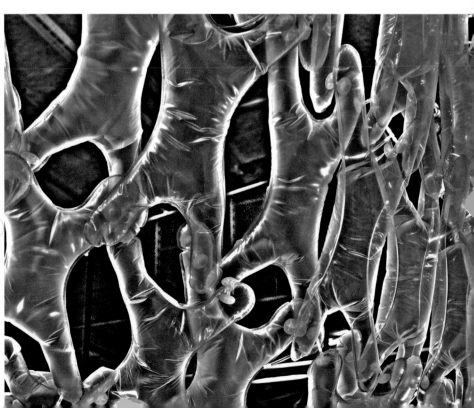

NERVOUS ETHER:
SHIVER OF BODIES

KATHY VELIKOV
AND GEOFFREY THÜN OF RVTR
WITH BENJAMIN RICE
OF MTTR MGMT

Nervous Ether is an installation that is developed as a full-scale responsive physical environment consisting of a cellular pneumatic skin, operating as an instrument to register and communicate remote environmental information while also generating specific sensations and effects within the immediate (inhabitable) environment. It aims to lever the agency of air and information to spatially and physically materialize the immaterial into a palpable and sensate environment.

The topology of Nervous Ether is developed through a tessellated array of tetrahedral forms, defined through the constraints of material behavior (polyethylene film under air pressure), manufacturing (laser contour welding bed dimensions) and aggregation. Two pneumatically interconnected layers of cellular cushions intertwine to create a membrane structure that is hung and tensioned within the space. The tessellated weave is inflated to a constant air pressure.

The weave forms an open framework supporting a number of actuatable membrane components that are integrated with the structure and air supply. Three types of responsive components are developed through iterative physical prototyping and testing: palpitating-cells and S-cells, that respond based on a translation of live weather station inputs of barometric pressure and wind speed, respectively; and wing-cells which respond to local proximity sensors, opening and fluttering when visitors approach the installation.

The title of the project is derived from the history of physics, where philosophers and scientists have speculated on the existence of nervous ether, a material atmosphere that is a conductor of the vibrations of heat, light, sound, electromagnetic impulses and mechanical frictions. In the late nineteenth century, the physicist John Tyndall theorized that the "transported shiver of bodies" of the cosmos and the stars could be intimately felt within our own physical bodies and consciousness. The installation explores material architectures of soft aggregate bodies, sensitive to frequencies and periodicity, to situated and extrinsic energies; yet spatial and experiential propositions in and of themselves.

This work forms part of a larger body of research by Kathy Velikov and Geoffrey Thün of RVTR and Benjamin Rice of MTTR MGMT into kinetic, environmentally-responsive envelope systems that develop continual information and material exchange, and dialogue between ourselves and the soft systems of architecture – such as light, thermal gradients, air quality and acoustics. Most recently, this research is testing the formal, material and operational possibilities of cellular pneumatic aggregates to function as deep building skins, imbued with environmental response, interaction and intelligence.

TEAM

Project Leaders: Kathy Velikov and Geoffrey Thün of RVTR with Benjamin Rice of MTTR MGMT

Project Assistants: Mary O'Malley and Dan McTavish

CCA 333 Students: Irma Acosta, Fernanda Bernardes, Welbert Bonilla, Harrison Chou, Jojit Diaz, Sirada Laomanutsak, Veronica Leung, Max Sanchez, Alexandre Silveira, Aaron Tam, Jia Wu, Mark Zannad

1 NERVOUS ETHER, COMPONENTS AND RESPONSE LOGICS
2 NERVOUS ETHER INSTALLED, OBLIQUE VIEW
3 INSTALLING NERVOUS ETHER
4 PNEUMATIC CONNECTION AND DISTRIBUTION DETAIL
5 PNEUMATIC TEXTILE DETAIL
6 MANUFACTURING AND TESTING OF PNEUMATIC COMPONENTS
7 NERVOUS ETHER INSTALLED, FRONT VIEW
8 PNEUMATIC TEXTILE DETAIL
9 LOGIC OF PNEUMATIC TEXTILE CONSTRUCTION
10 NERVOUS ETHER INSTALLED, SIDE VIEW

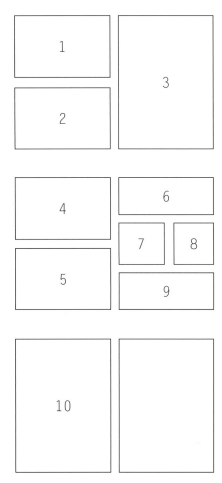

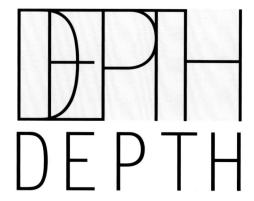

DEPTH

ALVIN
HUANG

SDA-
SYNTHESIS
DESIGN +
ARCHITEC-
TURE

daegu gosan public library

pure tension: volvo v60 pavilion

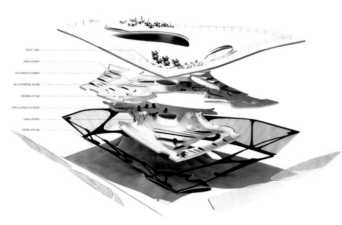

PROGRAM DIAGRAM

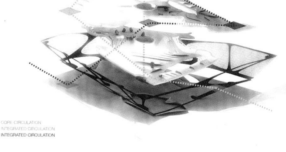

CORE CIRCULATION
INTEGRATED CIRCULATION
INTEGRATED CIRCULATION

CIRCULATION DIAGRAM

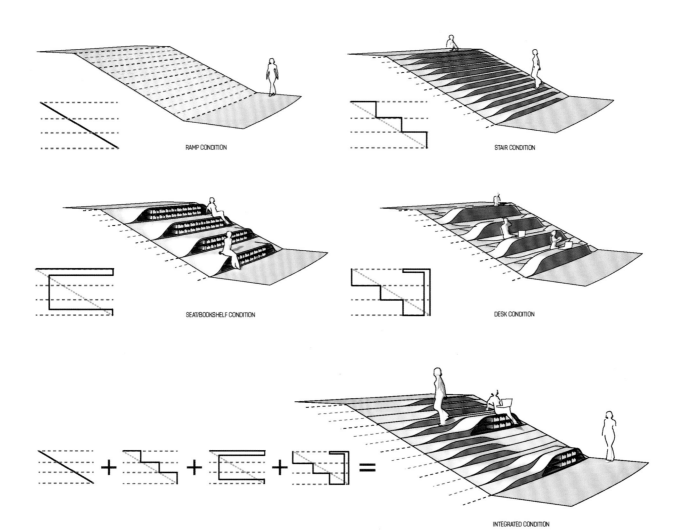

RAMP CONDITION

STAIR CONDITION

SEAT/BOOKSHELF CONDITION

DESK CONDITION

INTEGRATED CONDITION

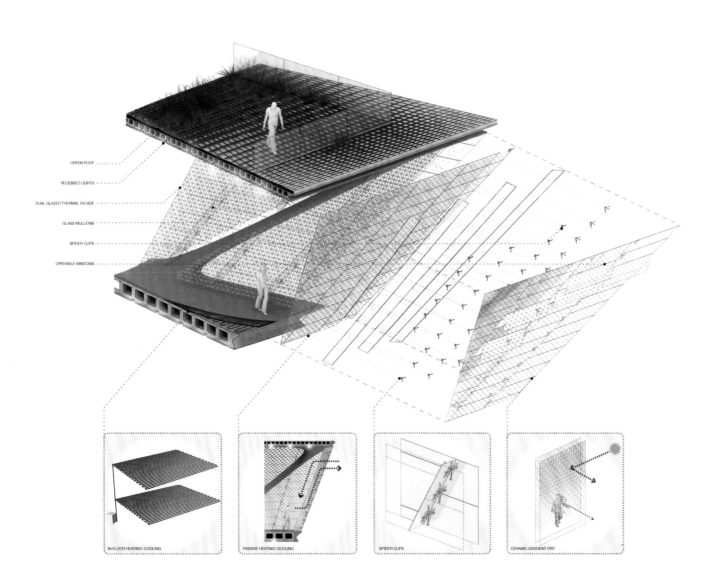

GREEN ROOF

RECESSED LIGHTS

DUAL GLAZED THERMAL FACADE

GLASS MULLIONS

SPIDER CLIPS

OPERABLE WINDOWS

IN-FLOOR HEATING/ COOLING

PASSIVE HEATING/ COOLING

SPIDER CLIPS

CERAMIC GRADIENT FRIT

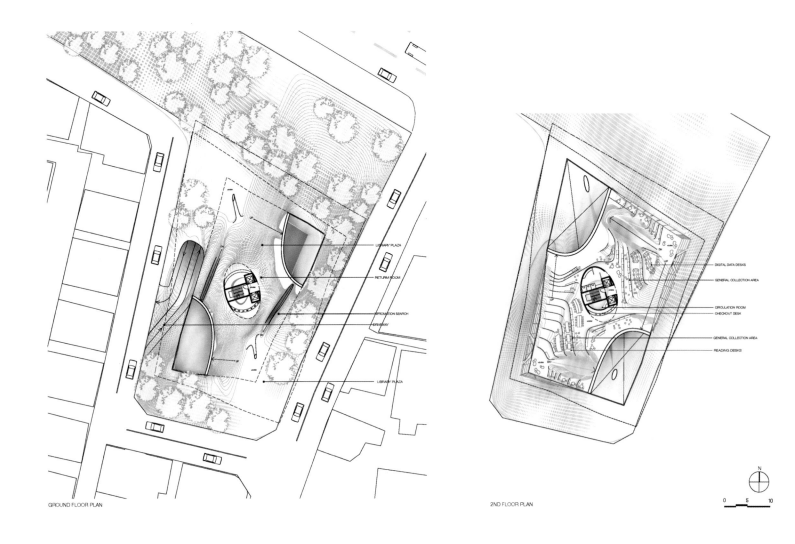

GROUND FLOOR PLAN

LIBRARY/ PLAZA

RETURN ROOM

INFORMATION SEARCH
DRIVEWAY/

LIBRARY/ PLAZA

2ND FLOOR PLAN

DIGITAL DATA DESKS

GENERAL COLLECTION AREA

CIRCULATION ROOM
CHECKOUT DESK

GENERAL COLLECTION AREA

READING DESKS

N

0   5   10

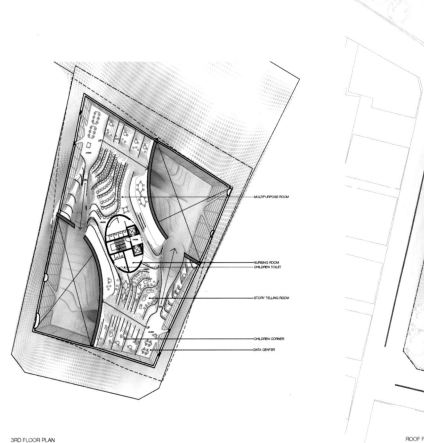

3RD FLOOR PLAN

MULTIPURPOSE ROOM

NURSING ROOM
CHILDREN TOILET

STORY TELLING ROOM

CHILDREN CORNER

DATA CENTER

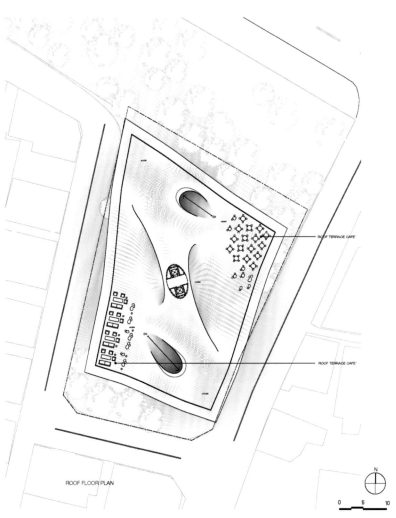

ROOF FLOOR PLAN

ROOF TERRACE CAFE

ROOF TERRACE CAFE

N

0   5   10

DAEGU GOSAN
PUBLIC LIBRARY

SDA
- SYNTHESIS DESIGN
+ ARCHITECTURE

The proposal for the Daegu Gosan Public Library challenges the conventional understanding of the spatial and social experience of a public library as a series of discrete reading rooms with defined thresholds and cluttered stacks. SDA proposes an intelligent, open, and integrated library experience, which supersedes the media storage methods of the past and changes the library space into a hybrid environment through ubiquitous information resources, integrated furnishings and active communal social spaces. The architecture is designed to enable and embody the spirit of open-source exchange and collective knowledge through free-form geometries, open plans and integrated amenities. SDA minimized the thresholds between spaces, floors, and functions to consider the library as an active, continuous, and fluid field of social, cultural, and intellectual discourse.

Conceptually and literally, the ground field of the site swells, peels, and multiplies vertically as a continuation of the adjacent park and urban fabric. This constant sectional change is articulated as a smooth vertical gradient, which merges floors, ramps, stairs, terraces and furnishings into an inhabitable and ergonomic landscape culminating in an open-air roof-scape lounge and terrace overlooking the city of Daegu. The boundaries between floors are blurred, as the continuously walk-able surface, which unifies the many spaces of the library, facilitates circulatory, physical and visual connections both internally within the network of spaces and externally with the surrounding context.

The building is materialized as an in-situ reinforced concrete structure, which like all other aspects has been designed to be fully integrated with the geometry of the library. The central core of the building provides its primary structural point of reference connecting vertically through the entire structure. The free-form geometry that defines the walk-able surfaces and unifies the building cantilevers out from this central core and is supported by its internal interconnections (ramps), perimeter interconnections (columns) and the lifted ground plane (foundation). The geometric logic of the form has been developed through a computational method known as "dynamic mesh relaxation" which relaxes planar mesh networks to "form-find" a continuously minimal surface. As developed in the 1950's and 60's through the seminal work of Frei Otto, minimal surfaces articulate the natural force paths of structural loads thus providing the optimal shape for maximum structural performance with minimal material. The shape of the surface, thus allows for relatively thin structure, which in our case is materialized as cast-in-place high performance reinforced concrete. This concrete would be cast on CNC-milled EPS foam formwork, coated with polyurethane. The geometry of the building has been rationalized so that each piece of formwork could be reused at least four times in order to maximize the efficiency and economy of the process.

PROJECT TEAM

Alvin Huang (Principal) David O. Wolthers, Filipa Valente,
Chia-ching Yang, Joey Sarafian, Mo Harmon, Behnaz Farahi

CONSULTANTS:

Buro Happold LA (Structural/MEP/Facades)

EVOLO 06
DEPTH
DAEGU GOSAN PUBLIC LIBRARY
SDA – SYNTHESIS DESIGN + ARCHITECTURE

PAGE 228 + PAGE 229

PAGE 230 + PAGE 231

PAGE 232

1 READING HALLS INTERIOR VIEW
2 MAIN ENTRANCE AERIAL VIEW
3 WHOLE COMPLEX AERIAL VIEW
4 OUTDOOR AREAS
5 PROGRAM DIAGRAM AXONOMETRIC
6 NIGHT VIEW READING HALLS
7 CIRCULATION INTEGRATION DIAGRAM
8 FAÇADE DETAIL
9 PLANS LEVEL 1 AND 2
10 PLANS LEVEL 3 AND 4

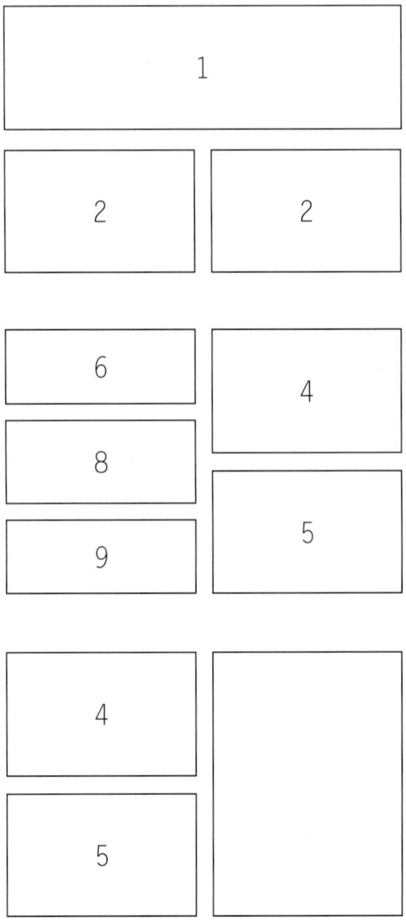

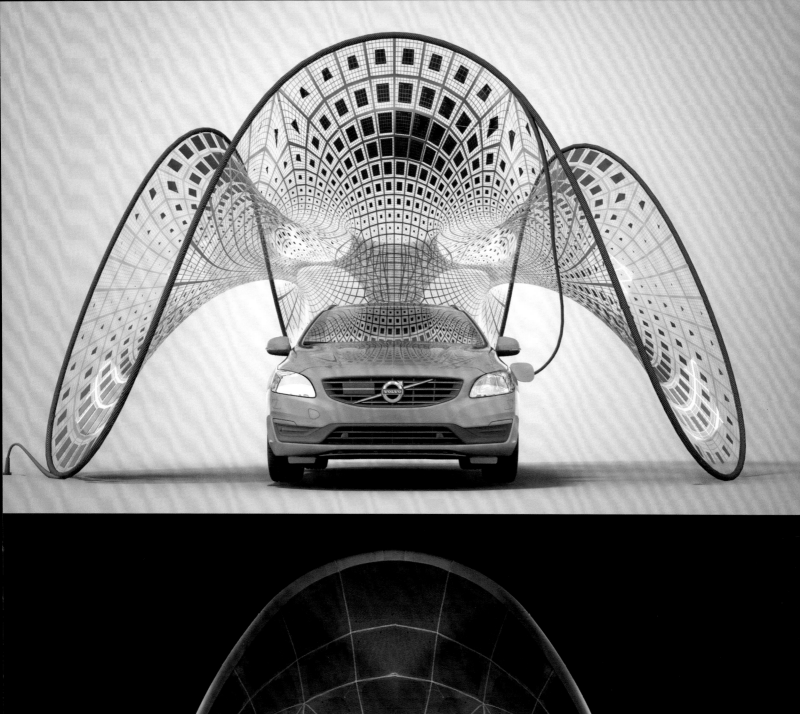

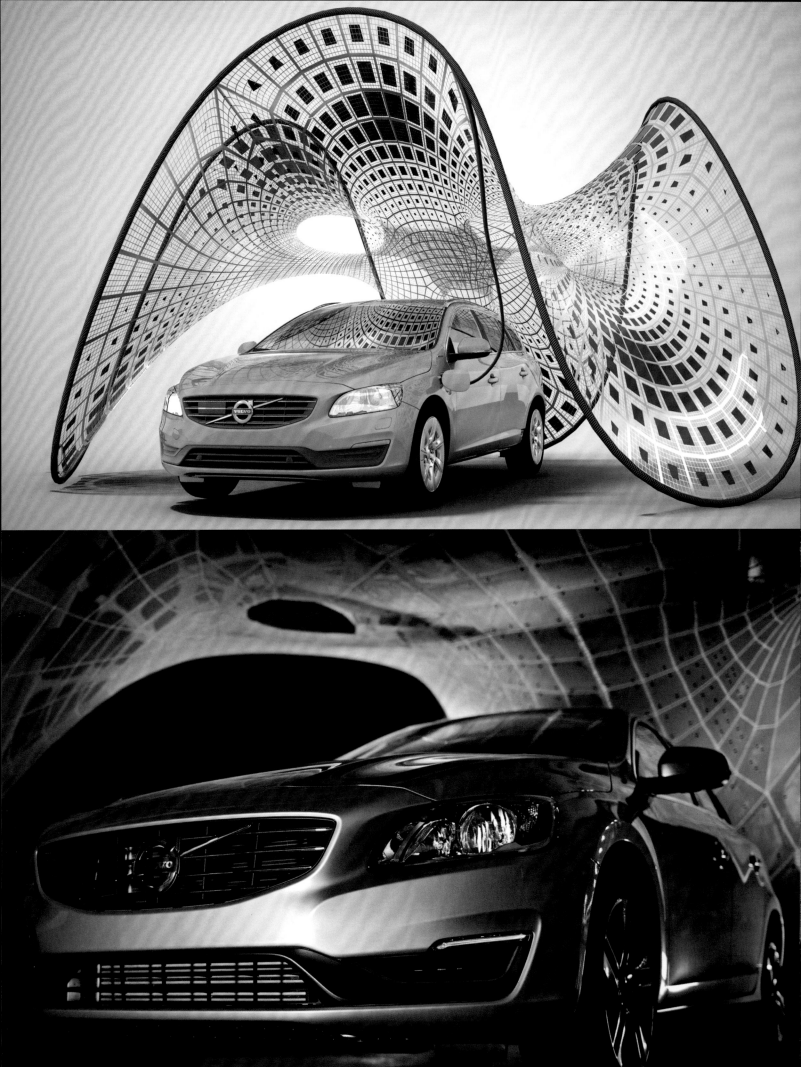

I.

Arrive with Volvo V60 and unload elements
from trunk of car

II.

Place anchor base in defined locations

III.

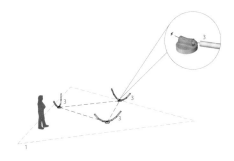

Insert lower pre-bent tubes into anchor plates

IV.

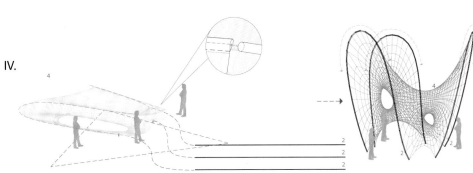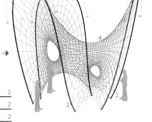

Feed in bent rods through sleeves in pre-fabricated mesh membrane

Bent rods through mesh membrane to
achieve tensioned form

V.

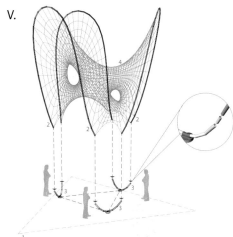

Insert tensioned structure to anchor plates

01. Assembly Material

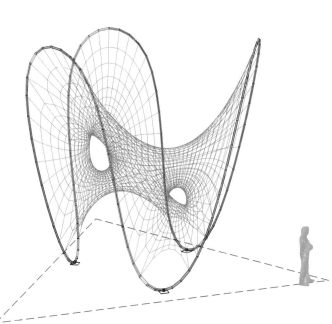

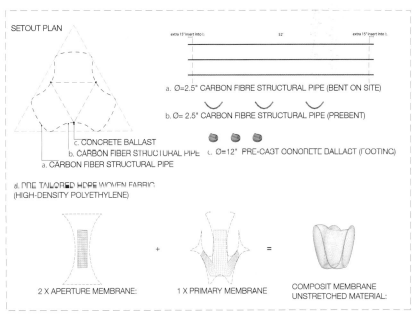

SETOUT PLAN

extra 15" insert into b.   52'   extra 15" insert into b.

a. Ø=2.5" CARBON FIBRE STRUCTURAL PIPE (BENT ON SITE)

b. Ø= 2.5" CARBON FIBRE STRUCTURAL PIPE (PREBENT)

c. CONCRETE BALLAST
b. CARBON FIBER STRUCTURAL PIPE
a. CARBON FIBER STRUCTURAL PIPE

c. Ø=12" PRE-CAST CONCRETE BALLAST (FOOTING)

d. PRE TAILORED HDPE WOVEN FABRIC
(HIGH-DENSITY POLYETHYLENE)

2 X APERTURE MEMBRANE: +   1 X PRIMARY MEMBRANE   =   COMPOSIT MEMBRANE
UNSTRETCHED MATERIAL:

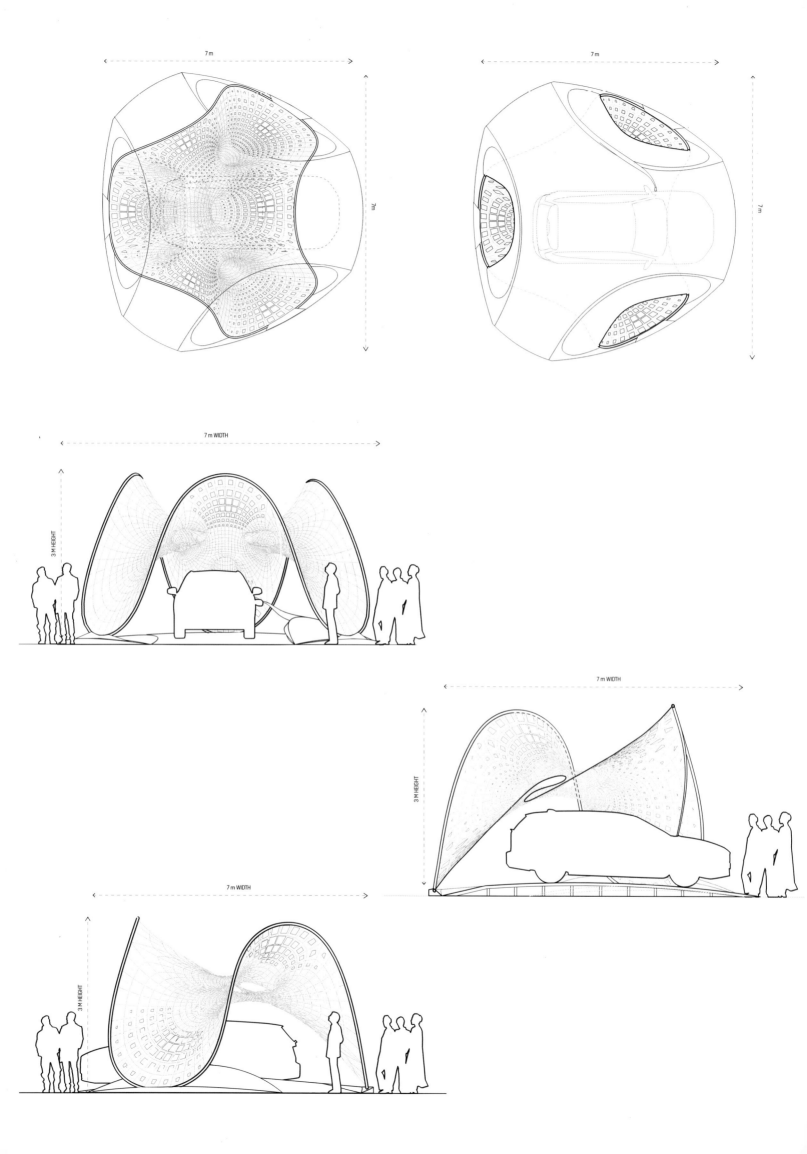

PURE TENSION
– VOLVO V60 PAVILION

SDA
– SYNTHESIS DESIGN
+ ARCHITECTURE

The Pure Tension Volvo Pavilion, a collaborative effort between Synthesis Design + Architecture, Buro Happold, and Fabric Images, is a lightweight, rapidly deployable, free-standing tensioned membrane structure and portable charging station commissioned by Volvo Car Italia to showcase the new Volvo V60 Hybrid Electric Diesel car. Officially launched in Rome, Italy in September 2013, this experimental structure was developed through a process of rigorous research and development that investigated methods of associative modeling, dynamic mesh relaxation, geometric rationalization, paneling, and material performance. These explorations illustrate the dialogue between design, engineering, and fabrication that define this project.

The project aspires to reinvent the typical trade show pavilion through its combination of dynamic form, optical effects and flexibility and adaptability to the space. The structure for the pavilion is highlighted by a uniquely sensual and continuous form composed of a tensioned HDPE Mesh skin with embedded PV panels and a perimeter ring made of carbon fiber rods. The effect of the structure's organic form, perforated mesh, and PV transparent panels provides a striking graphic identity to Volvo's V60 model which encourages visual and spatial interaction while simultaneously enabling different configurations to accommodate a variety of activities including: vendors, demonstrations, car trade shows.

The uniqueness of the design comes from a organic form which is both iconic and efficient while the moiré effect of a fabric mesh also will encourage visual interaction. Conceived as an extension of the legacy of Frei Otto's seminal lightweight tensioned membrane structures, it is the unique form that makes the structure both efficient and effective. The form was developed through a parallel process of both analogue and digital form finding to explore the material behaviors of composite tensioned membrane skins (relaxed meshes) and bending active frames. The carbon fiber tube ring is deformed into shape by the tailoring of skin, which binds it. In response, the frame pushes out while the skin pulls in, creating a form-force equilibrium that is lightweight, cost-efficient, and easy to assemble and disassemble. The pavilion is designed so that when it is disassembled it will fit inside the V60's trunk dimensions for easy transportation.

The issue of sustainability is addressed in the form of a power strategy which uses fabric embedded Photovoltaic panels and light collected from the sun or indoor artificial lighting to power the pavilion and charge the V60 model on show. The car will 'plug' directly into the pavilion's skin, charging its battery with the energy collected over the day. The 'Switch to Pure Volvo' pavilion becomes a symbol of the V60's attitude to efficient energy consumption and a showcase of the Hybrid V60's characteristics.

DESIGN TEAM

Synthesis Design + Architecture
(Alvin Huang, Filipa Valente,Chia-ching Yang, Behnaz Farahi, Yueming Zhou, Joseph Sarafian)

STRUCTURAL ENGINEERING

Buro Happold Los Angeles (Greg Otto, Sanjeev Tankha,
Stephen Lewis, Ron Elad)

COLLABORATORS

Fabric Images Inc., FTL Global, Ascent Solar Technologies Inc.

1 PAVILION FRONT VISUALIZATION
2 PAVILION COMPLETED. FRONT
3 PAVILION PERSPECTIVE VISUALIZATION
4 PAVILION COMPLETED. SIDE
5 ASSEMBLY STEPS
6 MATERIALS
7 ROOF PLAN
8 PLAN
9 FRONT ELEVATION
10 SECTION
11 SIDE ELEVATION

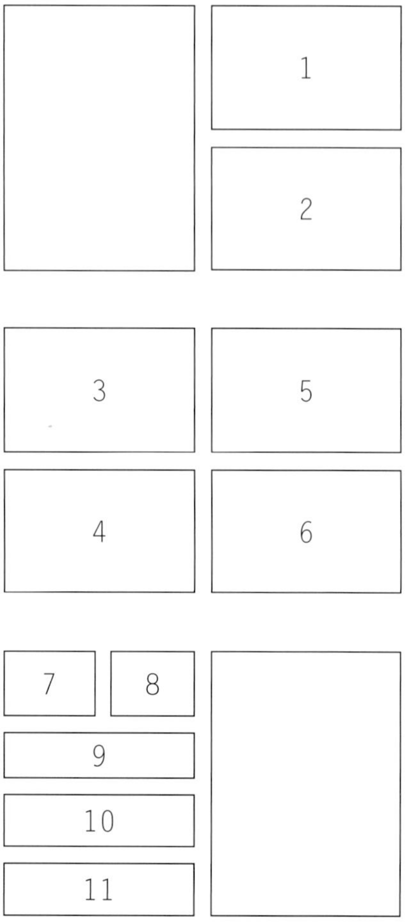

240
EVOLO 06
DEPTH
PURE TENSION – VOLVO V60 PAVILION
SDA – SYNTHESIS DESIGN + ARCHITECTURE

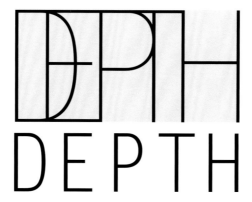

DEPTH

OCEAN

auxiliary architecture: membrane spaces

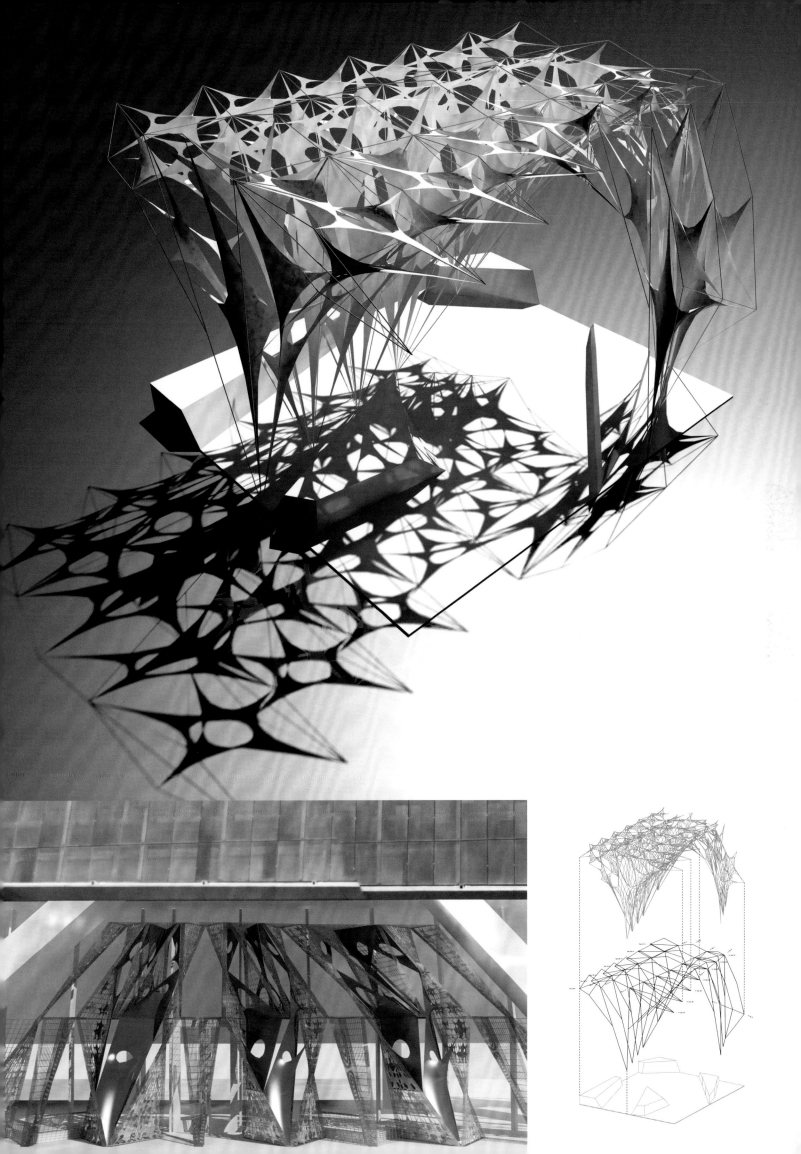

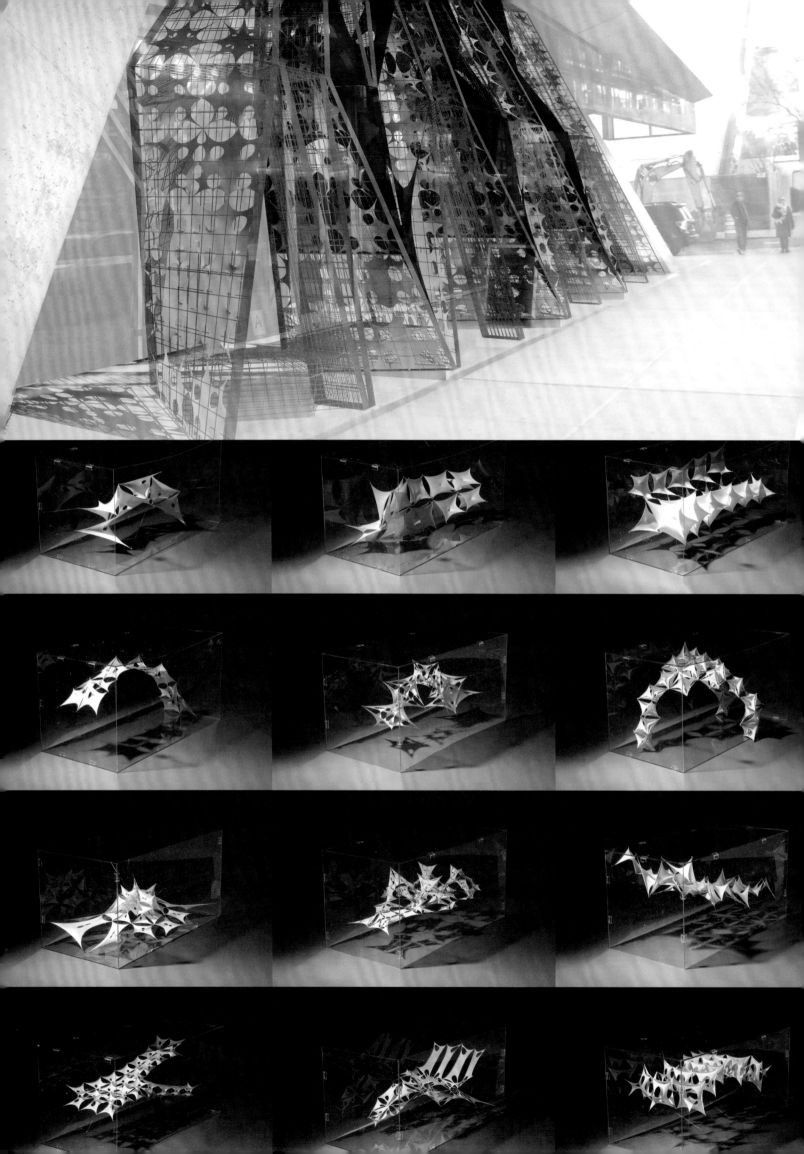

AUXILIARY ARCHITECTURES – MEMBRANE SPACES

OCEAN

OCEAN's Auxiliary Architectures research focuses on supplementary architectural interventions that seek to provide a spatially and atmospherically more heterogeneous environment. One of the ways this can be accomplished is by way of differentiated membrane arrays, often in combination with cable-nets. Such systems can be physically and computationally form-found. The correspondence between material and digital experiments facilitates the elaboration of complex configurations that can be analyzed through physical models and full-scale constructions and by way of computer-aided analysis. Of the ongoing research four examples were selected for this publication.

The Bylgia membrane installation at FRAC in Orleans, France (2008) and the Membrane installation at the University of Economy in Izmir constitute systematic experiments into differentiated membrane and cable-net systems that are driven by combined physical and computational form-finding linked with computational environmental analysis. Both projects led to the construction of a full-scale system. The MM-Tent Membrella (2008) and M-Velope (2012) projects are design studies that are mainly based on computational methods of form-generation coupled with computational environmental analysis. While the construction oriented projects deliver insights in the way in which such complex systems can be constructed and the environmental modulation capacity verified, the more computationally driven projects serve to advance the generative design process and the integration of augmented reality application to simulate and visualize the environmental modulation capacity of designs that can not immediately be implemented.

BYLGIA MEMBRANE INSTALLATION @ FRAC ORLEANS, FRANCE, 2008

OCEAN Team: Michael Hensel, Defne Sunguroğlu Hensel, Jeffrey Turko,
Daniel Coll I Capdevila, Toni Kotnik
Construction: Michael Hensel, Defne Sunguroğlu Hensel, Francois Jupin (FRAC)

MM-TENT MEMBRELLA, 2008

OCEAN Team: Jeffrey Turko, Pavel Hladik, Daniel Coll I Capdevila, Gudjon Erlendsson, Mattia Gambardella
Engineering: Buro Happold London

IZMIR MEMBRANE INSTALLATION, 2009

OCEAN Team: Michael Hensel and Defne Sunguroğlu Hensel

M-VELOPE, 2012

OCEAN Team: Jeffrey Turko, Christina Doumpioti, Pavel Hladik
Engineering: ARUP London – Giulio Antonutto, Luca Dellatorre

1 BYLGIA MEMBRANE INSTALLATION @ FRAC ORLEANS, FRANCE, 2008.
  DIGITAL MODEL
2 AUXILIARY ARCHITECTURES - MEMBRANE SPACES WORKSHOP
  @ IZMIR UNIVERSITY OF ECONOMY, 2009. FULL-SCALE CONSTRUCTION.
  PHOTOGRAPHY: MELIH UÇAR, 2009
3 AUXILIARY ARCHITECTURES - MEMBRANE SPACES WORKSHOP
  @ IZMIR UNIVERSITY OF ECONOMY, 2009.
  PHYSICAL FORM-FINDING AND CONSTRUCTION PROCESS
4 BYLGIA MEMBRANE INSTALLATION @ FRAC ORLEANS, FRANCE, 2008.
  FULL-SCALE CONSTRUCTION
5 MM-TENT MEMBRELLA, 2008. RAPID-PROTOTYPE MODEL OF THE COMPRESSION
  SYSTEM AND THE EDGE CABLES OF THE MEMBRANES
6 MM-TENT MEMBRELLA, 2008. DIGITAL MODEL
7 MM-TENT MEMBRELLA, 2008. RENDERED VIEW OF THE PROJECT IN CONTEXT.
8 MM-TENT MEMBRELLA, 2008. EXPLODED AXONOMETRIC:
  [I] BASE, [II] COMPRESSION SYSTEM, AND [III] MEMBRANES
9 MM-TENT MEMBRELLA, 2008. RENDERED VIEW OF THE PROJECT IN CONTEXT.
10 AUXILIARY ARCHITECTURES - MEMBRANE SPACES WORKSHOP
   @ IZMIR UNIVERSITY OF ECONOMY, 2009. 16 SCALED MODELS OF DIFFERENT
   MEMBRANE AND CABLE-NET SYSTEMS. PHOTOGRAPHY: MELIH UÇAR, 2009

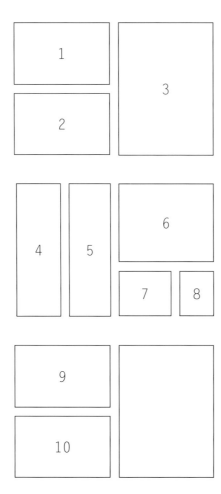

248
EVOLO 06
DEPTH
AUXILIARY ARCHITECTURES - MEMBRANE SPACES
OCEAN

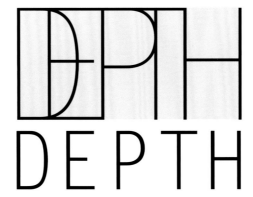

DEPTH

CRISTINA
DÍAZ
MORENO

AMID.
CERO9

EFRÉN
GARCÍA
GRINDA

cherry blossom pavilion

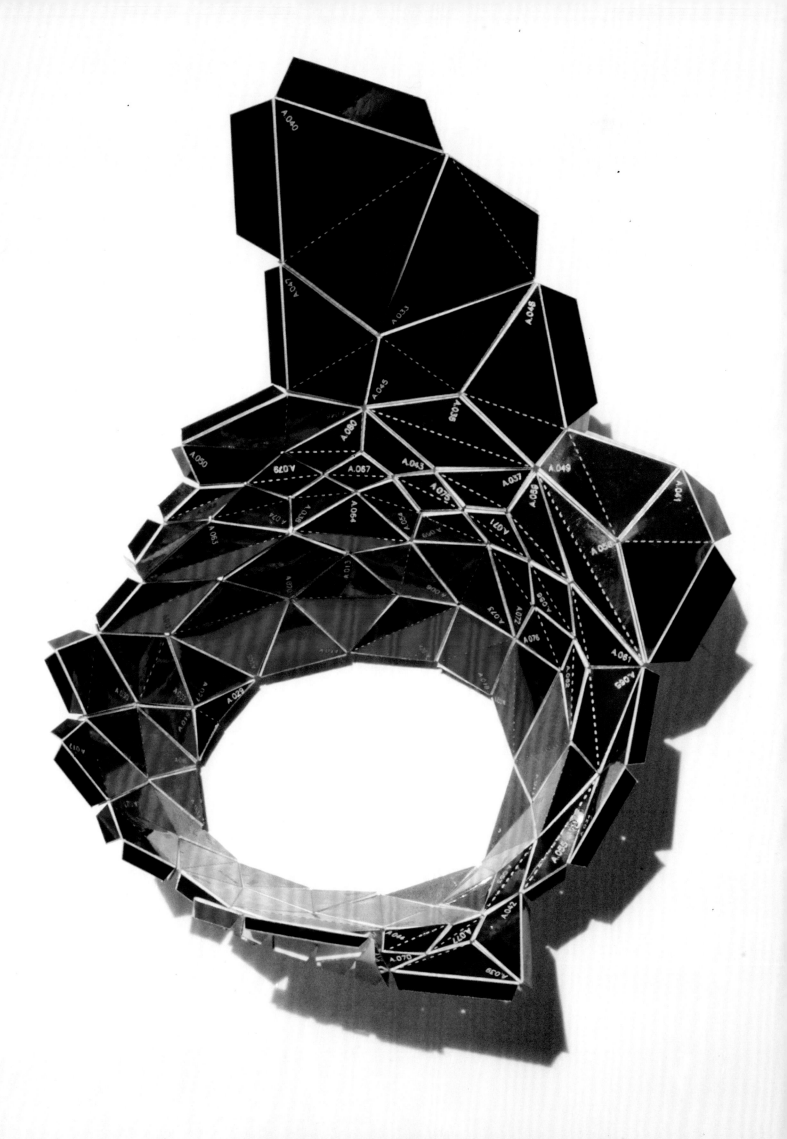

CHERRY BLOSSOM
PAVILION

AMID.CERO9
(CRISTINA DÍAZ MORENO +
EFRÉN GARCÍA GRINDA)

There is nothing more absurd for the Centre of the Fiesta del Cerezo (Cherry Tree Day) in Valle del Jerte, Spain than blindly importing models designed for other locations and purposes. Words such as 'Theatre', 'Auditorium', 'Convention Centre' or 'Conference Hall' lack any meaning whatsoever in the context of the celebration of a popular holiday involving agriculture, in an artificialized setting with a long history that dates back to at least the 18th century. Neither the urban typological models for halls nor the events that take place therein nor their organization or formal or material definitions mean anything in this case.

AMID.cero9's proposal for the Fiesta del Cerezo involves the development of a contemporary chapel, a building that establishes a close bond with the environment through its presence, position, volume and material. An assertive building, one that does not refuse to relate with the entire valley and whose scale provides a reference point. A church for pilgrims, a chapel, a lay Ronchamp, a San Baudelio de Berlanga that floats among the landscape, a Saint Chapelle that is raised from the ground and that makes the ascension to the main hall a spectacle for the senses and a tool to become one with the surrounding landscape. It is a hybrid between a man-made cavern with large openings to let light in, amongst cherry trees in bloom, and high technology scenic machinery, both solid and inexpensive, in plain view for everybody. The pavilion is a rock with biological and natural associations in the midst of the specialisation of the surrounding terrain of terraces and cherry trees - a strange hybrid that cannot be called a theatre or an auditorium any longer. It is a building that can remain closed for months and opened for the day or for the Otoñada (autumn season), in the same way as a church on a pilgrimage day.

The proposal for this landscape that shifts colors during the year is a ceramic building whose large glistening tiles overlap the fog and provide a contrast with the changes in colour of the valley, from green to red to white.

The main room explores the greatest possible versatility with conventional and technically tested means. The purpose of the configuration selected is to create a room with a flat floor that is compatible with the required occupancy level. The typology of the European concert halls of the 18th century, with their flat stall, short top amphitheater and high stage, has thus been used as a basis.

The enclosing shell is a three-dimensional structure of interwoven steel plate girders with high depth and slenderness. They form lozenges, triangles, and pentagons and ensure a similar behavior to that of a dome. The shell is lined with flat scales formed by ceramic pieces that fit the initial geometry with different sizes, as a function of the curvature of the surface. This is replicated towards the inside mosaics that serve to fine-tune the acoustics of the hall.

There is nothing more natural in this environment than building terraces to house the activities of this open-air holiday. These terraces adapt to the size of the groups of people and to the activities that take place within them in the same way as they now adapt to the size of the cherry trees and to the slopes. These new terraces shall apply the construction laws of the valley itself and shall be a visual, material, and spatial extension of the existing terraces.

PAGE 250 + PAGE 251

PAGE 252

1 FOLDED MODEL
2 UNFOLDED MODEL
3 VIEW FROM VALLEY
4 INTERIOR VIEW
5 INTERIOR WALLS DETAIL AND SKYLIGHTS

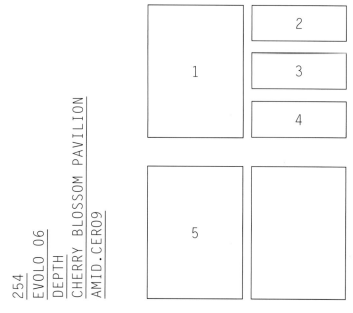

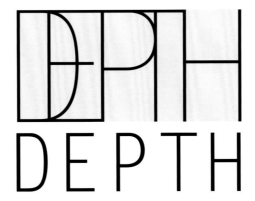

DEPTH

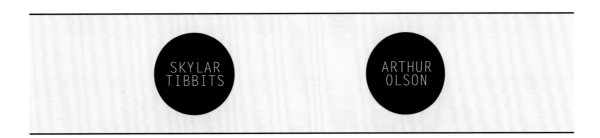

SKYLAR TIBBITS

ARTHUR OLSON

the self-assembly line

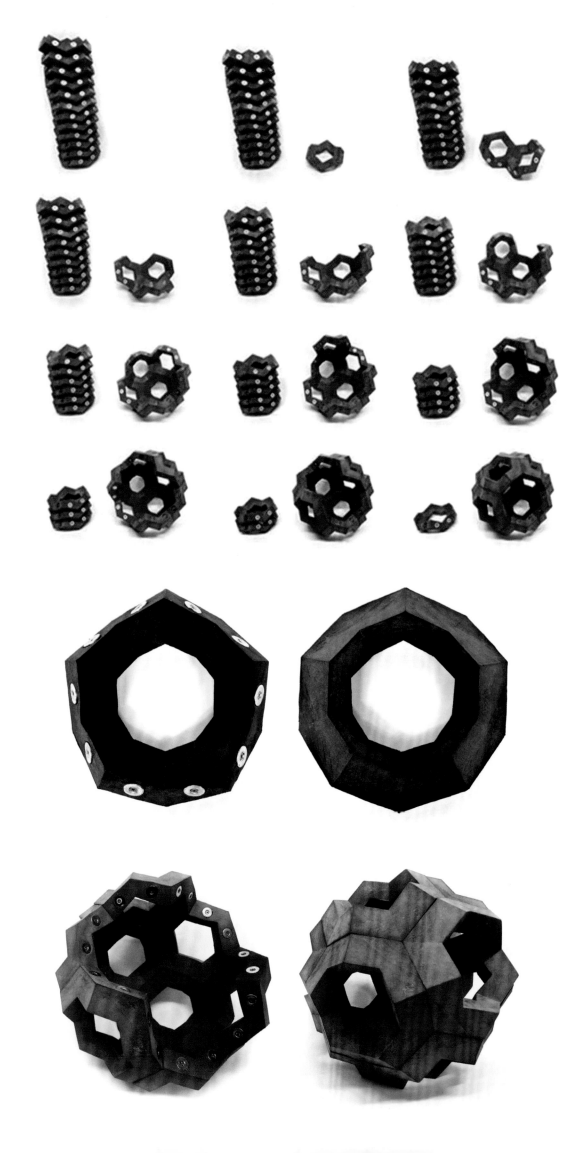

THE SELF-ASSEMBLY LINE

SKYLAR TIBBITS
+ ARTHUR OLSON

The Self-Assembly Line is a large-scale version of a self-assembly virus module, demonstrated as an interactive and performative structure. Discrete sets of modules are activated by stochastic rotation from a larger container/structure that forces the interaction between units. The unit geometry and attraction mechanisms (magnetics) ensure the units will come into contact with one another and auto-align into locally correct configurations. Overtime as more units come into contact, break away, and reconnect, larger, furniture scale elements, emerge. Given different sets of unit geometries and attraction polarities various structures could be achieved. By changing the external conditions, the geometry of the unit, the attraction of the units and the number of units supplied, the desired global configuration can be programmed.

Architecturally, this installation approaches the scenario of self-assembly as a vision for constructing large-scale structures - furniture, buildings or infrastructure - as opposed to most current endeavors in self-assembly at micro and molecular scale-lengths. Self-Assembly as a method of construction relies on discrete and programmable components, simple construction/design sequences, energy input and structural redundancy – fundamental elements that are demonstrated in the installation. This installation demonstrates the intersection of macro and micro worlds as well as translation from molecular and synthetic phenomena to large-scale physical implementation. There is an intention to fuse the worlds of design, computation, and biology through a process of scaling up. While implementing the known structure of molecular systems, this installation also proposes the implementation of design/engineering to natural phenomena as a hybrid system. Part scientific research, part design speculation – it is not restricted to the exact specifications of the biological realm, nor the limitlessness of the design world. The two can speak to each other while forming an interactive discovery of blown-up biological principles. Patterns emerge from within the interaction of the parts and unknown formations/hierarchies are developed through explicit programmability and simple energy input.

The installation presents, at the architectural-scale, biomimetic processes that span from molecules to organisms. Making these processes explicit in a large-scale, dynamic, aesthetic context provides a universally accessible demonstration of phenomena that are usually hidden from common experience. The underlying mechanisms that promote self-assembly and the generation of structural complexity from stochastic input are fundamental to our understanding of living systems. Experiencing the dynamics of such mechanisms provides the conceptual scaffolding for understanding scientific ideas that range from thermodynamics to evolution, without necessarily framing it in those terms. The installation itself demonstrates how such concepts can be adapted to uses that encompass human ingenuity and expression.

DESIGNERS

Skylar Tibbits, Founder of SJET LLC & Lecturer at MIT, Department of Architecture.
Arthur Olson, The Molecular Graphics Laboratory, The Scripps Institute, CA

PROJECT TEAM

Martin Seymour, Andrew Manto, Erioseto Hendranata, Justin Gallagher, Laura Salazar, Veronica Emig, Aaron Olson

BIOGRAPHIES

Skylar Tibbits is a trained architect, designer, and computer scientist whose research currently focuses on developing self-assembly technologies for large-scale structures in our physical environment. Skylar graduated from Philadelphia University with a 5 yr. Bachelor of Architecture degree and minor in experimental computation. Continuing his education at MIT, he received a Masters of Science in Design + Computation and a Masters of Science in Computer Science.

Skylar is currently a lecturer in MIT's Department of Architecture, teaching graduate and undergraduate design studios and co-teaching How to Make (Almost) Anything, a seminar at MIT's Media Lab. Skylar was recently awarded a TED2012 Senior Fellowship, a TED2011 Fellowship and has been named a Revolutionary Mind in SEED Magazine's 2008 Design Issue. His previous work experience includes: Zaha Hadid Architects, Asymptote Architecture, SKIII Space Variations and Point b Design. Skylar has exhibited work at a number of venues around the world including: the Guggenheim Museum NY and the Beijing Biennale, lectured at MoMA and SEED Media Group's MIND08 Conference, Storefront for Art and Architecture, the Rhode Island School of Design, the Institute for Computational Design in Stuttgart and The Center for Architecture NY. He has been published in numerous articles and built large-scale installations around the world from Paris, Calgary, NY to Frankfurt and MIT. As a guest critic, Skylar has visited a range of schools from the University of Pennsylvania, Pratt Institute and Harvard's Graduate School of Design.

Arthur Olson is the Anderson Research Chair Professor in the Department of Molecular Biology at The Scripps Research Institute and founder and director of its Molecular Graphics Laboratory. He received his B.S. (Honors) in Chemistry from the University of Michigan and his Ph.D. in Physical Chemistry from the University of California, Berkeley. He was a Damon Runyon Postdoctoral Fellow at Harvard University, working on the first atomic resolution structure of an intact viral capsid.

He is a pioneer in the analysis and visualization of biological assemblies spanning length scales from atoms to cells. His laboratory has developed, applied and distributed a broad range of molecular modeling and visualization software tools over the past 25 years, including AutoDock, which is used in over 20,000 laboratories around the world and is the most highly cited protein docking code in the scientific literature. In 2000, he started the first Internet distributed biomedical computing project, FightAIDS@Home, which is now supported by the IBM World Community Grid and is running on over two million computers worldwide, and for which he was honored by resolution in the California State Legislature. His latest work in molecular graphics focuses on the development of novel and intuitive human interfaces for research and education in structural molecular biology utilizing solid printing and augmented reality technologies. Olson's visualizations and animations have reached a broad audience through public venues such as the Disney EPCOT center, PBS television, and a number of arts and science museum exhibits around the world.

He has recently founded Science Within Reach, a company whose goal is to produce and distribute cyber-enabled tangible learning materials for both classroom and informal science education.

PAGE 256 + PAGE 257

1 COMPOSITE SELF-ASSEMBLY PROCESS
2 UNIT
3 COMPOSITE
4 COMPONENTS AND REVOLVING MACHINE
5 COMPONENTS AND REVOLVING MACHINE

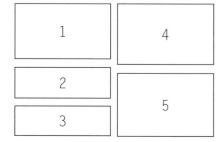

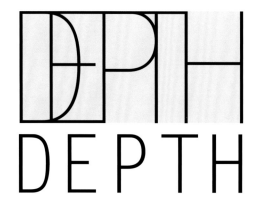

DEPTH

MING
TANG

TANG &
YANG
ARCHI-
TECTS

DIHUA
YANG

urban rhizome: agriculture network in milan 2030

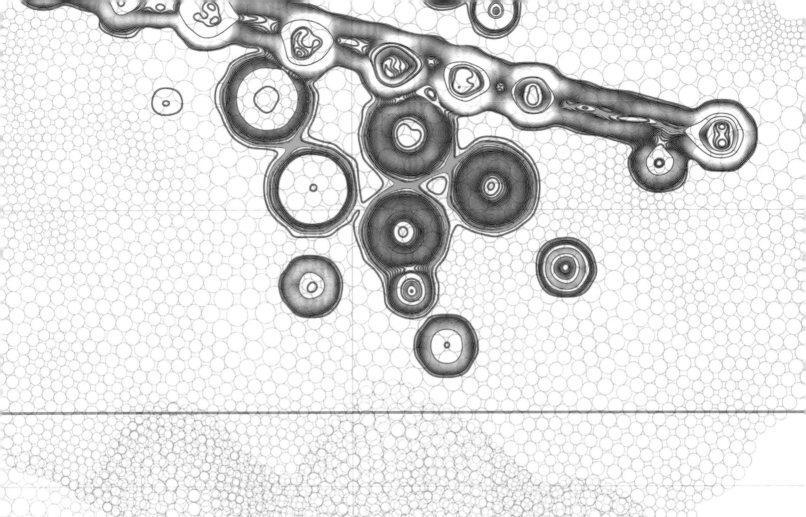
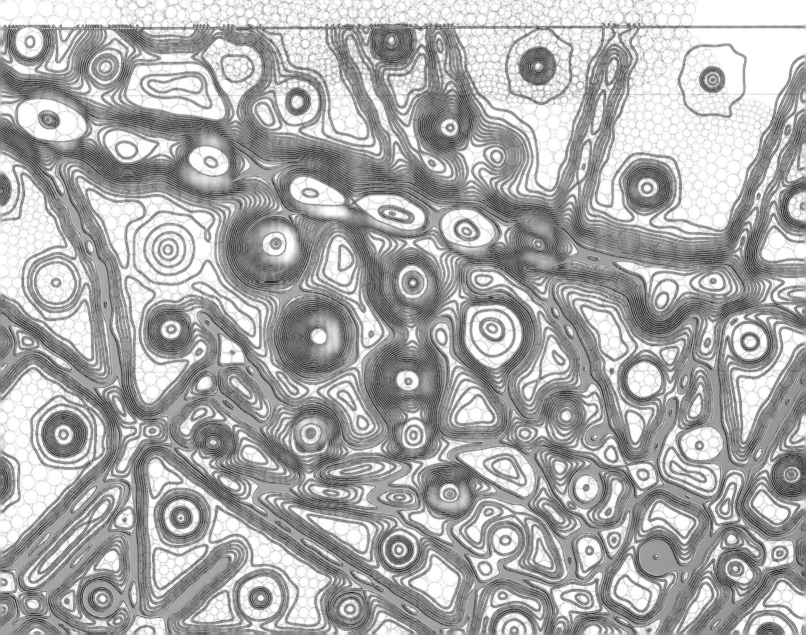

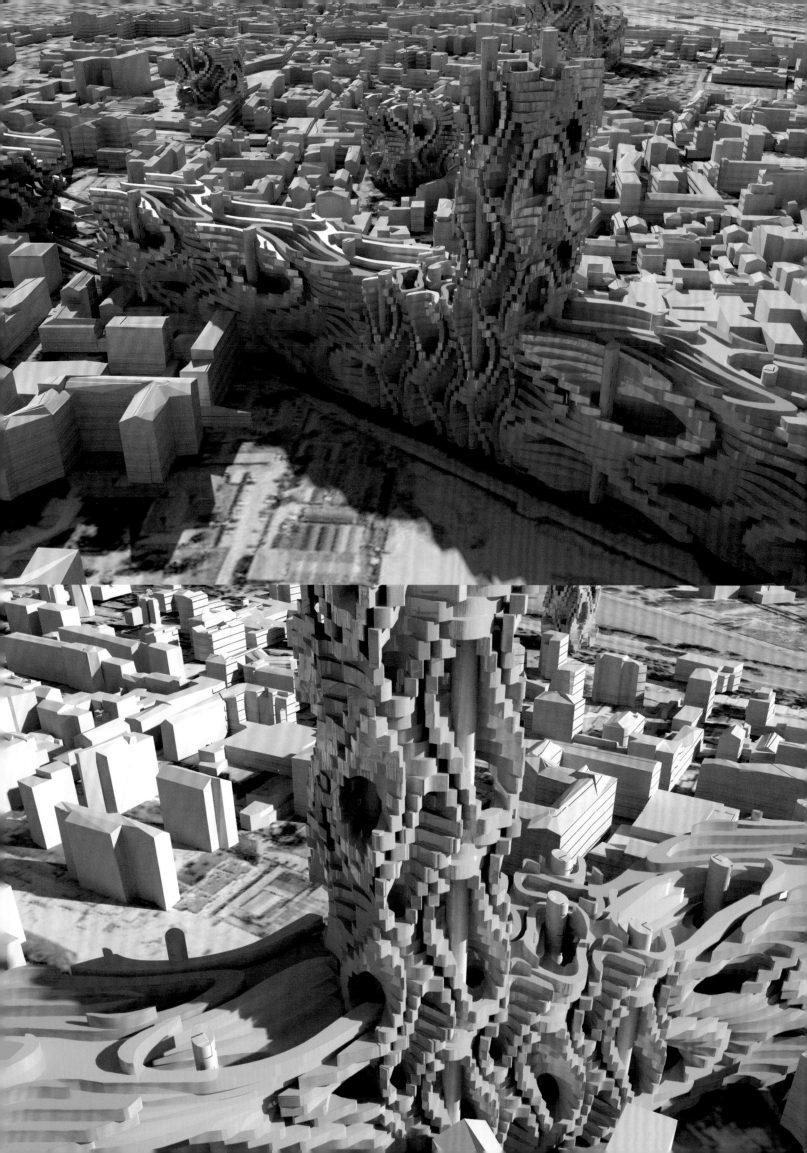

URBAN RHIZOME: AGRICULTURE NETWORK IN MILAN 2030

TANG & YANG ARCHITECTS

The central intention of the Urban Rhizome project is to transform the district of Dergano in Milan, Italy as a place for everyone - an attractive urban development of broad social diversity. The project recognizes the rapid development of the district and the current need to outsource the majority of the inhabitants' food and other required products. Urban Rhizome proposes the creation of vertical farms with integrated markets, transportation, and recreational programs. The surrounding areas are imagined as cultural and entertainment nodes attached to a green tissue that spreads and filters through the entire district.

This green loop of tree-lines boulevards includes express bicycle paths and elevated pedestrian promenades that connect the individual farms, housing units, commercial, and recreational spaces. A zigzag river metro line is suggested to serve the across river traffic while parking facilities are concentrated in the underground level of each vertical farm to achieve sustainable mobility and reduce car traffic.

Urban Rhizome is designed in phases; a number of green open areas and two bridges will initially be established on the north side in which the vertical farms can later adapt to. The landscape and water may adopt many different forms in the south part of the river, but will not find its final form until the area has been fully developed.

The first green area is at the cruise terminal to the north, and a continuous recreational wetland area will serve as a buffer against the noise from the highway and riverfront. Six vertical farms representing six different cultures and ethnical groups will be built along the river.

TANG & YANG ARCHITECTS

Founded by Ming Tang and Dihua Yang, Tang & Yang Architects is a multidisciplinary research/design firm with projects covering architecture design, interior design, landscape design and urban design. Its multi-disciplinary research includes parametric design, digital fabrication, building information modeling, performance driven design, digital computation, virtual reality, algorithm & programming, geography information system, simulation, mathematical form, interactive design and visual effects. The firm has been published in various international conferences, journals, books and exhibitions. The firm has published the book, Urban Paleontology: Evolution of Urban Forms in 2008, the second book, Parametric Building Design with Autodesk Maya, will be published by Rougtledge in 2014.

PAGE 261

PAGE 262 + PAGE 263

PAGE 264

1 URBAN DIAGRAM AND URBAN MASTERPLAN
2 MASTERPLAN WITH VERTICAL FARMS AND GREEN TISSUE
3 PLAN VIEW OF MAIN CORRIDOR
4 MAIN CORRIDOR WITH TRANSPORTATION HUB AND PEDESTRIAN PROMENADES
5 AERIAL VIEW
6 MAIN CORRIDOR AERIAL VIEW
7 VERTICAL FARM

URBAN RHIZOME: AGRICULTURE NETWORK IN MILAN 2030
TANG & YANG ARCHITECTS

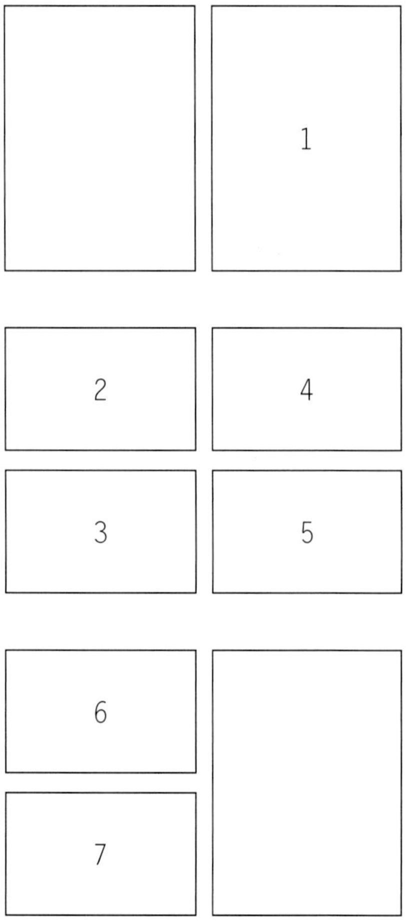

DEPTH

JASON KELLY JOHNSON

NATALY GATTEGNO

BENJAMIN RICE

future cities lab

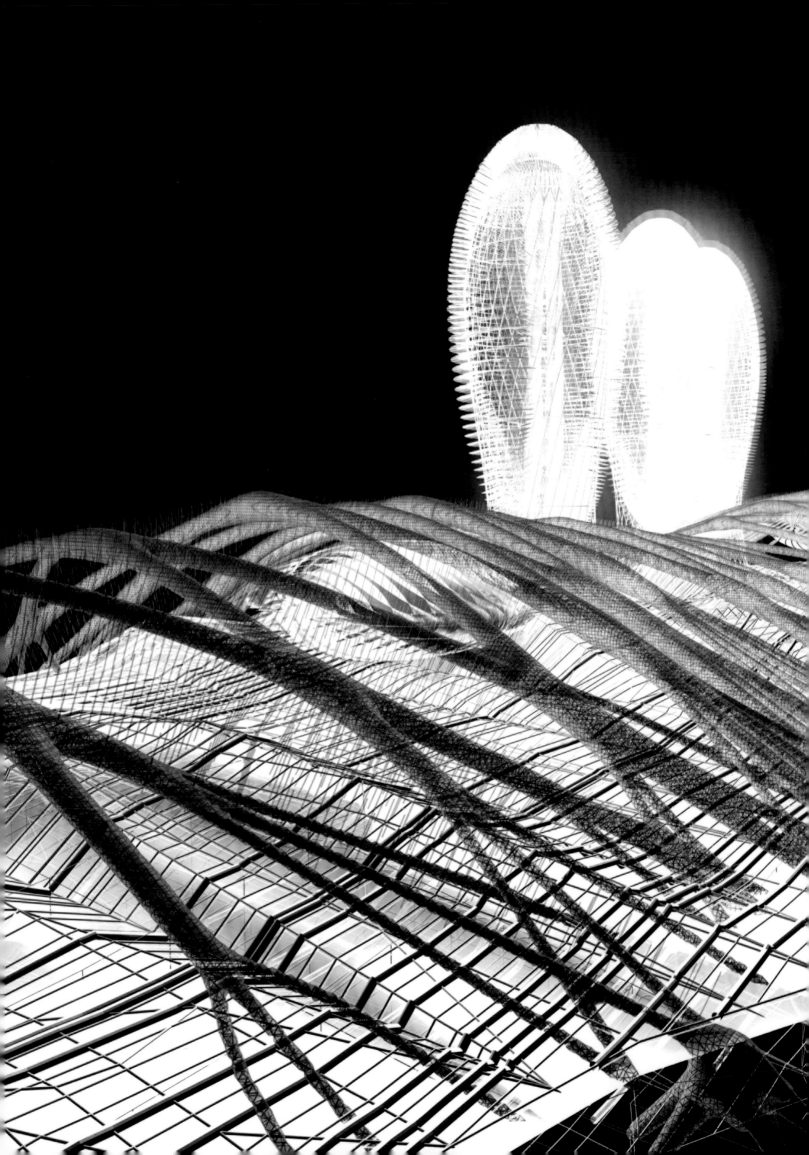

FUTURE CITIES LAB

INTERVIEWER: BENJAMIN RICE / MATTER MANAGEMENT (BR)
INTERVIEWEE: JASON KELLY JOHNSON (JKJ), NATALY GATTEGNO (NG)
PLACE: DOGPATCH, SAN FRANCISCO, CA. 2013
TRANSCRIPTION: BRYCE BECKWITH & SOO HAN

When discussing architecture in America the cities that tend to dominate the conversation are New York and Los Angeles. But there is a growing trend for innovative architects interested in exploring the realm of non-standard practice to pursue their agendas in alternate locations. Future Cities Lab is one of the firms leading this approach. Located in the Dogpatch neighborhood of San Francisco, their advanced research of the integration of advanced fabrication technologies, robotics, and responsive systems into the constitutive material of architecture becomes increasingly relevant, as well as surprisingly realizable, with each passing day. I met with Jason and Nataly at their office on a sunny day in 2013 to discuss their approach, projects, and why San Francisco was the ideal location to situate their practice.

BR: When discussing the work of Future Cities Lab it's impossible not to discuss the topic of installations. It seems to not only be a format that you receive commissions to do frequently, but also a scale you are quite comfortable working within. What role do these installations play in the office? Are they simply projects that you approach like any other, or do they operate as avenues of research for the generation of larger scale projects within the office?

JKJ: I think they are, in a lot of ways, avenues to test ideas and experiment with a multitude of formal and material possibilities. The most successful ones, like our Cirriform robotic wall proposal in Seattle, perform optimally at the scale of the installation and are suggestive of other potentials. That isn't to say that the ideas couldn't become scalable, just that they don't necessarily have to act as proposals for something larger. Once installed, these pieces, as well as how people interact with them, do begin to suggest alternative possibilities. For example, the Aurora and Glaciarium installations that we completed in New York were constructed in a way that people could primarily interact only with the perimeter of the piece. The result was a definite sense that the piece would benefit from being scaled up to become a larger immersive enclosure that would perform differently, and potentially more effectively, at another scale. We are working on several new projects that will hopefully do that.

NG: We've recently been describing these projects as 'live models' in order to explore these unique conditions that belong to neither the scales of a building nor the stand-alone gallery piece. The term 'live model' itself works through multiple scales due to the connotations associated with it: 'live' – meaning capable of vital processes, and 'model' - which is both a representation or simulation of something, and also an exemplar or optimal condition to strive for. That duality gives us this kind of other zone of operation, which exists between scales. That being said, I think we do see in most of these installations the possibility exploring other scales.

BR: These conditions that you're referring to, I'm assuming, exist on multiple levels, but participants can only interact with conditions occurring at certain levels or scales. For example, if you are embedding proximity sensors into an installation it is easy to interact with it, but what happens when that gets scaled up to a tower façade? How does the input data scale up with the project?

JKJ: Some of the ways in which we use sensors in these installations become stand-ins for larger scale forces or interactions. In the Hydramax project we completed for SF MoMA, because it is a scale model of a much larger urban proposal, we positioned the gallery visitors to act as, and be sensed by the model as, incoming weather. This begins to involve the participants as part of a simulation of environmental effects at a much larger global scale. The model was constantly changing its shape and light intensity depending on how visitors moved around the model. With a lot of the other installations it isn't so much about some kind of direct

EVOLO 06
DEPTH
FUTURE CITIES LAB
275

translation, but rather creating a kind of dynamic reciprocity between a person and the construction, similar to the way an electronic DJ might perform through both improvised live sampling and algorithmic playback. It's about creating something that you could begin to have a relationship with, perhaps something that's cybernetic in nature. That's really what we are getting interested in, especially with projects like Cirriform where people can begin to interact physically with the model. An interesting crossover effect begins to emerge through this kind of interaction, where the physical and digital worlds become one.

BR: Do you see any of these projects beginning to move beyond the thing itself? I read the Aurora project as a kind of indexing of larger phenomena – the way participants interact with the project reflects humanities interaction with the polar cap and visa versa. Do you see these projects intentionally beginning to index the motions, or conditions, that they produce or experience over time, place, etc.?

NG: Originally what we had wanted to do with Aurora was to have the actual geometry of the installation change relative to distant data collected at the ice cap using remote sensors. This distant data would have been fed into the installation simultaneously to the localized data of the gallery visitors. They would be in New York participating with what was seemingly a static object that was actually changing over time due to both local and global data streams.

JKJ: The goals of the Aurora project were not to take the data sets as literally as the word index suggests. Originally we were inspired by some of the Flash animations that we saw being produced about the receding ice caps in the Arctic. We thought that was an interesting moment where you could actually simulate past, present and potential futures through the animation medium. But we didn't want the installation to be that literal – we wanted to produce the condition where the participant, due to their interaction with the piece, began to understand their own negative or positive effect. The more you interacted with the piece, the more energy you would drain from it. The Glaciarium operated in a very similar way – the more the piece was viewed the warmer it would become, melting the ice cylinder contained within. We were trying to use interactions to trigger effects that weren't about global warming literally, but rather were about the effect of you and your relationship with something highly synthetic and possibly cybernetic, as well as the cycles, technological and social, that then begin to emerge.

NG: I do think that, on one hand, it is an index, but on the other hand it becomes a framework that then allows other things to emerge architecturally through it. I think it may start with an indexical reading, but it quickly takes on these other guises or disguises as it moves forward.

BR: Do you see the work that you're producing as attempting to challenge the traditional idea of architectural permanence? It seems like architects have often accepted permanence as the default condition of their work, but in a lot of ways it appears as though your firm is purposely undermining that.

JKJ: We are trying to critically participate in a world increasingly defined by impermanence – whether it be rapid technological or ecological change, or human adaptation. That is the contemporary condition that we are now witnessing. What happens when places that had meaning in the past – for example public libraries and schools – are replaced by mobile devices, online communities and cloud computing? Take social networking as an example: it's seen as something that is constantly in flux, something that is constantly taking inputs and outputs, constantly shifting relative to various trends, geopolitical events, etc. At times it seems to rest, almost become static or permanent, and at other times it moves towards forms of maximum fluctuation. We are trying to pursue an architecture that might actually participate with these things while simultaneously attempting to understand what the resultant spatial, material or immaterial implications are. Those who resonate most with the work are people that can relate to that. Whether it's someone who is into social media, programming or hacking, biosciences or robotics, they can begin to read in the work overlaps and potentials between architecture and these different fields. I also believe that the coming generation will literally expect everything to be dynamically informed by networked computation and artificial intelligence. It suggests that in the future we – architects, engineers, designers - will routinely be challenged to construct objects, buildings and landscapes to be entirely responsive, kinetic and heuristic.

NG: I don't necessarily think our work is a resistance to a status quo or existing condition. It is, instead, an understanding of a larger, expanded territory that architecture has to address. I don't really see it as a dilemma – we aren't developing things that are impermanent in order to resist permanence. I think it is more of an understanding of this expanded territory of operation. For example, in our Datagrove installation project in Silicon Valley, we wove local trending Twitter text feeds into a public space using small LCD screens and text-to-speech modules. We set out to create a contemporary social media "whispering wall" that would give form and meaning to a normally invisible, yet ubiquitous stream of data. We tried to do this in a manner that was both spatial and expressive, explicitly trying to resist the minimalist anti-aesthetic that seems to define Silicon Valley design culture right now.

BR: So, would you describe your work as polemical?

NG: I don't think that it necessarily starts there, but it does become polemical.

JKJ: It's polemical, but we don't necessarily begin these projects with some sort of big 'fuck you' to thousands of years of architectural history. Instead, we are trying to pursue a world in which design and everything around it is live – from energy cycles that are constantly shifting, to material cycles that aren't stable, to networks that are in constant flux. The idea that the world is stable is very shortsighted because everything around us is actually moving, changing, and/or degrading, and entropy is a topic we come back to a lot while talking about these issues because it begins to take them on. Contemporary planned cities tend to be disappointing due to this belief that things are stable, while cities such as contemporary Athens and Rio de Janeiro have some degree of flexibility built into them that allows them to expand and contract based on localized constraints. Through our work we are trying to amplify some of these conditions and tease out potential forces and counter forces. Our most successful projects embody this kind of dynamism, and we try to embed these qualities so that they become active participants in the complexity of the city, rather than just neutral backdrops.

BR: How do you think that San Francisco has influenced this pursuit? It is a city that is the seat of development for many emerging industries, with one notable exception: architecture. Has this amplitude of industries other than architecture led you to look beyond our disciplinary boundaries for issues to take on?

JKJ: When we arrived three years ago I wasn't really prepared to drink the Bay Area 'Kool-Aid' right away. But there is this sense here that anything is possible. Technologically speaking, everything truly is possible here. You don't routinely meet people here who would say 'No we can't do that.' You're right that this is probably less the case in the building and construction industry, but that is changing. Take the building our lab is located in: there is an amazingly diverse group of researchers here that are setting up labs. Across the hall is a biotech lab and an LED artist, upstairs is a lab focused on fuel cell production, and down the hall is a start-up company developing shape-memory alloy products. These are just a few of the artists, designers, and researchers doing amazing stuff in this one building. It produces this interesting techno-utopian spirit where ideas seem doable, especially if you look out into the neighborhood and see companies like Adobe, Zynga and Twitter. Whether or not they are willing to fund built environments is another question, though.

NG: There's always been this assumption that the development of these innovation leaders would lead to a desire to explore these ideas through other mediums - architecture, art or public space. But I agree: that hasn't necessarily been the case upon arriving here. I remember when we told people we were moving to California the assumption was that we were going to Los Angeles, because it tends to be more architecturally driven than San Francisco. But it seems like there is a lot of room here for the work we are interested in doing and the kind of collaborations we are interested in setting up. We obviously are interested in building, but we came to San Francisco knowing that we wanted to collaborate with a whole series of people and industries that you wouldn't necessarily be able to in other locations.

BR: It's interesting that you bring that up, because everyone always talks about it being difficult, as an architect, to be outside of New York or Los Angeles. But you guys purposefully aren't in those locations and you've managed to leverage the value of this place into something that is consequential. How have these collaborations played into that? How have they affected the work?

JKJ: With the Xeromax robotic skin installation, for instance, we worked with a programmer who, during the day, worked for the NASA Jet Propulsion Lab. She would come into the office and do these crazy hack-a-thons with us which were really interesting experiences. We've also recently been collaborating with the folks from Miga Motors who received funding from both the NSF and NASA to develop miniature shape memory alloy motors, which they have spent several years working on. They also helped fund our recent installation at SF MoMA. Ripon DeLeon, who has worked as a lead project manager in our lab for two years now, also has a computer science background which makes him a very versatile designer and collaborator. These are people who have serious research agendas that ground their work, but are also interested in how those agendas can begin to inform the world around them. They are interested in the potential architectural side and the collaboration that could exist between the various disciplines. A lot of this goes back to educating people and challenging them to begin thinking about how their research might open up possibilities in other fields. I think that architects and designers are in this amazing position to begin giving people a better sense of how emerging technologies could become applicable in much broader arenas, such as urban settings or in the developing world. This is something that we are trying to tap into.

NG: And I think, in some ways, while we are tapping into expertise at the local level we are also able to provide a more visionary or conceptual framework that allows these researchers to come together and impact the environments that we're designing. So I would say that expertise is definitely something we are tapping into, but at the same time there is a rewiring, or reconnecting, of various components or industries that wouldn't otherwise be working together.

BR: It sounds almost like architectural, or social, hacking. It's really fascinating.

JKJ: Definitely.

BR: So we have these two types of projects that are extremely visible in the practice – installations and urban proposals. What is going on in-between those two scales?

NG: We are attracted to projects that have multiple inputs or triggers, things that have the potential for transforming. Urban situations generally offer pretty straightforward, multiple input conditions. The installation scale is often at the opposite end of that spectrum, but still has the potential for unexpected interactions through direct human involvement. I would say that we have touched upon the middle scale through some of our projects without being overly explicit. For example, Energy Farm is this large-scale proposal that captures and transforms light and brings it down to the ground. So that becomes a fostering of environments at that middle scale and begins to suggest possible building interactions. Also, the Supergalaxy project attempts to integrate a more intimate reworking of the ground plane in an effort to affect that middle scale of interaction within the larger urban organization.

JKJ: I would also say that the Trilux pavilion begins to interact with this middle scale as well. It is one of the first projects we have done that is occupiable in a traditional sense. That was a really encouraging experience and we are interested in doing more projects where people aren't simply looking at the results from afar, but are actually immersed, literally, in the geometry. In some ways it is a difficult scale to work at because it is just beginning to cross the line where building codes start to take effect, but it is also exciting because it is a scale where people really begin to engage with what you're doing in a more spatial and visceral way. Not to say that simply building bigger is better, but rather that interactions become more intense when spaces are immersive and urban.

BR: Wasn't this your first piece in San Francisco? How did that affect your view on, or your experience of, the project?

NG: In some ways this was the first project that we built for the city we inhabit. So, that was really interesting because we weren't just showing up to install it, flying home, and then showing back up to take it all down and leave again. We were actually able to see the project through multiple views by visiting it throughout its life cycle. This was not only an interesting experience, but an important one as well. We were surprised with some of the behaviors we witnessed the project exhibit, because we didn't embed any kind of interactive, technological component, yet it still acted and reacted to the environmental conditions it encountered. It rained the entire first week the installation was up, which caused all of these carefully steam bent quills to flatten out entirely. So these three domes that we had carefully designed and simulated slumped into these eggplant shapes that sat heavy on the constructed base. Then there were two weeks of sunshine that dried everything out and the eggplants began to rise up into domes again, although never to return to the original, designed height.

JKJ: Essentially the project went from this sleek 20-year old physique to an old guy with a bellicose stomach. Then, when it got sunny out, it would shape back up. It was one of those projects where we spent a lot of time designing and simulating within these sophisticated software suites, and we thought we totally understood the project and its material behaviors. But, once we began steam-bending and working with the imperfections of the lumber, coupled with some extreme weather, these presumptions began to get challenged. So, for us this was a fascinating project and we look forward to exploring these challenges in future projects.

NG: There are also combinations of digital-fabrication techniques that we've obviously used in a lot of our projects, but in this case, apart from the CNC-milled base, everything was basically stock pine lathe hand drilled from templates. We were convinced that the challenge was going to come from mistakes made in this analog process, but, surprisingly, the difficulties emerged from the material itself.

BR: There is a lot of talk now around the loss of traction regarding digital models when there is a vacuous condition surrounding them. At the end of the day there are many things that our digitally generated models cannot predict, and often times these issues have to be taken on through physical craft. From the outside the topic of craft seems to be a consistent theme within your work. What role do you feel craft plays within the firm?

JKJ: I think that, for us, craft plays an important role in what we do. But what does craft mean today? I suppose it is a kind of "high performance" craft. In a single project we might use five or more unique software packages or programming languages, laser cutters, CNC machines, a 3D printer, electronics, microcontrollers, and then hand sew it all together with a needle and thread! I think there are several layers to this and it is important to stress just how synthetic our particular approach is, and how much dexterity and patience it takes. For example, for all our projects we design, fabricate, program and debug all our own circuit boards. By crafting even the most basic building components we are able to iterate and explore to the max. A lot of that stuff normally gets hidden but we're interested in trying to pull that stuff out and explore its expressive potential. Another example – unless we are working with composites - we general resist using glue, even in our models – everything is thought through and connections get designed through various methods, including notching, folding, and hand sewing to name a few. This creates a quality in the projects at the detail level that attempts to encourage the kind of intimate interaction we are interested in.

NG: I also don't think that the idea of craft excludes digital fabrication techniques. I would say that craft includes both digitally and analog fabricated components, and we often explore the combination of the two. Primarily this all comes down to the knowledge about materials and how they come together. This certainly applies to 3D printing and the emerging field of advanced composites. 3D printing also has immense potential especially when it is coupled with other skills such as custom printer building and structural optimization software. For instance, there is certainly hardware and software craft involved in printing a heterogeneous structural component using varying densities of a material. You only print material where it is absolutely necessary, or you vary the printed material based on whether it is structural, electrical, plumbing, etc. We view this as craft as well, and it takes an immense amount of skill to do it well.

BR: Considering how much simulation the firm does, where does materiality begin to fit into the design process? Do you simulate and then choose materials based on that direction, or do you simulate based upon the material that you have at your disposal?

NG: I think it's a combination of the performance and effect in terms of what we want it to do and how we want it to behave, and then that begins to give us clues as to what types of materials to start using and then that gets fed back into the process.

JKJ: With most of these projects we will use fairly crude materials to quickly build the prototypes and develop more specificity as we iterate through the design process. A lot of the structural and Kangaroo physics simulation that we've done recently is much more related to membrane and canopy structural tests, and a lot of that happens before materials have been chosen and can fluidly inform the design and prototyping process. Firefly, the plug-in for Grasshopper that I developed with Andy Payne, allows you to integrate sensors, control actuators and a lot more, directly from within the Rhino modeling environment. This way you can simulate and control a physical model with a digital model, and vice versa. Using Grasshopper's various built-in programming component you can also explore a range of life-like behaviors, intensities, and thresholds in real-time. People around the world are now using Firefly at all stages of project development – from initial digital and physical modeling and sketching, to interaction design, energy analysis, a means to visualize and actuate 3d printers, etc. I think Firefly, and several new plug-ins are opening up incredible possibilities in terms of linking form to performance, to context, to behavior, or other types of live inputs including social media, internet feeds and machine vision.

BR: Do you work scale-less often? Most of the prototypes I see around your office have specific design directions, and I'm wondering if scale-less technique development is something the office focuses on in order to instigate directions.

JKJ: We do a lot of scale-less experimentation. It is how we begin to develop an understanding of how all of these various components come together. We gain a lot of intuition on how structures are going to work this way, and I think it's really important to go back and forth between tests that are scaled and scale-less as a way of iteratively investigating things. Parametric modeling is so integrated in our practice now that we can fluidly explore a range of scales in a very short period of time. For our generation the computer is not merely a tool to perform a prescribed task or to speed up manual operations. Computation has become a generative and creative tool used to explore ideas. It becomes really interesting when you gain a fluency – as if it were your native language – and you begin to feel that you can, pretty much, do anything. We can integrate anything, we can evaluate any set of data, we can simulate anything – but, at the end of the day, what's the big idea? What are we trying to communicate with this project? A lot of our conversations in the lab are about how we need to pursue architecture and engineering simultaneously. How do we fuse ideas about the contemporary city, about society and culture, with ecology and technology? We are inspired by the collaborations of Xenakis and Le Corbusier, and the experimental projects of Nervi, Candela, Le Ricolais and Buckminster Fuller certainly come to mind. But we are also keenly aware that there are shortfalls to this kind of work, and hopefully as we move forward we can avoid the big ones.

BR: Well now that anything's possible, what's next? Which is the hardest part, right?

NG: Well, we know what's next on our boards and screens, but I do think, for us, the next step is beginning to test these ideas at that next scale. In terms of technology, it is something that is always changing, so I think that is simply about evolving with it and pushing the boundaries of what we do.

JKJ: I think technologically there are a few things we are interested in pursuing next. The use of micro-controllers, sensors and actuators is now pretty well established and will likely guide the next decade of robotic fabrication, smart building research, etc. I think that what we're trying to figure out next is how to make – or perhaps "grow" is a better word – new materials that will essentially be sensing-actuator composites. So, moving much more into engineering synthetic materials and exploring how these things can become more intelligent, self-energized, and renewable. Scale-wise, I think we're definitely trying to push the practice to engage the city in a much more explicit way. For instance, the Hydramax project we just completed for SF MoMA is embedded in, and interacting with the city, and the energy cycles of the Bay. I think there are currently only a handful of designers attempting to produce work that synthesizes digital craft, integrates advanced technologies and that also attempts to engage ecological, social or political ideas. That's what we are attempting to explore and what is helping frame where we are going as a lab – trying to understand how we produce future projects that are rigorous and well-crafted, and also relevant to the unique conditions of our place and time.

BIOGRAPHY

Future Cities Lab is an experimental design and research office based in San Francisco, California and Athens, Greece. Design principals Jason Kelly Johnson and Nataly Gattegno have collaborated on a range of award-winning projects exploring the intersections of design with advanced fabrication technologies, robotics, responsive building systems and public space.

Their work has been published and exhibited worldwide. Most recently they were awarded the 2011 Architectural League of New York Young Architects Prize, and were the 2008-09 Muschenheim and Oberdick Fellows at the University of Michigan TCAUP, the 2009 New York Prize Fellows at the Van Alen Institute in New York City, and exhibited work at the 2009-10 Hong Kong / Shenzhen Biennale. Both Johnson and Gattegno are graduates of Princeton University. They currently teach at the California College of the Arts and UC Berkeley, and lead workshops around the world, including the Architectural Association (AA) Global Summer Program Biodynamic Structures, Hydra-Cities Lab in Athens, Greece, and the Urban Islands workshop in Sydney, Australia.

Benjamin Rice is a principal of the award-winning firm MTTR MGMT. His work has been published and exhibited widely, including shows at the Storefront for Art and Architecture, the A+D Museum, Project 4, and the Denver Art Museum, as well as articles in On Ramp, Pidgin Magazine, The Huffington Post, and TARP. He is currently a Lecturer at the UC Berkeley College of Environmental Design and a Senior Lecturer at the California College of the Arts. He received his Bachelor of Architecture from the Southern California Institute of Architecture and his Master of Architecture from Princeton University.

PAGE 268 + PAGE 269

PAGE 270 + PAGE 271

PAGE 272 + PAGE 273

PAGE 274

1 AURORA
2 CIRRIFORM
3 CIRRIFORM
4 DATAGROVE
5 DATAGROVE
6 HYDRAMAX
7 SUPER GALAXY
8 THERMASPHERES
9 THERMASPHERES
10 TRILUX
11 XEROMAX
12 ENERGY FARM

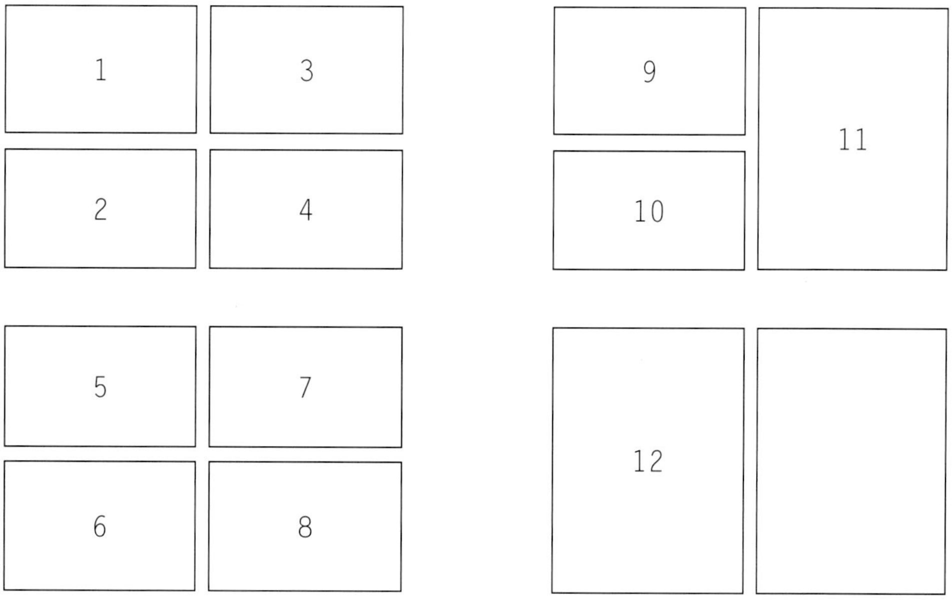
1
3
2
4
9
11
10
5
7
6
8
12

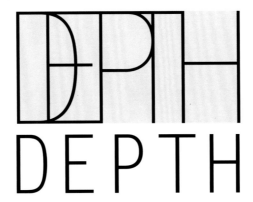

DEPTH

KRISTINE
MUN

USC
SCHOOL OF
ARCHITEC-
TURE

vitalized geometry

CODE AND MACHINING
RULES FOR RESPONSIVE BEHAVIOR

Meaning of Code related to Priniciple

The fitness of the scrunching geometry of latex must be analyzed as two sets of layers with two sets of information, the second being dependent on the input of the first layer. The nature and character of the scrunching deformation occurs according to the very forces exerted onto the material and therefore is a product of the material's ability to resist the forces with its inherent "fitness."

Varying forces upon the same surface creates an uneven distribution of forces resulting in varying forms. An analysis of the fitness capacity of the developing geometry allows for a kind of functional optimization. New resulting forms emerge as "aesthetically effcient" parts progress and "weak" or "bad" parts are removed or altered.

Action Diagram
(Input > Processing > Output feedback)

There are two layers of information: the primary (relaxed) layer and the secondary (stretched) layer. The coding below shows the coding of the primary layer (the scrunches) that respond to information from the secondary layer.

The input is the set of forces that determine the degree of stretching of the secondary (stretched) layer. The degree of the stretch of each member will accordingly adjust the sin curve of each and produce a grid-like pattern that represents the input.

The input of the sin curves is overlaid onto a uniform grid of points. The points which are closest in distance to the curves are offset in the Z direction relative to the plane of the material. The points coplanar to the surface are weaved with those that are offset to generate the geometry of the scrunch.

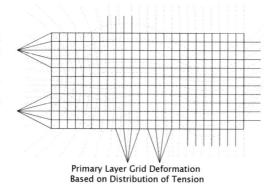

Primary Layer Grid Deformation
Based on Distribution of Tension

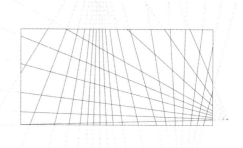

Evolution of Grid Based on Distribution of Tension

Basic Sin Curve

Points Within Offset Boundary

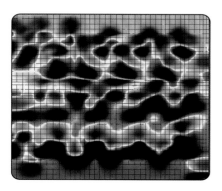

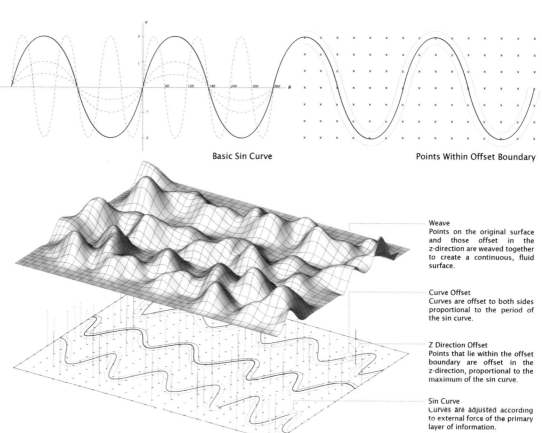

Weave
Points on the original surface and those offset in the z-direction are weaved together to create a continuous, fluid surface.

Curve Offset
Curves are offset to both sides proportional to the period of the sin curve.

Z Direction Offset
Points that lie within the offset boundary are offset in the z-direction, proportional to the maximum of the sin curve.

Sin Curve
Curves are adjusted according to external force of the primary layer of information.

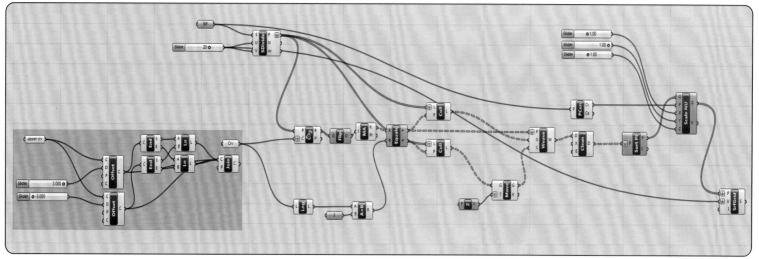

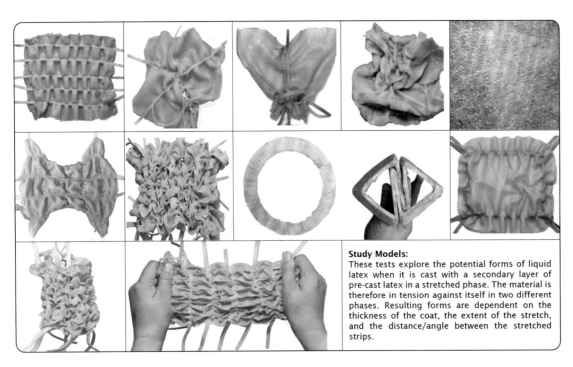

Study Models:
These tests explore the potential forms of liquid latex when it is cast with a secondary layer of pre-cast latex in a stretched phase. The material is therefore in tension against itself in two different phases. Resulting forms are dependent on the thickness of the coat, the extent of the stretch, and the distance/angle between the stretched strips.

Casting Process
Liquid latex painted over pre-cast, latex strips in a stretched state, laid out in a uniform and altered grid.

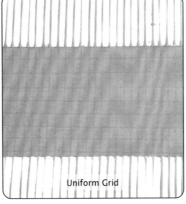

Uniform Grid

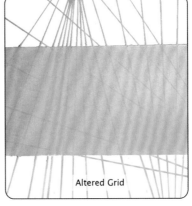

Altered Grid

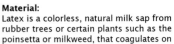

Material:
Latex is a colorless, natural milk sap from rubber trees or certain plants such as the poinsetta or milkweed, that coagulates on exposure to air. Upon coagulation, it becomes a highly elastic material with high tensile strength.

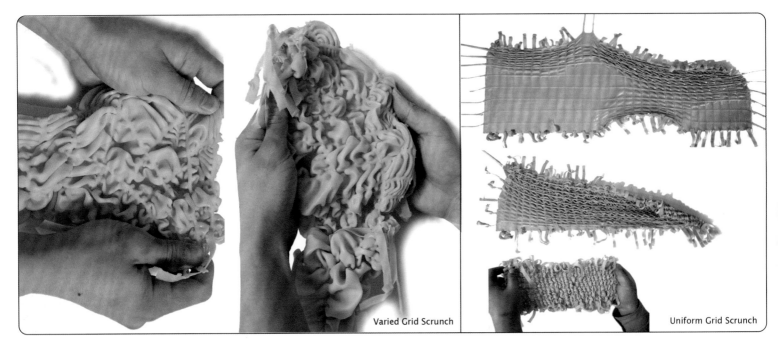

Varied Grid Scrunch

Uniform Grid Scrunch

Logic Diagram

  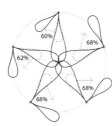 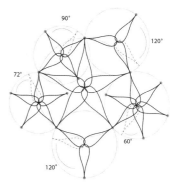

The petal is formed with a single wire, where both ends meet at the same fixed point.

The petal rotates around its midpoint in a complete circle, duplicating itself every 72 degree to create a 5-point radial component.

Each petal duplicates itself and rotates along its fixed point to create a new 3, 4, 5, or 6-point component, where the petals are scaled accordingly so that two of each component's fixed points meet another component's fixed point.

If 3-point, rotate 120°, 240°
If 4-point, rotate 90°, 180°, 270°
If 5-point, rotate 72°, 144°, 216°, 288°
If 6-point, rotate 60°, 120°, 180°, 240°, 300°

 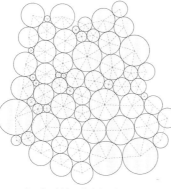 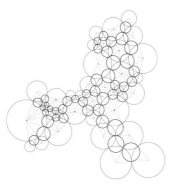 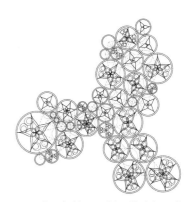

Growth pattern of the radial geometries

Imposition of circle packing logic creates a new order and new grid, making each component tangent to its neighboring component. Where there is an error in this relationship, an empty cirle if formed to fill in the gaps and allow the pattern to continue.

Selected portion of the pattern to model physically, where the construction lines become the structural framework for the radial components.

A second radial component is layered into the framework in places where space is in excess abundance. Circles that have a radius larger than 3.5" and contain the original radial component will be layered with the second radial component, where the number of nodes matches that of the original radial component. Empty circles that have a radius larger than 2" will be layered with the second radial component, where the number of nodes varies between 4, 5, and 6.

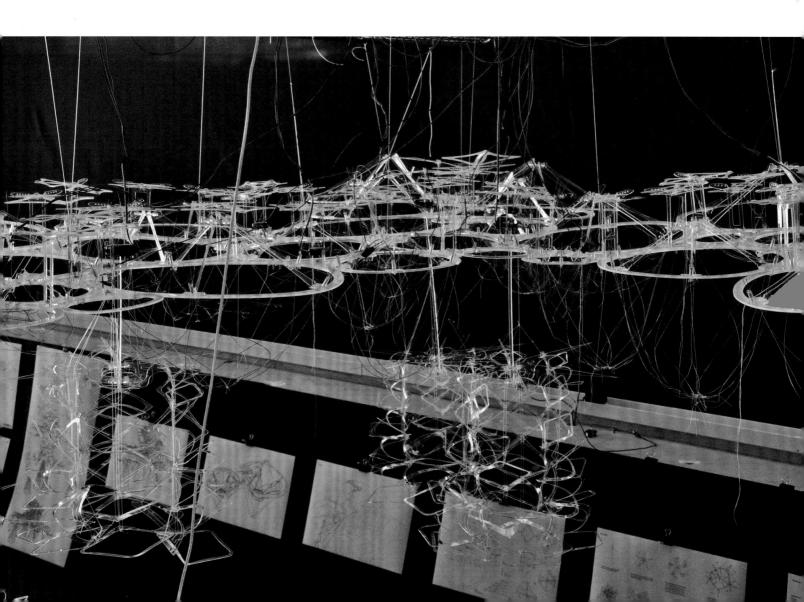

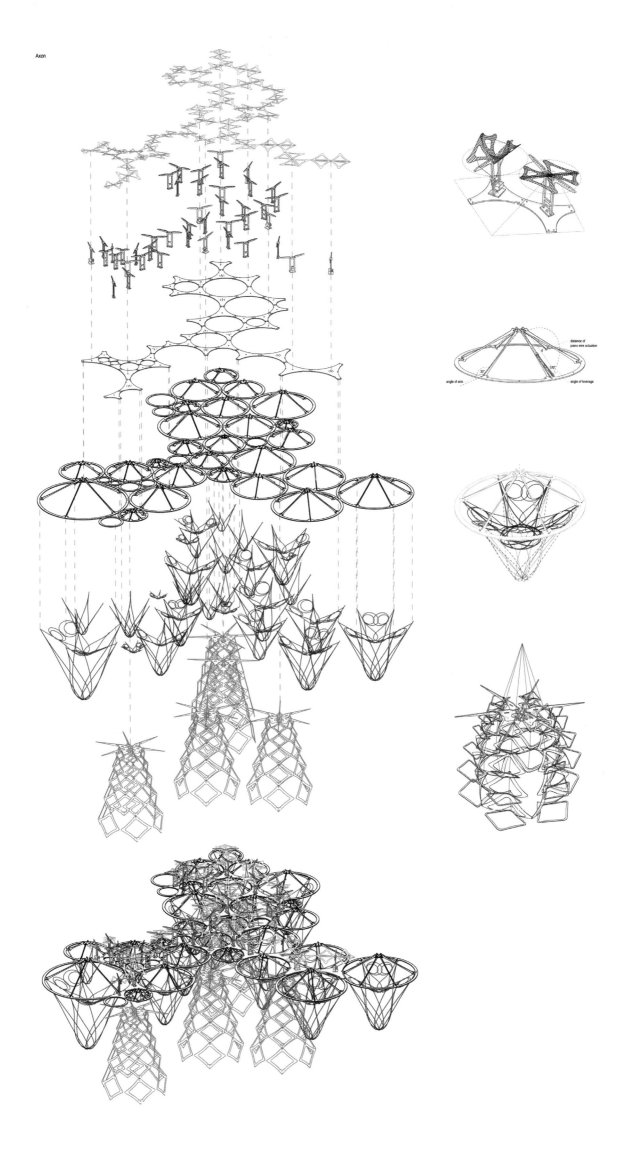

Axon

distance of
piano wire actuation

angle of arm   angle of leverage

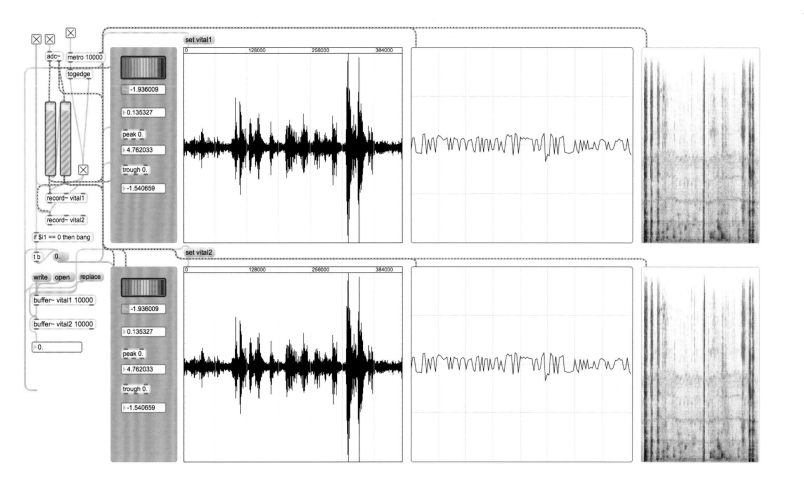

Actuation

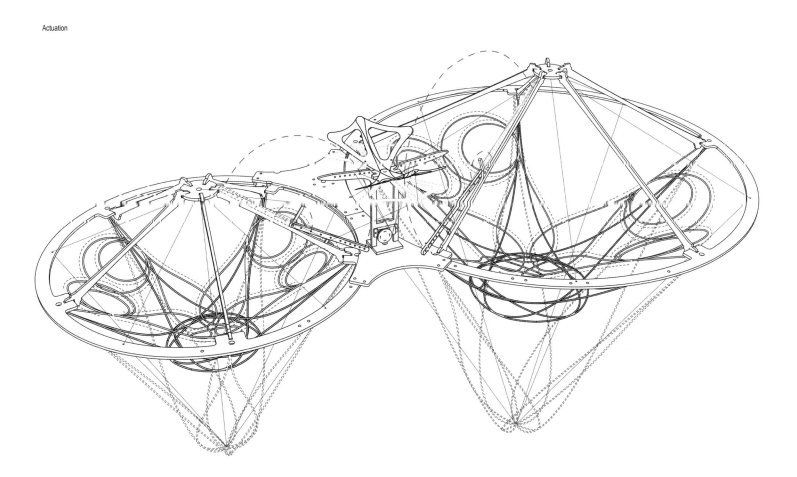

PRINCIPLE OF BEAUTY
SYMMETRY & VARIATION
RULES FOR GEOMETRY BEHAVIOR

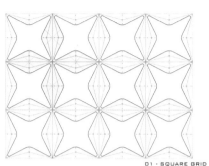

01 - SQUARE GRID

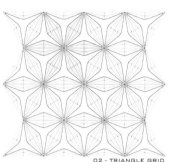

02 - TRIANGLE GRID

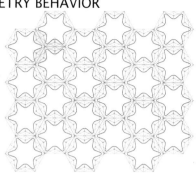

03 - HEXAGON GRID

04 - RADIANT GRID

MEANING OF PRINICIPLE

HOGARTH: OF SYMMETRY

IF THE UNIFORMITY OF FIGURES, PARTS, OR LINES WERE TRULY THE CHIEF CAUSE OF BEAUTY, THE MORE EXACTLY UNIFORM THEIR APPEARANCES WERE KEPT, THE MORE PLEASURE THE EYE WOULD RECEIVE: BUT THIS IS SO FAR FROM BEING THE CASE, THAT WHEN THE MIND HAS BEEN ONCE SATISFIED, THAT THE PARTS ANSWER ONE ANOTHER, WITH SO EXACT AN UNIFORMITY, AS TO PRESERVE TO THE WHOLE THE CHARACTER OF FITNESS TO STAND, TO MOVE, TO SINK, TO SWIM, TO FLY, ETC. WITHOUT LOSING THE BALANCE: THE EYE IS REJOICED TO SEE THE OBJECT TURNED, AND SHIFTED, SO AS TO VARY THESE UNIFORM APPEARANCES.

OF VARIETY

THE SHAPES AND COLOURS OF PLANTS, FLOWERS, LEAVES, THE PAINTINGS IN BUTTERFLIES WINGS, SHELLS, ETC. SEEM OF LITTLE OTHER INTENDED USE, THAN THAT OF ENTERTAINING THE EYE WITH THE PLEASURE OF VARIETY.

ALL THE SENSES DELIGHT IN IT, AND EQUALLY ARE AVERSE TO SAMENESS. THE EAR IS AS MUCH OFFENDED WITH ONE EVEN CONTINUED NOTE, AS THE EYE IS WITH BEING FIXED TO A POINT, OR TO THE VIEW OF A DEAD WALL.

INTERPRETATION:

SYMMETRY, A METHODOLOGY OF MANIPULATION, WILL PERFORM AS THE RULE FOR THE DEVELOPMENT OF GEOMETRIES, AS WELL AS AGGREGATION. HOWEVER, SYMMETRY SHOULD NOT BE A LIMITATION FOR SHAPES. ULTIMATELY, HARMONIOUS FORMS WILL ALL QUALIFIED. ADDITIONALLY, THE LOGIC CAN TAKE ADVANTAGE OF A SYMMETRY SYSTEM, LIKE SOUND AND SIGNALS.

INTERLLEGENT MATERIALS WITH VERY LITTLE RULES WILL EMERGENT VARIOUS OUTCOME, DUE TO ITS OWN PROPORTIES. THE EMERGENT FORM IS UNPREDICTABLE, AND GIVING MUCH UNCERTAINTY TO THE HARMONIOUS FORM. THEN, VARIETY CAN BE INTERPRETED AS THE COMPOSED DYNAMICS.

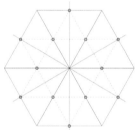
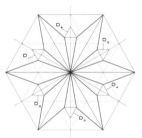
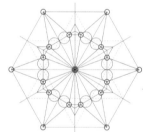
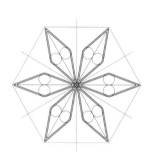

D_x = DYNAMIC VALUES CONTROL GEOMETRY

MANIPULATION OF PLANE GEOMETRY IN TRIANGULAR GRID

STRETCHING TO 300%

ASSEMBLE WITH A FRAME

SPREAD GRAPHITE

ATTACH CONNECTORS ON OPPOSITE SIDE OF EACH FACE

LOW VOLT POWER SUPPLY WITH CONVERTER

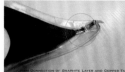

CONNECTION OF GRAPHITE LAYER AND COPPER TAPE

SHORT CAUSES SPARK, AND BURNED OFF GRAPHITE

SHORT CAUSES SPARK, AND BURNED OFF GRAPHITE

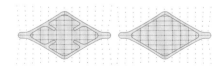

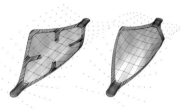

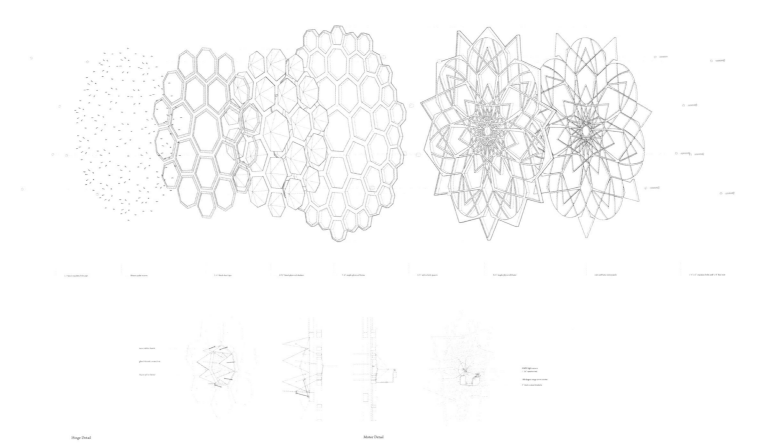

Hinge Detail

Motor Detail

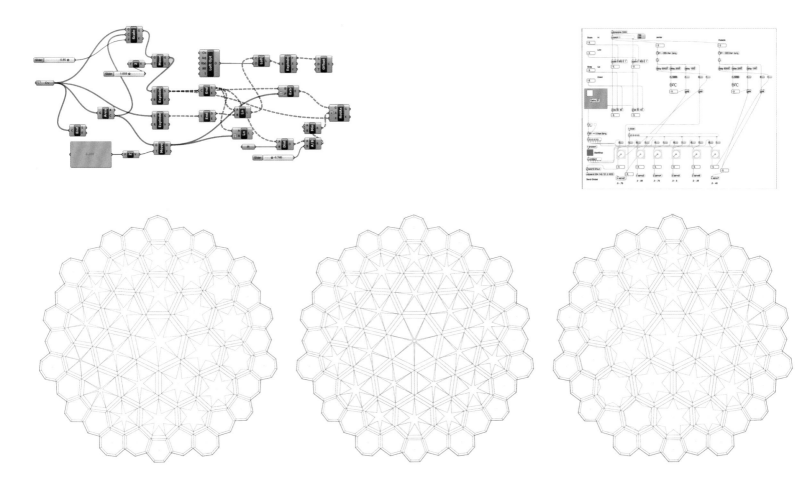

fig. 1   fig. 2   fig. 3   fig. 4

fig. 5   fig. 6   fig. 7   fig. 8

fig. 9   fig. 10   fig. 11   fig. 12

fig. 1   fig. 2   fig. 3   fig. 4

fig. 5   fig. 6   fig. 7   fig. 8

fig. 9   fig. 10   fig. 11   fig. 12

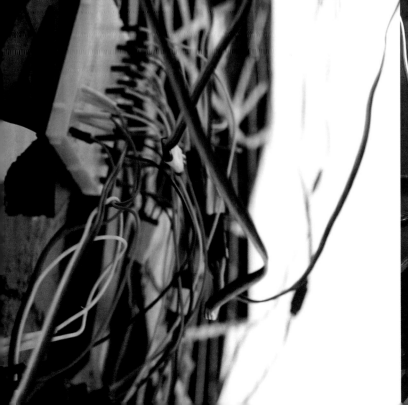
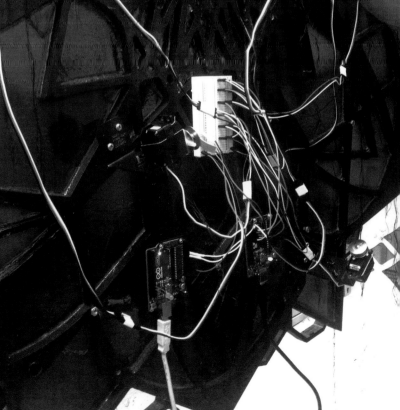

Caustic Frame Geometry

Immersive Interaction

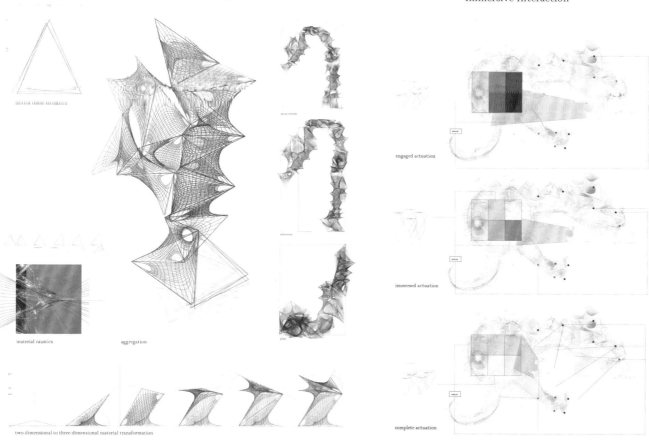

material caustics

aggregation

engaged actuation

immersed actuation

complete actuation

two-dimensional to three-dimensional material transformation

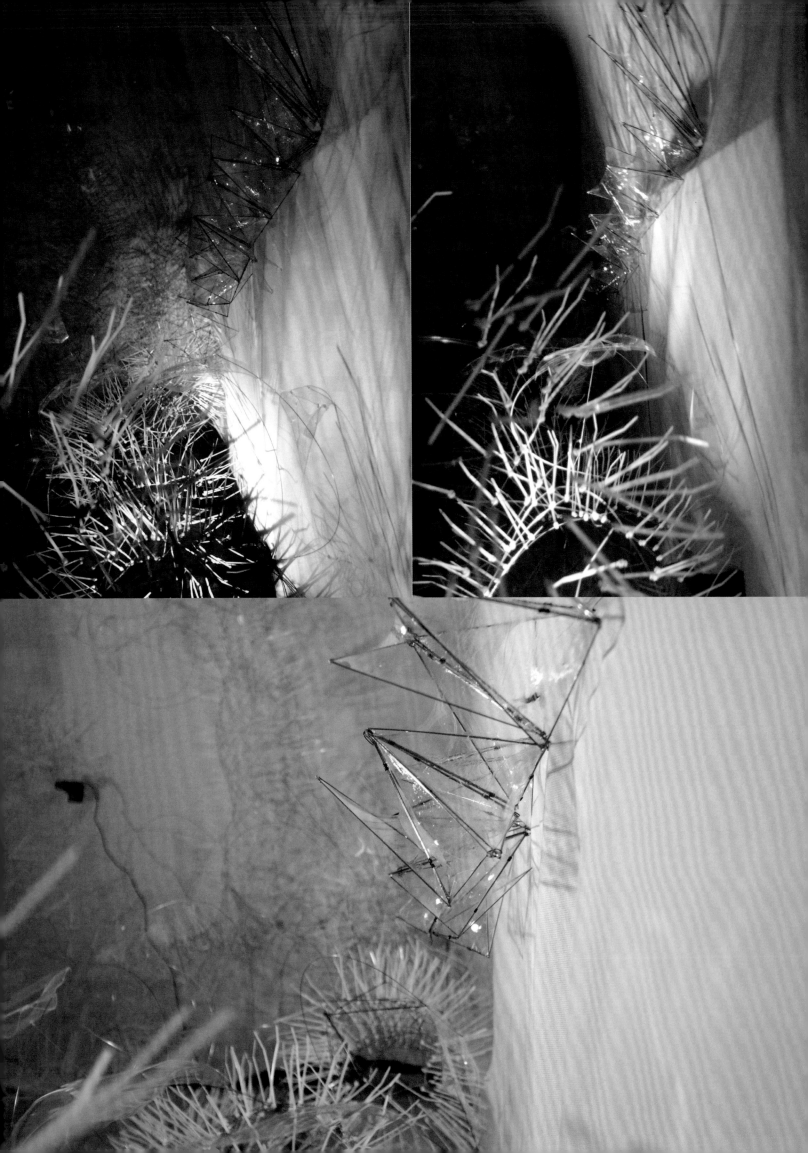

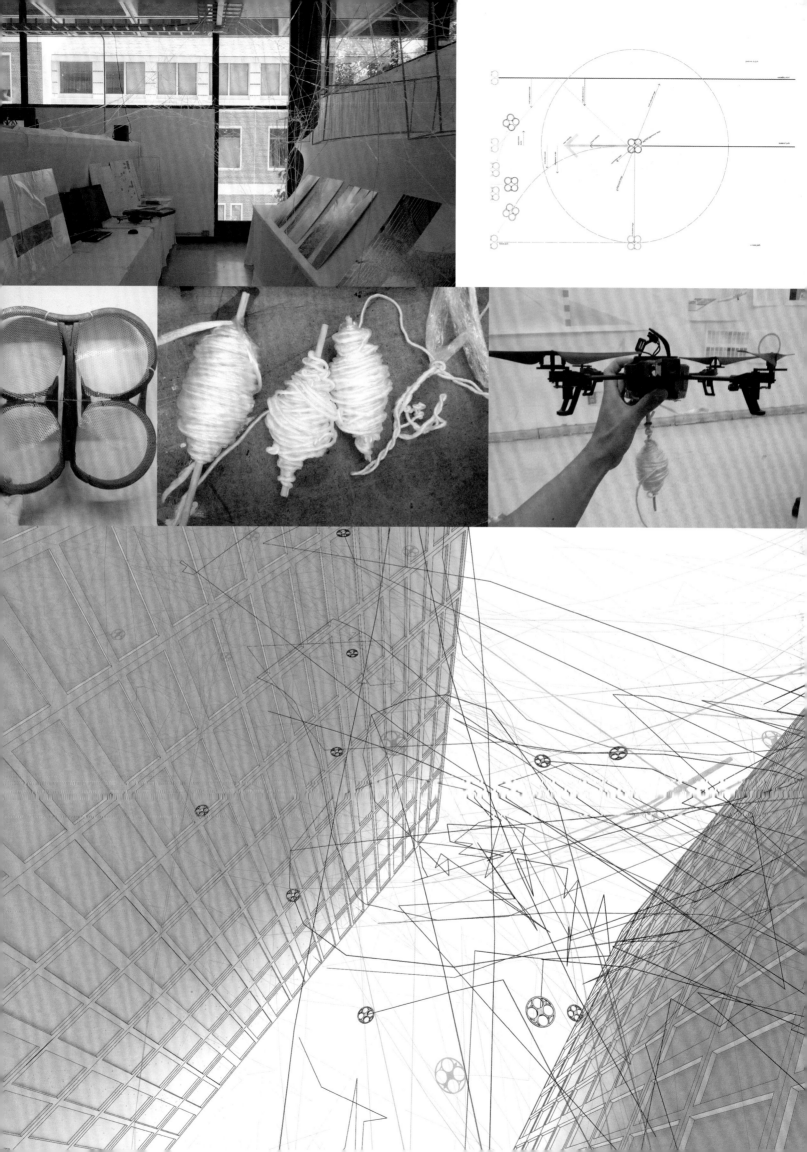

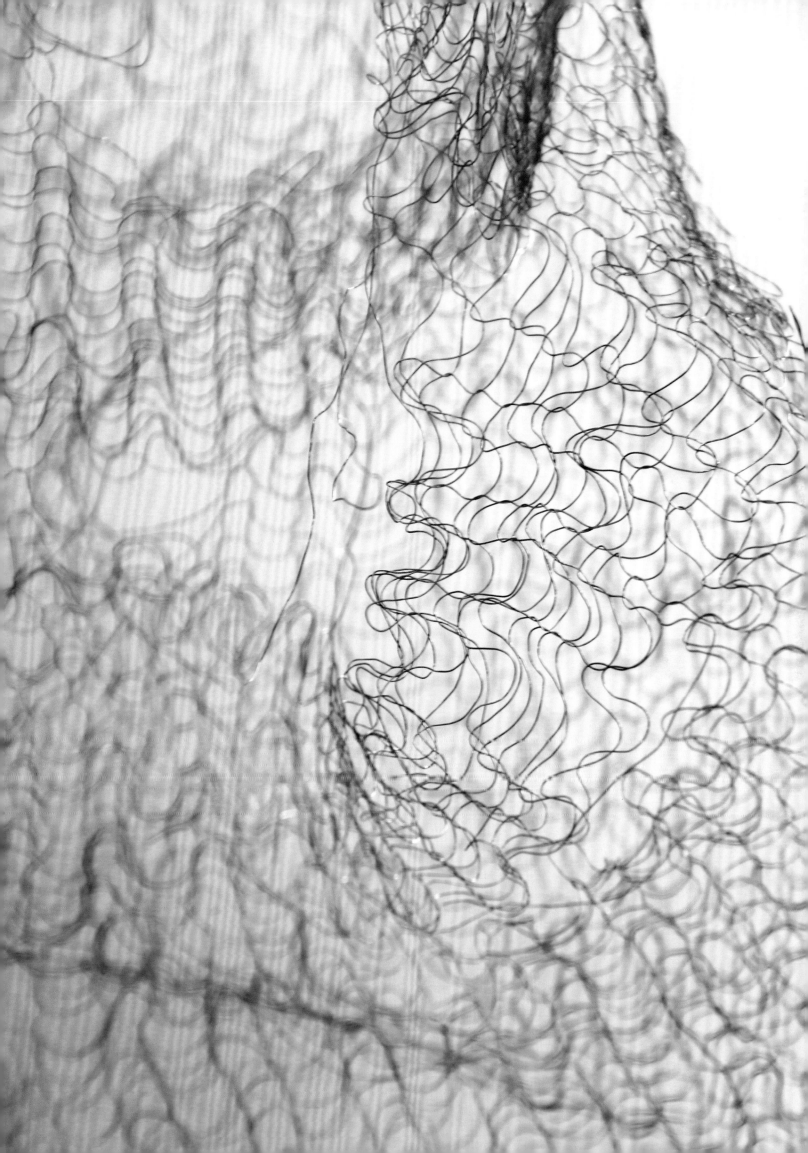

Weaving Diagram: Material: Yarn

REPEAT
12345678 (NO 9 10) repeat 40,   125678 (NO 3 4 9 10) repeat 20,
Expansion: 6 15 12 37 18 35...
Expansion: 12345678__12345678__12345678__ ...
EXTEND
123456 -> 80 Expansion: 12345612312456,   XTEND-RANDOM repeat 20

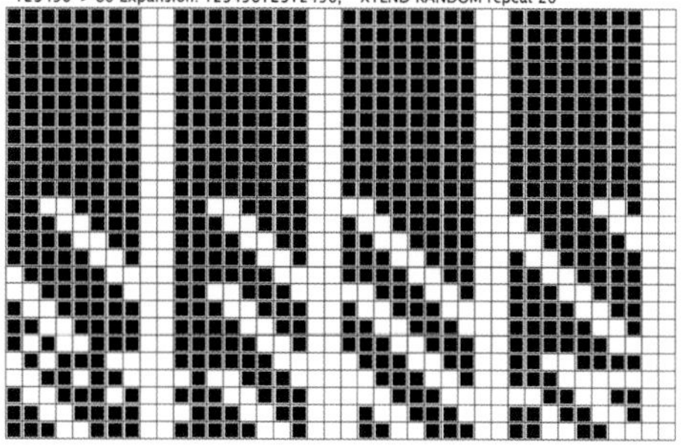

CODE:

```
// Constant
int TailorDelay1=300 ;
int TailorDegree =50;
int RotationalSpeed = 20;

// Tailor
    Tailor.write(90 + TailorDegree);
    Rotation.write(90 + RotationalSpeed);
    delay(TailorDelay1);
    Tailor.write(90 - TailorDegree);
    Rotation.write(90 + RotationalSpeed);
    delay(TailorDelay2);
```

A white cell means the point is not connected.-
During weaving, a black cell places the warp
thread in front. A white cell places the weft
thread in front. Only the thread that is in front is
visible at that point in the weaving.

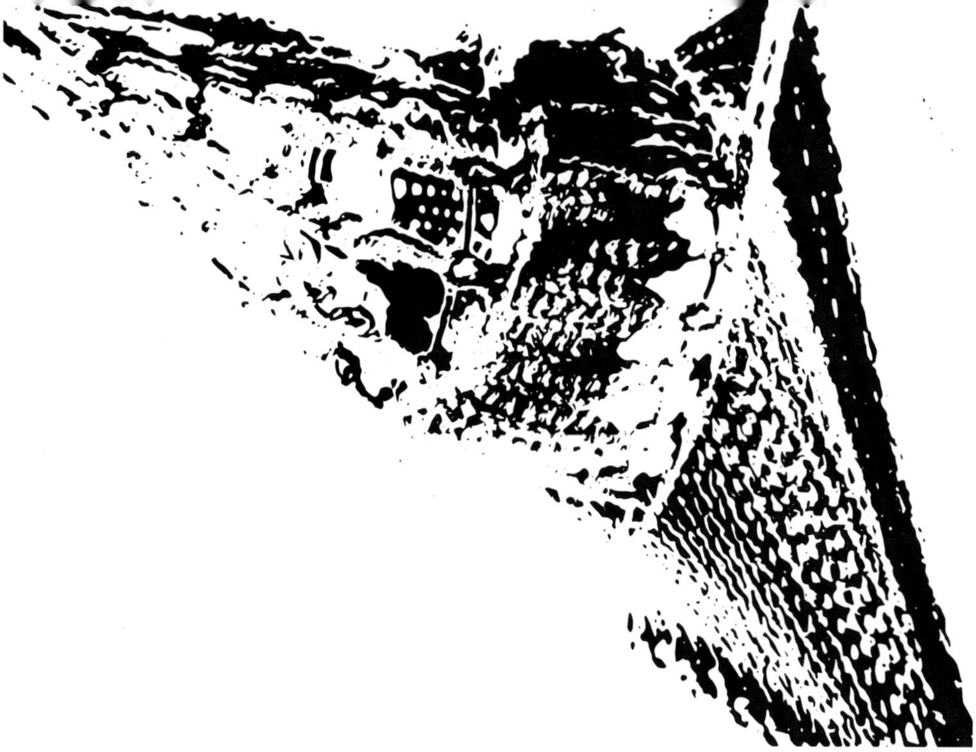

Weaving Diagram: Material: Carbon Fiber, Spray-Casted

FIRST MATERIAL ,REPEAT
12345678 (NO 9 10) repeat 80
Expansion: 12345678__12345678__12345678__ ...

SECOND MATERIAL, EXTEND-RANDOM
Expansion: 6 15 12 37 18 35...

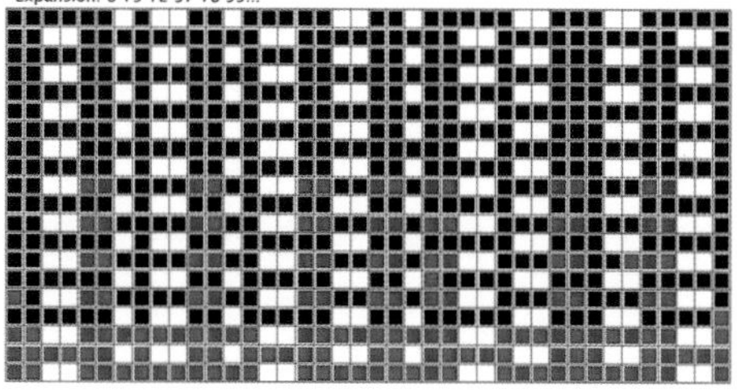

CODE:

```
// Constant
int TailorDelay1=230 ;
int TailorDegree =40;
int RotationalSpeed = 30;

// Constant
int TailorDelay2=RANDOM ;
int TailorDegree =RANDOM;
int RotationalSpeed = 40;

// Tailor 1,2
    Tailor.write(90 + TailorDegree);
    Rotation.write(90 + RotationalSpeed);
    delay(TailorDelay1);
    Tailor.write(90 - TailorDegree);
    Rotation.write(90 + RotationalSpeed);
    delay(TailorDelay2);
```

■ Carbon Fiber Tow 3K

■ Carbon Fiber Tow 50K

You can change the logic of sequences by edit-
ing the warp and weft expressions in the
weaving draft design window. To simplify the
process, machin allows you to work in a
pattern expression language.

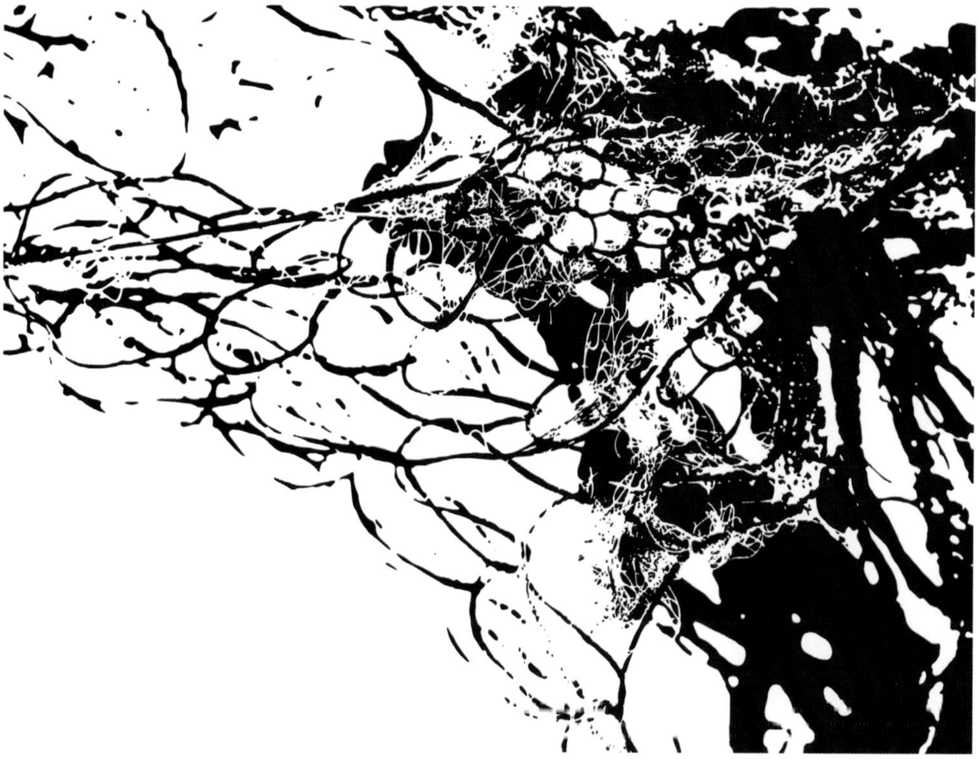

Hand Weaving Diagram: Material: Yarn

$\overrightarrow{\Sigma F=0}$

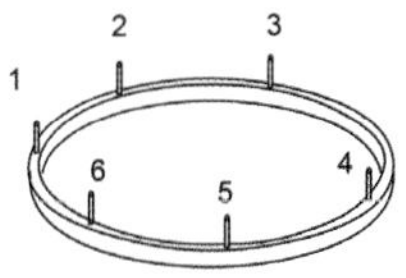

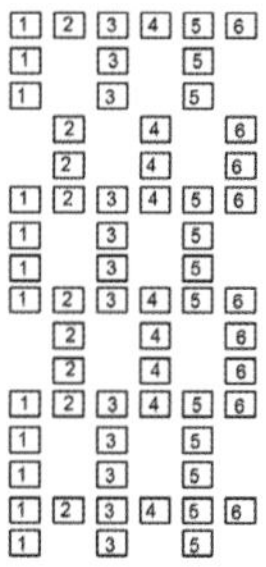

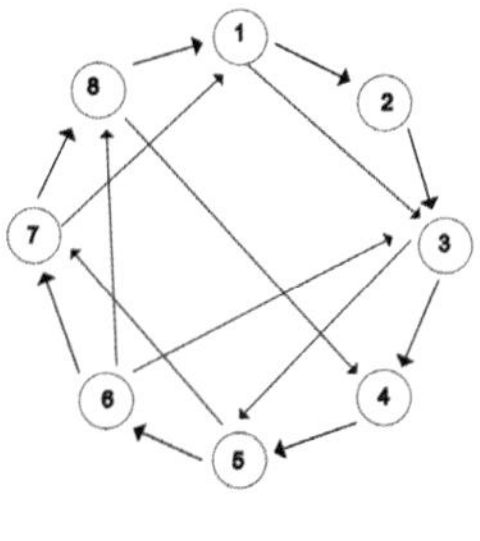

The ring has 6to infinity array that
describes which points (on the left) are
connected to which other point (across the
top). A black cell indicates that the harness is
connected for the corresponding treadle.

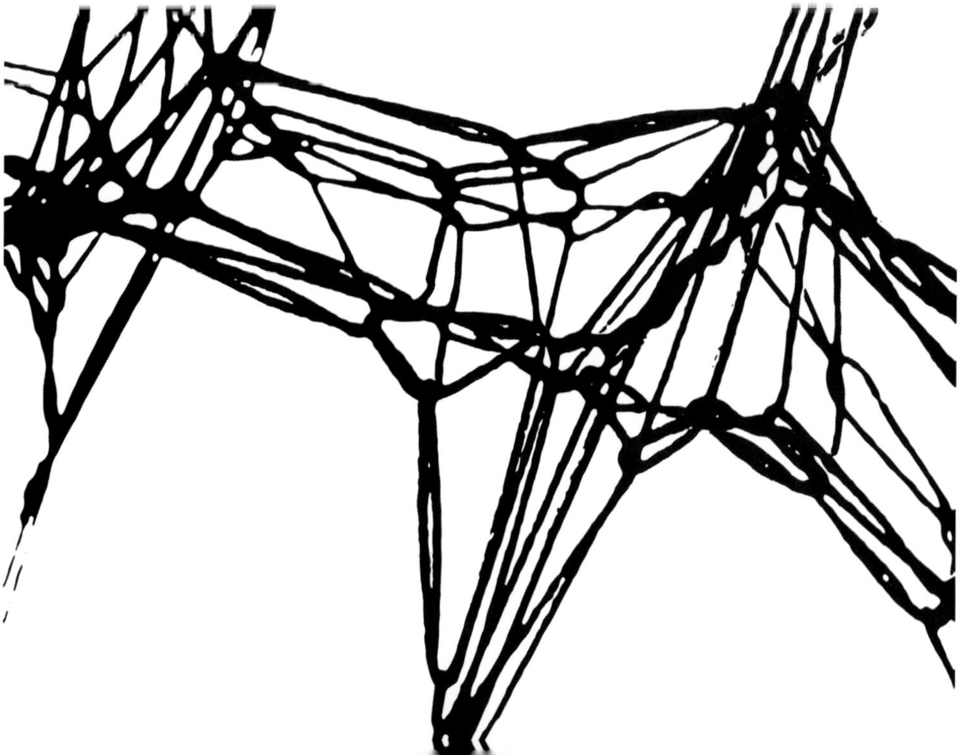

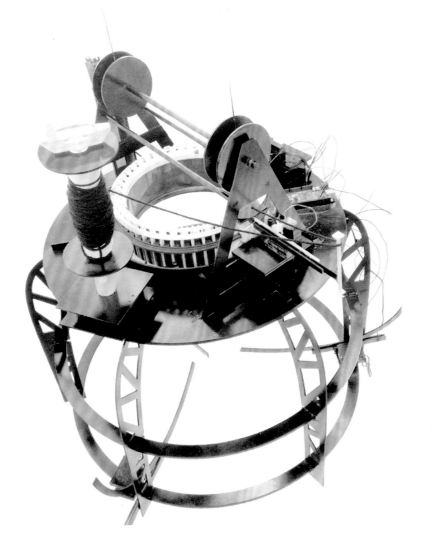

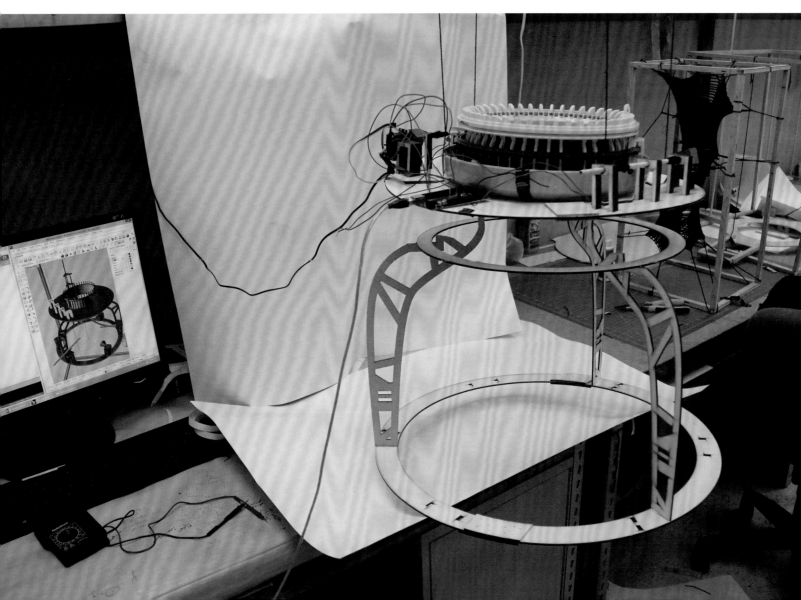

VITALIZED GEOMETRY

A WORLD OF INTENSIVE
AND EXTENSIVE FORCES IN CONSTANT
NEGOTIATION TOWARDS
THE PRODUCTION OF BEAUTY

DR. KRISTINE MUN
USC SCHOOL OF ARCHITECTURE SPRING 2013 THESIS STUDIO
ASSISTANTS: F.MYLES SCIOTTO, SAM KEVILLE

Vitalized Geometry understands geometry as forces and explores three areas of engagement to produce and engineer responsive, empathic systems. Robert Vischer initiated a discussion on *Empathy, Form and Space* as a 'psychological' aesthetics during the 19th century when the changes in society questioned the art's exhaustive tie to traditional themes and as such invigorated a modern foundation of artistic practice. Empathy in form brings questions to fore about how we can build *motifs* in design where aesthetics moves beyond representation and is actuated by experience of the user to their environment. Interactive spaces/forms begin to address how architecture can be redefined in this domain. These empathic forms - forms that sense, feel and respond to the environment - create haptic textures (visual, actual, experiential) that "...reflect very subtle agreements between the beholder's internal state and the change in context introduced by an object." ("Computation of Beauty" G. Flake)

The idea of the vital, or enlivened, is based on technologies of matter that are able to self-stimulate form from within. Although the discourse of matter philosophy and beauty goes back to antiquity, the 17thc Enlightenment era engaged in the prosthetics of technical devices that reawakened their knowledge of the world around them. Microscopes and telescopes extended our visions and thus the discovery of a new foundation of material order. Arts, science and technology inevitably became an unbreakable triad for techne by the 19th c. where new industrial technologies propelled Gottfried Semper to formulate the epic publication of *Der Stil "Style in the Technical and Tectonic Arts; or, Practical Aesthetics"* (1860). Style to Semper was not image but a process, an evolutionary transformation. Not a *processual* change in geometry or pattern but in matter. Understanding style as coming into form must then be predicated on a geometry that is vital. William Hogarth, an 18thc painter, satirist and critic published The Analysis of Beauty (1753) to show beauty as a system of variation. Stressing the (serpentine) line and variation as key components with principles of order, change was deemed necessary to beauty. These proponents express that matter/style/form were dynamic and involved through morphological changes.

We question with the same spirit how current technologies might create a new aesthetic derived from systemic operations that encourages a processual reality, creating exquisite forms ... a milieu of sensations. Contrary to traditional role of the architect who imposes form over matter, here matter is viewed as alive and intrinsic to this thought understands information as in-formation. It takes on the position that all matter (analog or digital) is in a state of continual becoming (continual individuation) and architecture as such, in the digital or processed out of the digital, becomes part of the processing activity; that is, the creative principle continues long after the architectural object had been built. As architecture comes out of the dynamic process and stays in the dynamic process, architecture assumes part of the technological process and becomes a technological object itself.

The studio began by reinterpreting Hogarth's position of beauty as a system of variation interlocked in the contemporary practice by deploying dynamic systems in form. Variety, uniformity, intricacy, distinctness are some of Hogarth's principles applied in these projects. Variation implies change, gradual shifts, and transformations, and dynamic operations are necessary for the eruptions of differentiated milieux. Vitalized Geometry is a tightly woven relationship between logic of paths, geometry, sensations and material performance that set up the milieux for an empathic architecture. The following are the works from this studio that created, fabricated, and coded dynamic responsive territories using advanced computational processes and machining technologies actuated with force feedback devices.

Reflexive Elastegrity, by Chris Chiou and Daniel Kim, negotiates *geometry of tension* through a material performativity initiated by the touch of a viewer. Hogarth's principle of *fitness* and *simplicity* activates the vital geometry as aesthetics of force, like Gothic lines (Worringer). According to Hogarth, fitness contributes to beauty in its representation of propriety and its materialization of function. The fitness capacity of Latex is developed by pinning it against itself in multiple distinct elastic states, and testing the capacities of each to resist the other. Painting one layer at a time, slight but controlled manipulations of the elastic state of one layer cause changing variations within the surface as a whole. Simplicity, the principle that enhances variety and pleases the eye, is reflected upon the minimal alteration of geometric figures used on the wood veneer to create an organic system of lines and voids which under compression yield varying results. Interaction is achieved through sensors detecting touch, exciting the form and expressing its attraction by extending towards the viewer.

PAGE 283

PAGE 284 + PAGE 285

PAGE 286

1 REFLEXIVE ELASTEGRITY. CODE
2 REFLEXIVE ELASTEGRITY. MATERIAL
3 REFLEXIVE ELASTEGRITY
4 REFLEXIVE ELASTEGRITY. WOOD
5 REFLEXIVE ELASTEGRITY. ACTUATORS

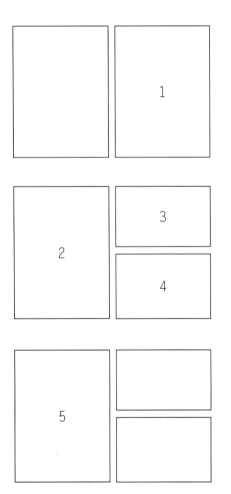

Sound Mood, by Jordan LaRue and Chao Wei, is an interactive soundscape, initiated by the sound of environment, that interacts with the visitors and learns from their response to generate the following process of interaction. Hogarth's principles variety, symmetry and intricacy are used to populate the geometry of frequency. All human senses delight in the beauty of variety, the composed dynamics. Drafted from the behavior of sound, a rhythmic series of geometry is presented to visualize the invisible sound. In return the change of environment entertains the eye and ear with the pleasure of variety. Driven by the study of Electro-active Polymer (EAP), a responsive material, the shape of leaf units follows the rule of symmetry. Meanwhile, a great sense of intricacy emerges from the integration of triangulation patterns and circle packing. In sum, its mobility and interactivity vitalizes a dynamic beauty.

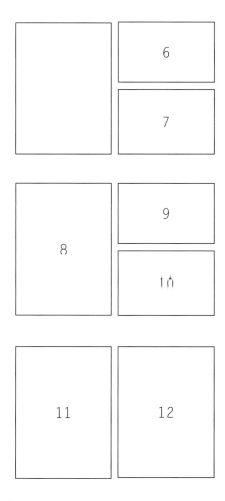

Responsive Apertures, by Shaun Skoog and Andrew Wang, is a responsive window that is regulated by the detection of environmental forces. The dynamism in the geometry is actuated by the material transformation interacting with intensive forces of heat and light. Utilizing principles of distinctness and intricacy, two layers of geometries overlay one another and interact based on light/heat data collected from the environment. Hogarth's says the form with most distinctness is pyramid because it is the only object made with straight lines that has the most variation with the least amount of parts. In this effort, to create a geometry that changes without losing its essence actuated radial geometry produced variety without losing its essential radial form. In two layers, the back geometry is in-filled with thermo-chromatic resin that shifts from black to white based on heat/light. The front layer of hexagonal shutters open and close based on a certain percentage difference of black/white ratio that is detected by a photo-sensor in each cell. This 'self-regulating heat window' has many implications related sustainability.

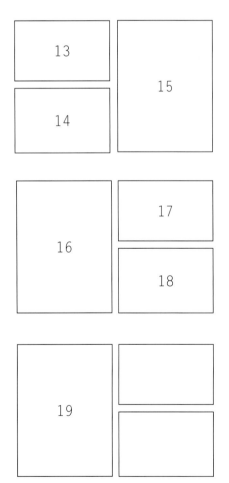

Immaterial Actuation, by Tristan Mcguire and Danielle Saunders, places the body into a chamber where the material is light. Machines and materials are vitally connected and reciprocally constrained. A dialogue created between light catchers and givers Hogarth's principle of intricacy and symmetry guided a system of overlapping and over layering of piano wire that was created through loose mechanical connections, which become stable through a weaving process and interlocked with viscous bioplastic that solidifies as triangulated light reflective film that recasts caustic frames into the environment. Arduino controlled servo motors housed within intricate wire form actuate acrylic modules, reflecting and refracting light as visitors disrupt the visual equilibrium established between the light catchers and the light givers.   The material surface of ac(tua)tion and the immaterial surface of projection fuse physical and visual sensations created in the interaction between the passerby and the space and forms an empathic relationship where movement affects space, which comes back to affect movement by its caustic registers.

PAGE 297

PAGE 298

20 IMMATERIAL ACTUATION
21 IMMATERIAL ACTUATION
22 IMMATERIAL ACTUATION
23 IMMATERIAL ACTUATION
24 IMMATERIAL ACTUATION

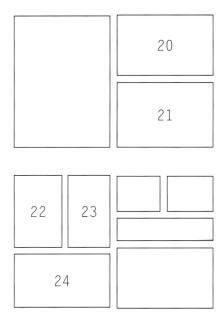

Aerial Construction Systems, by Augustine Liu, is an experimental process for creating a 3d networked structure untilizing a Quadrocopter for "drawing" out a material line. To analyze the potential of robotic systems as a fabrication method to produce physical structure, Quadds and Pathlogic based on Hogarth's principle of quantity and multiplication work in tandem to outline the systemic process of constructing beauty. Hogarth describes beauty as the "manners in which pictures are painted". Hogarthian philosophy of beauty as a multiplication of lines "adds greatness to grace". As such scale could be achieved simply by multiplying the number and size of lines. Aerial Construction Systems exploits quantity as a method of transforming a small thread into a collective surface. The form is created when agents react to their surroundings and each other. As the agent moves, the lines left by the threads indicate local movement, whereas the proportion of the form describes universal logic.

PAGE 299

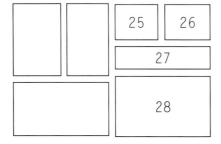

Automated Weaver, by Shahab Rahimi, is a 3d weaving/knitting machine that is programmed to feed a continuous line to form variety of 3d shapes relative to the material. The robot is programmed with algorithm that produces regular and irregular patterns. Hogarth's principle of regularity is developed in the process of weaving (knitting). Regularity is beautiful because it is uniform though variety is still necessary. "We find regularity necessary, in some degree, to give the idea of rest and motion, without the possibility of falling. But when any such purposes can be as well effected by more irregular parts, the eye is always better pleased on the account of variety." (Hogarth) The Automated Weaver creates the variance of patterns from regular to irregular with different materials (from yard, rope, wire, to carbon fiber/resin) associated with automated patterns that naturally produce differentiated aesthetic.

PAGE 300 + PAGE 301

PAGE 302 + PAGE 303

PAGE 304

29 AUTOMATED WEAVER
30 AUTOMATED WEAVER
31 AUTOMATED WEAVER
32 AUTOMATED WEAVER. CARBON FIBER
33 AUTOMATED WEAVER
34 AUTOMATED WEAVER
35 AUTOMATED WEAVER
36 AUTOMATED WEAVER
37 AUTOMATED WEAVER
38 AUTOMATED WEAVER

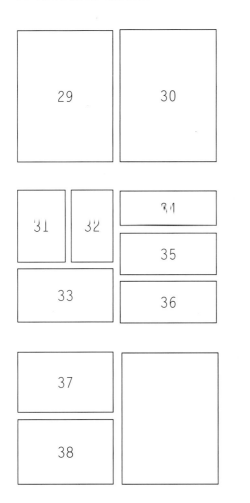

LIGNE ROSET

westedge
DESIGN FAIR

OCTOBER 16-19, 2014
THE BARKER HANGAR
SANTA MONICA, CA

CONNECT WITH US: ☑ westedgedesignfair ☑ westedgedesign ☑ westedgedesign ☑ westedgedesign